American Minute

to Fr. Witt

[signature]

Notable Events
of American Significance
Remembered on the Date They Occurred

William J. Federer

American Minute

Notable Events
of American Significance
Remembered on the Date They Occurred

William J. Federer

Cover Photos - Description and Credits:
Columbus disembarking the Santa Maria - October 12, 1492, (Percy Moran, 1892, U.S. Naval Academy Museum); Pilgrims - November 11, 1620 ("Signing of the Mayflower Compact" by Edward Percy Moran, Pilgrim Hall Museum, 75 Court Street, Plymouth, MA 02360, Pilgrim Society); Benjamin Franklin - c1776 (Chicago Historical Society); Betsy Ross sewing the American Flag - June 1776 ("Birth of Our Nation's Flag" by Charles H. Weisgerber, www.ushistory.org, Independence Hall Association); Washington kneeling in prayer at Valley Forge - December 1777 ("The Prayer at Valley Forge" by Arnold Friberg); Thomas Jefferson (Painting by Rembrant Peale, 1805); The Alamo Mission in San Antonio, Texas - February 24, 1836; Native American Indian Chief - c1880; Teddy Roosevelt and the Rough Riders after the Battle of San Juan Hill in Cuba - July 1, 1898; Booker T. Washington, president of Tuskegee Institute - c1920, (Tuskegee, Alabama); Charles A. Lindbergh with his plane "Spirit of St. Louis," - May 20, 1927 (U.S. Postage Stamp); Raising of the American Flag at the Battle of Iwo Jima during World War II - February 23, 1945 (Photograph by Joe Rosenthal, United Press); NASA Space Shuttle Challenger at lift-off before explosion - January 28, 1986.

Amerisearch, Inc., P.O. Box 20163, St. Louis, MO 63123,
1-888-USA-WORD, 314-487-4395 voice/fax
www.amerisearch.net, wjfederer@aol.com

This book is dedicated to our four children, whom I would drive to gradeschool each day. To liven the ride, Jessica Joy would sing "Today is my favorite day..." Will, half-asleep, would sing "This is the day that the Lord has made..." Melody would surprise us with a song from her heart, and Michael, the youngest, would sing an enthusiastic "Whose the King of the jungle, whose the King of the sea, whose the King of the universe, and whose the King of me?" Now my children are grown and I reminisce how time flies!

"Work as if you were to live 100 years;
pray as if you were to die tomorrow."
- Benjamin Franklin
Poor Richard's Almanac, May 1757

Introduction

The American Minute was orginally written as a sixty-second radio feature broadcast across America. With the expansion of the Internet, the American Minute began to be emailed out daily to thousands.

Now tens-of-thousands of individuals read the American Minute on numerous web sites which post them daily or listen to them on radio and television. After many requests, these short, inspiring and challenging historical vingettes have been put into a book for your enjoyment.

It is our hope that you will find refreshing insight as you take time each day for an American Minute.

American Minute
January 1st

The Emancipation Proclamation went into effect on this day. It stated: "I, Abraham Lincoln, President of the United States, by virtue of the power in me vested as commander-in-chief...do, on the first day of January, in the year of our Lord one thousand eight hundred and sixty-three...publicly proclaim...that all persons held as slaves...are, and henceforward shall be, free....And I hereby enjoin upon the people so declared to be free to abstain from all violence...and...recommend...they labor faithfully for reasonable wages." Lincoln concluded: "And upon this act...I invoke...the gracious favor of Almighty God."

American Minute
January 2nd

*T*oday, January 2nd, is Betsy Ross Day. She was born a day earlier on January 1, 1752, to a Quaker family in Philadelphia, the 8th of 17 children. She apprenticed as a seamstress, where she fell in love with an upholsterer named John Ross, son of an Episcopal rector and nephew of George Ross, who signed the Declaration of Independence. As Quakers forbade interdenominational marriage, John and Betsy eloped. They attended Christ's Church and their pew was next to George Washington's. During the Revolution, John died when a munitions depot he was guarding blew up. Shortly after, General Washington asked Betsy Ross to sew the American Flag.

American Minute
January 3rd

*F*rederick the Great of Prussia called these ten days "the most brilliant in the world's history." After winning the Battle of Trenton, Christmas night, George Washington's small force dodged General Cornwallis' 8,000 man British army. The night before the battle, Washington left his campfires burning and silently marched his army around the back of the British camp at Princeton, New Jersey. At daybreak, this day, January 3, 1777, Washington attacked, capturing three regiments of British troops. Enthusiasm swept America. Ezra Stiles, president of Yale College, stated: "Who but a Washington, inspired by Heaven, could have conceived the surprise move upon the enemy at Princeton?"

American Minute
January 4th

    Called the "Father of American Medicine," he signed the Declaration of Independence, was Surgeon General of the Continental Army, and was a staff member of the Pennsylvania Hospital, where he opened the first free medical clinic. His name was Benjamin Rush, and he was born this day, January 4, 1745. Rush also founded a Bible Society, a Sunday School Union and a Society for the Abolition of Slavery. Dr. Benjamin Rush stated: "The only foundation for... education in a republic is... religion. Without this there can be no virtue, and without virtue there can be no liberty, and liberty is the object... of all republican governments."

American Minute
January 5th

*R*aised by an elderly white couple after his mother was kidnapped following the Civil War, he left home at age eleven and began school in Neosho, Missouri, paying his own tuition. He drifted from there to several towns across Kansas, supporting himself by working as a cook, doing laundry and odd jobs. He eventually received his bachelor's and master's degrees from Iowa State College of Agriculture. Booker T. Washington recruited him to teach at Tuskegee Institute, where he introduced hundred of uses for the peanut, soybean and sweet potato, creating a multi-million dollar industry - revolutionizing the South's economy. His name was George Washington Carver, and he died this day, January 5, 1943. Turning down offers to work for Henry Ford and Thomas Edison, George Washington Carver said: "God is going to reveal to us things He never revealed before if we put our hands in His."

American Minute
January 6th

In 567 AD, at the Council of Tours, the church tried to reconcile a dispute between Western Europe and Eastern Europe. The West celebrated the feast of Christ's birth on Christmas day, December 25th as its major holiday, and the East celebrated this day, January 6th as Epiphany, remembering the visit of the Wise Men and Jesus' baptism. Since no agreement could be reached on a specific date, the decision was made to have all 12 days between December 25th and January 6th designated "holy days" or as it was later pronounced "holidays." These became known as the "Twelve Days of Christmas."

American Minute
January 7th

*H*e became the 13th President when President Zachary Taylor died unexpectedly. He sent Commodore Perry to Japan and admitted California, which had just begun the Gold Rush, into the Union. His name was Millard Fillmore and he was born this day, January 7, 1800. When the Library of Congress caught fire, he and his Cabinet formed a bucket brigade to extinguish the flames. Millard Fillmore stated: "On commencing my Presidential career, I found the Sabbath had frequently been employed...for private interviews with the President....To...end to this I ordered my doorkeeper to meet all Sunday visitors with an indiscriminate refusal."

American Minute
January 8th

*T*hough the War of 1812 had ended two weeks earlier, news had not yet reach New Orleans and on this day, January 8, 1815, five thousand British soldiers charged in a frontal assault against General Andrew Jackson's Tennessee and Kentucky sharpshooters. French pirate Jean Lafitte and his men aided the Americans. In just a half-hour, over two thousand British were killed and only 8 Americans. General Jackson wrote: "It appears that the unerring hand of Providence shielded my men from the shower of balls, bombs, and rockets, when every ball and bomb from our guns carried with them a mission of death."

American Minute
January 9th

Richard Milhous Nixon was born this day, January 9, 1913. A Lieutenant Commander in the Navy during WWII, he was a Congressman, Senator, and Vice-President under Eisenhower. He lost his first presidential race to John F. Kennedy by the smallest margin in a presidential election up to that date. He served as America's 37th President before resigning. In his Inaugural Address, President Nixon stated: "No man can be fully free while his neighbor is not.... This means black and white together as one nation, not two.... What remains is...to insure...that as all are born equal in dignity before God, all are born equal in dignity before man."

American Minute
January 10th

*H*is daughter was Harriet Beecher Stowe, who wrote the abolitionist novel "Uncle Tom's Cabin." His son was Henry Ward Beecher, a famous New York preacher who was known for denouncing slavery and government corruption, and for being in support of a woman's right to vote. His name was Lyman Beecher and he died this day, January 10, 1863. A renowned New England clergyman, Lyman Beecher wrote: "If this nation is, in the providence of God, destined to lead the way in the moral and political emancipation of the world, it is time she understood her...calling... For mighty causes...are rushing with accumulating power to their consummation of good or evil."

American Minute
January 11th

*H*e was the grandson of Princeton president Jonathan Edwards, whose preaching began
the Great Awakening revival. He became the president of Yale, serving for twenty-two years. His
name was Timothy Dwight, and he died this day,
January 11, 1817. Finding many of Yale's students
enamored with French enlightenment, Timothy
Dwight often visited with students on campus,
logically answering questions of faith. By the end
of his tenure, not only did the majority of the
student body profess Christianity, but many became ministers. Timothy Dwight wrote: "Where
there is no religion, there is no morality,..the ultimate foundation of...life, liberty and property is
buried in ruins."

American Minute
January 12th

"The only thing necessary for evil to triumph is for good men to do nothing." This famous quote was from British statesman Edmund Burke, who was born this day, January 12, 1729. Considered the most influential orator in the House of Commons, Burke stands out in history, for, as a member of the British Parliament, he defended the rights of the American colonies and strongly opposed the slave trade. Edmund Burke stated: "What is liberty without...virtue? It is...madness, without restraint. Men are qualified for liberty in exact proportion to their disposition to put moral chains upon their own appetites."

American Minute
January 13th

*E*ducated at Oxford, James Oglethorpe joined the Austrian army and was fighting the invading Muslim Turks at age 17. Upon return to England, he entered Parliament and presided over prison reform. There he got the idea of founding a colony in America where the poor and destitute could start afresh and where people persecuted for their faith could find refuge. James Oglethorpe secured a charter for the Colony of Georgia and on this day, January 13, 1733, his ship, the Ann, arrived with one hundred and fourteen settlers, a doctor and a minister, Herbert Henry, who offered a prayer at the ship's arrival. A year later, a shipload of Salzburgers, Protestant refugees, arrived and, led by Oglethorpe, they settled the town of Ebenezer. Oglethorpe then sailed for England and returned with more immigrants, including Moravian missionaries, John Wesley, founder of Methodism, and his brother Charles, who served as Oglethorpe's secretary. The great preacher and friend of Ben Franklin, George Whitefield, also came to Georgia and founded an orphan school in Savannah.

American Minute
January 14th

Albert Schweitzer was born this day, January 14, 1875, in a village in Alsace, Germany. A Lutheran pastor's son and acclaimed for playing the organ, he earned doctorates in philosophy and theology, was pastor of St. Nicholai's Church, principal of St. Thomas College, and professor at University of Strasbourg. Then, at age 30, he read a Paris Missionary Society article on the desperate need for physicians in Africa. To everyone's dismay, he enrolled in medical school and became a medical missionary, founding a hospital in the jungle village of Lambarene, Gabon, west central Africa. A friend of Albert Einstein, Albert Schweitzer won the Nobel Peace Prize and used the prize money to build a leper colony. He visited the United States in 1949 and his daughter married an American doctor volunteering at the hospital. Overcoming innumerable difficulties, Dr. Albert Schweitzer wrote: "One day, in my despair, I threw myself into a chair in the consulting room and groaned out: 'What a blockhead I was to come out here to doctor savages like these!' Whereupon his native assistant quietly remarked: 'Yes, Doctor, here on earth you are a great blockhead, but not in heaven.'"

American Minute
January 15th

Martin Luther King, Jr. was born January 15, 1929. A Baptist minister, like his father and grandfather, he pastored Dexter Avenue Baptist Church in Montgomery and Ebenezer Baptist Church in Atlanta, before forming the Southern Christian Leadership Conference. In April 1963, Rev. King wrote: "As the Apostle Paul carried the gospel of Jesus Christ...so am I compelled to carry the gospel... I must make two honest confessions to you, my Christian and Jewish brothers...I stand in the middle of two opposing forces...One is a force of complacency....The other force is one of bitterness and hatred, and it comes perilously close to advocating violence. It is expressed in the various black nationalist groups...the largest being Elijah Muhammad's Muslim movement. Nourished by frustration over racial discrimination, this movement is made up of people who have lost faith in America...I have tried to stand between these two forces...for there is the more excellent way of love... One day the South will know that when these disinherited children of God sat down at lunch counters they were standing up for what is best in the American dream and for the most sacred values in our Judeo-Christian heritage.

American Minute
January 16th

*T*homas Jefferson had it commemorated on his tombstone, along with the Declaration of Independence. What was it? It was Jefferson's Article of Religious Freedom, passed this day, January 16, 1786, in the Virginia Assembly. In it, Jefferson wrote: "Well aware...that Almighty God hath created the mind free...all attempts to influence it by temporal punishments...tend only to begat habits of hypocrisy and meanness, and are a departure from the plan of the Holy Author of religion, who being Lord both of body and mind, yet chose not to propagate it by coercions on either, as was in his Almighty power to do, but to extend it by its influence on reason alone."

American Minute
January 17th

On January 17, 1781, Washington's southern army defeated the British troops at Cowpens. In hot pursuit, Lord Cornwallis reached the Catawba River just two hours after the American troops had crossed, but a storm made the river impassable. He nearly overtook the Americans again at the Yadkin River, just as they were getting out on the other side, but a torrential rain flooded the river. This happened a third time at the Dan River. British Commander Henry Clinton wrote: "Here the royal army was again stopped by a sudden rise of the waters, which had only just fallen (almost miraculously) to let the enemy over." General George Washington had previously written to Brigadier General Thomas Nelson of Virginia, August 1778: "The Hand of Providence has been so conspicuous in all this (the course of the war) that he must be worse than an infidel that lacks faith, and more wicked that has not gratitude to acknowledge his obligations; but it will be time enough for me to turn Preacher when my present appointment ceases."

American Minute
January 18th

By a resolution of the Senate, he was esteemed as one of the five greatest senators in U.S. history. An outstanding orator, his political career spanned almost four decades, serving as Secretary of State for Presidents William Henry Harrison, John Tyler and Millard Fillmore. His name was Daniel Webster, born this day, January 18, 1782. From a plain New Hampshire farm background, he was educated at Dartmouth College and went on to become the highest paid attorney of his time. Webster fought to end the slave trade, settled the Northeast boundary of the United States with the Webster-Ashburton Treaty, and defended the Constitution, when South Carolina threatened nullification, with the now famous words: "Liberty and Union, now and forever, one and inseparable!" Daniel Webster stated: "If our posterity neglects religious instruction...no man can tell how sudden a catastrophe may overwhelm us and bury all our glory in profound obscurity."

American Minute
January 19th

William Orville Douglas died this day, January 19, 1980. He was a Justice of the U.S. Supreme Court for 36 years, after teaching law at Yale and Columbia University. In the 1952 case of Zorach v. Clauson, Justice William Douglas asserted: "The First Amendment, however, does not say that in every respect there shall be a separation of Church and State...Otherwise the state and religion would be aliens to each other - hostile, suspicious, and even unfriendly." Justice Douglas continued: "We are a religious people and our institutions presuppose a Supreme Being.... When the state encourages religious instruction...it follows the best of our traditions... We find no constitutional requirement makes it necessary for government to be hostile to religion and to throw its weight against the efforts to widen the scope of religious influence... We cannot read into the Bill of Rights such a philosophy of hostility to religion...The state may not establish a 'religion of secularism' in the sense of affirmatively opposing or showing hostility to religion, thus preferring those who believe in no religion over those who do believe."

American Minute
January 20th

35th President John F. Kennedy stated in his Inaugural Address, January 20, 1961: "The same revolutionary beliefs for which our forebears fought are still at issue around the globe - The belief that the rights of man come not from the generosity of the state but from the hand of God." Kennedy's Address was followed with prayers by a rabbi, a Protestant minister, a Catholic cardinal, a Greek Orthodox bishop, and a poem by Robert Frost. 2nd President John Adams stated in his 1797 Inaugural: "I feel it to be my duty to add, if a veneration for the religion of a people who profess and call themselves Christians...to consider a decent respect for Christianity among the best recommendations for the public service" 9th President William Henry Harrison stated in his 1841 Inaugural: "I deem the present occasion sufficiently important and solemn to justify me in expressing to my fellow citizens a profound reverence for the Christian religion." 16th President Abraham Lincoln stated in his 1861 Inaugural: "Intelligence, patriotism, Christianity, and a firm reliance on Him who has never yet forsaken this favored land, are still competent to adjust in the best way all our present difficulty."

American Minute
January 21st

*H*e produced epic films in Hollywood for almost five decades and started Paramount Pictures. His name was Cecil B. DeMille and he died this day, January 21, 1959. His best-known films include: Samson and Delilah, The Ten Commandments and The Greatest Show on Earth, for which he won an Academy Award. At the opening of The Ten Commandments, Cecil B. DeMille stated: "Man has made 32 million laws since the Commandments were handed down to Moses on Mount Sinai...but he has never improved on God's law.... They are the charter and guide of human liberty, for there can be no liberty without the law."

American Minute
January 22nd

On January 22, 1973, the Supreme Court's decision in the case of Roe v. Wade allowed abortions in the first six months of pregnancy. Twenty-three years later, Norma McCorvey, who was the "Jane Roe" in the Roe v. Wade suit, was interviewed by USA Today. She stated that once, while employed at a clinic when no one was in: "I went into the procedure room and laid down on the table...trying to imagine what it would be like having an abortion... I broke down and cried." On ABC's World News Tonight, Norma McCorvey said: "I think abortion's wrong. I think what I did with Roe v. Wade was wrong."

American Minute
January 23rd

January 23, 1789, John Carroll founded Georgetown University. He was brother of Daniel Carroll, who signed the U.S. Constitution and gave the land where the Capitol is built. He was cousin to Charles Carroll, the wealthiest man in America and the Declaration's longest living signer. John's nephew Robert Brent, was Washington, D.C.'s first mayor, reappointed by Jefferson and Madison. John Carroll, America's first Catholic bishop, founded the nation's first Catholic seminary and parochial school system. He persuaded Elizabeth Seton to start a girls school in Baltimore. In 1776, the Continental Congress asked John Carroll to go with Ben Franklin to try to enlist Canada's support of the Revolution. His influence helped some of States to allow Catholics equality. Bishop John Carroll wrote: "Freedom and independence, acquired by...and cemented with the mingled blood of Protestant and Catholic fellow-citizens, should be equally enjoyed by all." President Washington wrote to him in 1790: "I presume that your fellow-citizens will not forget the patriotic part which you took in their Revolution...or the important assistance which they received from a nation in which the Roman Catholic faith is professed."

American Minute
January 24th

James Madison's strong position of defending religious freedom began when, as a youth, he stood with his father outside a jail in the village of Orange and listened to several Baptists preach from their cell windows, having been imprisoned for their religious opinions. Madison wrote of his disapproval of this practice to a friend named William Bradford, on this day, January 24, 1774, stating: "There are at this time in the adjacent Culpepper County not less than 5 or 6 well meaning men in jail for publishing their religious sentiments which in the main are very orthodox." Two years later, Madison helped write the Virginia Bill of Rights, which stated: "That Religion, or the Duty which we owe our Creator, and the Manner of discharging it, can be directed only by Reason and Convictions, not by Force or Violence; and therefore all Men are equally entitled to the free exercise of Religion, according to the Dictates of Conscience; and that it is the mutual Duty of all to practice Christian Forbearance, Love, and Charity towards each other."

American Minute
January 25th

President Ronald Reagan delivered his State of the Union Address to Congress on this day, January 25, 1984, making reference to the fact that they open each session of Congress with prayer. President Reagan stated: "Each day your members observe a 200-year-old tradition meant to signify America is one nation under God. I must ask: If you can begin your day with a member of the clergy standing right here leading you in prayer, then why can't freedom to acknowledge God be enjoyed again by children in every school room across this land?"

American Minute
January 26th

After commanding in World War I, he became superintendent of West Point, and in 1930 became a four star general and the youngest Chief of Staff of the U.S. Army. During World War II, he became Allied Supreme Commander in the Southwest Pacific and received the surrender of the Japanese. He was promoted to a five star general and served as Supreme United Nations Commander during the Korean War, until President Harry Truman made the very unpopular decision to removed him. His name was Douglas MacArthur, and he was born on this day, January 26, 1880. To the cadets at West Point, Douglas MacArthur stated: "The soldier, above all other men, is required to practice the greatest act of religious training - sacrifice."

American Minute
January 27th

After Spain's monarchs sent Columbus on his voyage, they not only drove Muslims out of Spain, but also Jews, many to Portugal then Amsterdam, from where some sailed with Dutch merchants to South America. When Spain attacked there, many fled, and in 1654, twenty-three refugees on the French ship *Sainte Catherine* arrived in New Amsterdam. Gov. Stuyvesant's tried to evict them, not letting them worship outside their homes. In 1664, New Amsterdam became New York and there the first synagogue in North America was built in 1730. Jews grew to 1,500 in the colonial era in seven synagogues from New York to Savanah. Beginning 1830, Ellis Island saw 100,000 Jews immigrate to escape persecution in Bavaria, and from 1881 over a million arrived fleeing Russia's pograms. Pres. Woodrow Wilson wrote: "Whereas in countries engaged in war there are nine million Jews, the majority of whom are destitute of food, shelter, and clothing; driven from their homes without warning...causing starvation, disease and untold suffering- Whereas the people of the U.S. have learned with sorrow of this terrible plight... I proclaim January 27, 1916, a day to...make contributions for the aid of the stricken Jewish people to the American Red Cross."

American Minute
January 28th

Seventy-three seconds after lift-off, on this day, January 28, 1986, the Space Shuttle Challenger exploded, killing its entire seven member crew, which included a High school teacher, the first private citizen to fly aboard the craft. In his address to the nation after this disaster, President Ronald Reagan stated: "The crew of the space shuttle Challenger honored us by the manner in which they lived their lives. We will never forget them, nor the last time we saw them, this morning, as they prepared for their journey and waved goodbye and 'slipped the surly bonds of earth,' to 'touch the face of God.'"

American Minute
January 29th

*H*e read a poem at President John F. Kennedy's Inauguration. He won the Pulitzer Prize for poetry and received the Congressional Gold Medal. Beginning as a farmer in New Hampshire, he became a teacher at Amherst College, the University of Michigan and a professor of poetry at Harvard. His name was Robert Frost, and he died this day, January 29, 1963. In an interview on radio station WQED, Pittsburgh, Robert Frost stated: "Ultimately, this is what you go before God for: You've had bad luck and good luck and all you really want in the end is mercy."

American Minute
January 30th

*F*ranklin Delano Roosevelt was born this day, January 30, 1882, in Hyde Park, New York. He was the thirty-second President of the United States, serving over 12 years, longer then any other President. His administration spanned the Great Depression and World War II. In a 1935 radio broadcast, Franklin D. Roosevelt declared: "We cannot read the history of our rise and development as a nation, without reckoning with the place the Bible has occupied in shaping the advances of the Republic.... Where we have been the truest and most consistent in obeying its precepts, we have attained the greatest measure of contentment and prosperity."

American Minute
January 31st

Jacob Duche' was born this day, January 31, 1738. He was the Anglican clergyman who, at the request of the Continental Congress, opened the first session of Congress with prayer. Conscious of the impending British attack, Rev. Jacob Duche' read Psalm 35, which begins: "Plead my cause, Oh, Lord, with them that strive with me, fight against them that fight against me... Let those be turned back and humiliated who devise evil against me." Of that reading, John Adams wrote in a letter to his wife: "I never saw a greater effect upon an audience. It seem as if heaven had ordained that Psalm to be read on that morning."

American Minute
February 1st

*F*ive dollars was all she was paid by the Atlantic Monthly Magazine for her poem, The Battle Hymn of the Republic, which was published this day, February 1, 1862. The Union's theme song during the Civil War Julia Ward Howe wrote it while visiting Washington, D.C., and seeing it teem with military, galloping horses and innumerable campfires. Sleeping unsoundly one night, Julia Ward Howe penned: "In the beauty of the lilies Christ was born across the sea; With a glory in his bosom that transfigures you and me: As he died to make men holy, let us die to make men free, While God is marching on."

American Minute
February 2nd

*F*ebruary 2, 1848, the United States Congress ratified the peace treaty which ended the Mexican War and, in exchange for 15 million dollars, brought the territories of California, Nevada, Utah, and parts of Arizona, New Mexico, Colorado and Wyoming, into the Union. The treaty began: "In the Name of Almighty God: The United States and the United Mexican States animated by a sincere desire to put an end to the calamities of the war....have, under the protection of Almighty God, the Author of Peace, arranged, agreed upon, and signed the following: Treaty of Peace."

American Minute
February 3rd

On the frigid night of February 3, 1943, the Allied ship Dorchester plowed through the waters near Greenland. At 1:00am, a Nazi submarine fired a torpedo into its flank, killing many in the explosion and trapping others below deck. It the ensuing chaos, four chaplains: a priest, a rabbi and two protestant ministers; distributed life jackets. When there were none left, the four chaplains ripped off their own jackets and put them on four young men. Standing embraced on the slanting deck, the chaplains bowed their heads in prayer as they sank to their icy deaths. Congress honored them by declaring this "Four Chaplains Day." In February of 1954, President Dwight Eisenhower remarked: "And we remember that, only a decade ago, aboard the transport Dorchester, four chaplains of four faiths together willingly sacrificed their lives so that four others might live. In the three centuries that separate the Pilgrims of the Mayflower from the chaplains of the Dorchester, America's freedom, her courage, her strength, and her progress have had their foundation in faith. Today as then, there is need for positive acts of renewed recognition that faith is our surest strength, our greatest resource."

American Minute
February 4th

*F*or a time he earned his living barnstorming and performing daring feats of aviation. He became a flying cadet in the U.S. Air Service Reserve, and flew mail routes to Chicago. In 1927, after 33 and a half hours, this twenty-five year-old became the first person to fly solo across the Atlantic Ocean. His name was Charles A. Lindbergh, son of a U.S. Congressman, and he was born this day, February 4, 1902. Years later, speaking at the Institute of Aeronautical Sciences, Charles Lindbergh stated: "It was not the outer grandeur of the Roman but the inner simplicity of the Christian that lived though the ages."

American Minute
February 5th

Persecuted in England for preaching religious liberty, Roger Williams fled to Boston, arriving this day, February 5th, 1631. He pastored a short time in the Massachusetts Bay Colony only to be sentenced to be sent back to England for his opposition to the state church. He escaped and lived among the Narragansett Indians, befriending them and learning their language. They gave him the land upon which he founded Providence Plantation, Rhode Island. This was the first place ever where the freedom to worship was separated from the control of the state. In 1639, he organized the first Baptist Church in the new world.

American Minute
February 6th

*H*e started his professional career as radio host in Iowa, served in the Army Air Corp during World War II, and became an actor, appearing in over 50 films. He was President of the Screen Actors Guild, switched from Democrat to Republican, and became Governor of California. At the age of sixty-nine, he was the oldest person elected President of the United States. In 1981, just sixty-nine days after his inauguration, he survived an assassination attempt. Who was he? Ronald Reagan, born this day, February 6, 1911. President Ronald Reagan stated at Reunion Arena, Dallas, Texas, 1984: "If we ever forget that we are One Nation Under God, then we will be a Nation gone under."

American Minute
February 7th

Frederick Douglass was born this day, February 7, 1817. A former slave, he had become an abolitionist and a commanding spokesman for slaves. His powerful orations exposed the injustices of slavery and championed their right to life and liberty. In retelling of his conversion, Frederick Douglass said: "I loved all mankind, slaveholder not excepted, though I abhorred slavery more than ever. I saw the world in a new light.... I gathered scattered pages of the Bible from the filthy street gutters, and washed and dried them, that...I might get a word or two of wisdom from them."

American Minute
February 8th

*T*he Boys Scouts of America was incorporated this day, February 8, 1910. Sir Robert Baden-Powell had begun the movement in England two years prior. A hero of the South African Boer Wars, Sir Baden-Powell's troops were besieged two hundred days by an overwhelming army, but due to his resourcefulness, his men survived. The Boy Scouts are now the largest voluntary youth movement in the world, with membership over 25 million. The Scout Oath states: "On my honor, I will do my best: To do my duty to God and my country, and to obey the Scout Law, To help other people at all times. To keep myself physically strong, mentally awake, and morally straight." In 1924, President Calvin Coolidge addressed a gathering of Boy Scouts in New York: "The three fundamentals of scouthood are reverence for nature...reverence for law...and reverence for God. It is hard to see how a great man can be an atheist. Doubters do not achieve...No man realizes his full possibilities unless he has the deep conviction that life is eternally important, and that his work, well done, is part of an unending plan."

American Minute
February 9th

*"T*ippecanoe and Tyler too." This was the campaign slogan of ninth President William Henry Harrison, born this day, February 9, 1773. He was the first President to die in office, serving the shortest term of only thirty days. A Major General, Harrison was commander of the Northwest, winning the Battle of Tippecanoe. He was the son of Benjamin Harrison, signer the Declaration, and grandfather of Benjamin Harrison, the 23rd President. In his Inaugural Address, 1841, President William Henry Harrison stated: "I deem the present occasion sufficiently important and solemn to justify me in expressing to my fellow citizens a profound reverence for the Christian religion, and a thorough conviction that sound morals, religious liberty, and a just sense of religious responsibility are essentially connected with all true and lasting happiness."

American Minute
February 10th

Cortez ordered his ships sunk. There was no turning back. With 500 men Cortez set out this day, February 10, 1519, toward Mexico City. Cortez' secretary, Francisco Lopez de Gomara, recorded that after they triumphantly entered the city, Montezuma proudly showed them the grand buildings, including a theater made of human bones, wherein was counted 136,000 skulls... a tower was made of skulls too numerous to count...walls and steps covered with human blood, pits where the human bodies were thrown after people had eaten off the arms and legs...black-robed priests with hair matted down with human blood. Soldier Bernal Diaz del Castillo recorded that Cortez' remarked: "'Senor Montezuma, I do not understand how such a great Prince and wise man as you are has not come to the conclusion...that these idols of yours are not gods, but...devils' ...He explained to him very clearly about creation of the world, and how we are all brothers, sons of one father and one mother who were called Adam and Eve....That a cross (when they asked why we worshipped it) was a sign of the other Cross on which our Lord God was crucified...for the salvation of the whole human race."

American Minute
February 11th

On February 11, 1861, newly elected President Abraham Lincoln left Springfield, Illinois for Washington, D.C., never to return. In his Farewell Speech he stated: "I now leave, not knowing when or whether ever I may return, with a task before me greater than that which rested upon Washington. Without the assistance of that Divine Being who ever attended him, I cannot succeed. With that assistance I cannot fail. Trusting in Him who can go with me, and remain with you, and be everywhere for good, let us confidently hope that all will yet be well.... Unless the great God who assisted him [President Washington] shall be with me and aid me, I must fail: but if the same omniscient mind and mighty arm that directed and protected him shall guide and support me, I shall not fail - I shall succeed. Let us all pray that the God of our fathers may not forsake us now. To him I commend you all. Permit me to ask that with equal sincerity and faith you will invoke his wisdom and guidance for me."

American Minute
February 12th

*C*an you believe it? Abraham Lincoln and Charles Darwin were born on the exact same day, February 12, 1809, but their lives had completely different effects. Lincoln is best known for freeing the slaves by issuing the Emancipation Proclamation, affirming that all men are equal. Darwin is best known for the theory of evolution, arguing that all men are not equal because some are more evolved. Darwin's theory has been used by atheists to explain away belief in God, whereas the last act of Congress signed by Lincoln, before he was shot, was to place the phrase "In God We Trust" on all our national coin.

American Minute
February 13th

"**M**an has forgotten God, that is why this has happened," was Solzhenitsyn's response when questioned about the decline of modern culture. A Russian author, Solzhenitsyn was imprisoned for eight years by Joseph Stalin. He wrote "The Gulag Archipelago" for which he was awarded the Nobel Prize for Literature in 1970, but the Communist government would not allowed him to leave the country to accept it. Finally, under international pressure, the Soviet Union expelled him on this day February 13, 1974. While in Washington, D.C., in 1975, Alexander Solzhenitsyn warned: "I...call upon America to be more careful...because they are trying to weaken you...to disarm your strong and magnificent country in the face of this fearful threat - one that has never been seen before in the history of the world."

American Minute
February 14th

*I*n the 3rd century, Emperor Claudius the Goth not only commanded that the Roman gods must be worshiped, but he temporarily forbade marriage, because he believed single men made better soldiers. Legend has it that Valentine, who was a bishop in Italy, risked the Emperor's wrath by refusing to worship idols and for secretly marrying young couples. Saint Valentine was dragged before the Prefect of Rome, who condemned him to be beaten to death with clubs and have his head cut off on February 14, 269AD. While awaiting execution, it is said he prayed for the jailers' sick daughter, who miraculously recovered. He wrote her a note and signed it, "from your Valentine."

American Minute
February 15th

Today, February 15th, in the year 1898, the U.S.S. Maine blew up in Havana Harbor. President William McKinley approved the Joint Resolution of Congress, which stated: "The abhorrent conditions which have existed for more than three years in the island of Cuba...have been a disgrace to Christian civilization, culminating, as they have, in the destruction of a United States battle ship with 266 of its officers and crew, while on a friendly visit in the harbor of Havana... Therefore, Resolved by...Congress assembled...That the people of the island of Cuba are and of a right ought to be free."

American Minute
February 16th

"*F*rom the halls of Montezuma to the shores of Tripoli." The Marine Corp anthem recalls when Muslims of North Africa, known as the Barbary Pirates, were committing terrorist acts on the high seas, seizing American ships and cargo, and selling crews into slavery. They offered to stop only if America paid "tribute." An attempted peace treaty stated in the original Arabic: "We...agreed that if American Christians are traveling with a nation that is at war with...Tripoli...neither he nor his goods shall be taken." Tripoli did not honor the treaty, as the Koran forbade making treaties with "infidels," so President Thomas Jefferson sent in the Marines. On February 16, 1804, in what Admiral Horatio Nelson described as the "most bold and daring act of the age," Lieutenant Stephen Decatur sailed his ship, the Intrepid, at night into the pirate harbor of Tripoli, burned a ship and escaped unharmed amidst fierce enemy fire. The Marines then captured the Muslim stronghold and forced them to make peace on U.S. terms.

American Minute
February 17th

A baseball star, Billy Sunday played for the Chicago White Stockings (Sox) in the 1890's. Born during the Civil War in a log cabin in Iowa, his father, a Union Army soldier, died of pneumonia when Billy was a month old. At age 15, he struck out on his own, working several jobs before playing baseball. His career took off and he became one of the most popular athletes in the nation. While recovering from a baseball injury in 1887, he heard a group of gospel singers after leaving a Chicago saloon. They invited him to their mission where he experienced a conversion. He began attending YMCA meetings, quit drinking and got married. A national sensation occurred this day, February 17, 1889, when Billy Sunday preached his first sermon as an evangelist in Chicago. He went on to pioneer radio broadcasting so enthusiastically that the FCC was formed in response. Over the next 46 years 100 million people would hear him. In his animated style, Billy Sunday said: "Going to church doesn't make you a Christian any more than going to a garage makes you an automobile."

American Minute
February 18th

*P*ilgrim's Progress was published this day, February 18, 1678. It was written John Bunyan, who was born in Bedford, England, and at age 29, became a Baptist minister. Bunyan was imprisoned over 12 years for preaching without a license. While in jail, he supported his family by making shoelaces. Pilgrim's Progress, which is an allegory of a Christian's journey to the Celestial City, has been translated into over 100 languages and, after the Bible, held the position as the world's best-seller for hundreds of years. It could be found in nearly every colonial New England home. In Pilgrim's Progress, John Bunyan wrote: "Christian ran thus till he came at a place somewhat ascending, and upon that place stood a cross...So I saw in my dream, that just as Christian came up with the cross, his burden loosed from off his shoulders, and fell from off his back..."

American Minute
February 19th

Born in Massachusetts, Adonirum Judson was educated at Brown University. On this day, February 19, 1812, being 23-years-old, he and his 22-year-old wife Ann, sailed from New England to Calcutta. They were America's first foreign missionaries. Settling in the strange land of Rangoon, they began to preach and write in Burmese. Enduring many hardships, Adoniram was imprisoned during the Burmese War. He later gained respect from the Burmese and British officials, translating his acclaimed English-Burmese Dictionary and the Bible. By his death, there were 63 churches, 123 ministers and over 7000 baptized Christians in Burma. As a young man, Adonirum wrote: "How do Christians discharge this trust committed to them? They let three fourths of the world sleep the sleep of death, ignorant of the simple truth that a Savior died for them."

American Minute
February 20th

A Colonel during the Revolutionary War, he fought in the battles of Long Island and Saratoga, built the fortifications at Breed's Hill and commanded the Colonial Militia at the Battle of Bunker Hill. His name was William Prescott and he was born this day, February 20, 1726. When the British blockaded the Boston harbor, William Prescott wrote to the city's inhabitants: "Providence has placed you where you must stand the first shock... We...must sink or swim together.... Let us...stand fast in the liberty wherewith Christ has made us free. And may He...grant us deliverance."

American Minute
February 21st

Washington's birthday and Lincoln's birthday, both in the month of February, have been celebrated for generations all across the United States, but the Uniform Holiday Bill, signed by President Lyndon Johnson in 1968, moved the celebration of Washington's Birthday to the third Monday in February. Sometime after this, the name of the holiday was changed to "Presidents Day." Of note is that virtually every President swore into office with their hand upon a Bible, ended their oath with the phrase "So help me God" and acknowledged a Supreme Being in their address upon assuming the Presidency. Eisenhower, Reagan and George H.W. Bush are among those who included a prayer in their Inaugural Addresses. President Eisenhower stated: "My friends, before I begin...would you permit me the privilege of uttering a little private prayer of my own. And I ask that you bow your heads. Almighty God, as we stand here at this moment..."

American Minute
February 22nd

*G*eorge Washington was born February 22, 1732. He was unanimously chosen as Commander-in-Chief of the Continental Army, unanimously chosen as President of the Constitutional Convention, and unanimously chosen as the first U.S. President. After the Declaration of Independence was read to his troops, General Washington's orders placing chaplains in each regiment, ended: "The General hopes and trusts, that every officer and man, will endeavour so to live, and act, as becomes a Christian Soldier, defending the dearest Rights and Liberties of his country." After his Inauguration, President Washington attended a service led by Congress' chaplains in New York City's St. Paul's Chapel. In his Inaugural Address, Washington said: "It would be peculiarly improper to omit, in this first official act, my fervent supplications to that Almighty Being who rules over the universe... No people can be bound to acknowledge and adore the Invisible Hand which conducts the affairs of men more than the people of the United States. Every step by which they have advanced to the character of an independent nation seems to have been distinguished by some token of Providential agency."

American Minute
February 23rd

The Panama Canal Zone was acquired for ten million dollars by the United States on this day, February 23, 1904. Years later, in 1912, President William Taft referred to it in an address to Congress: "Our defense of the Panama Canal, together with our enormous world trade and our missionary outposts on the frontiers of civilization, require us to recognize our position as one of the foremost in the family of nations." President Taft continued, we must "clothe ourselves with sufficient naval power...to give weight to our influence in those directions of progress that a powerful Christian nation should advocate."

American Minute
February 24th

"**R**emember the Alamo" was the cry of the Texas army. The battle began today, February 24th, 1836, when three thousand Mexicans attacked 182 Texans. Within thirteen days, all defenders were killed, including Davy Crockett and James Bowie. The Texas Declaration of Independence stated: "General Antonio Lopez Santa Ana, who having overturned the constitution of his country, now offers, as the cruel alternative, either abandon our homes...or submit to the most intolerable of all tyranny.... He denies us the right of worshiping the Almighty according to the dictates of our own conscience."

American Minute
February 25th

"Our institutions of freedom will not survive unless they are constantly replenished by the faith that gave them birth" stated Secretary of State John Foster Dulles, who was born this day, February 25, 1888, in the home of his grandfather, a former Civil War general. A graduate of Princeton, John studied law at George Washington University, served as U.S. Army Major in WWI and was elected U.S. Senator, before serving as advisor to Truman and Secretary of State for Eisenhower. The son of a Presbyterian pastor, John Dulles helped negotiate the Peace Treaty with Japan after World War II and served as U.S. Ambassador to the UN. Washington Dulles International Airport is named for him. John Foster Dulles remarked: "Man has his origins and his destiny in God.... Our institutions reflect the belief of our founders that all men were endowed by their Creator with inalienable rights....that human institutions ought primarily to help men develop their God-given possibilities."

American Minute
February 26th

"**G**"God is behind everything, but everything hides God," wrote Victor Hugo in his classic Les Miserables, Book 5, Chapter IV. Born this day, February 26, 1802, Victor Marie Hugo was hailed as the greatest of the Romanticists poets. He is best know for writing Cromwell, 1827, The Hunchback of Notre Dame, 1831, and Les Miserables, 1862, an epic story of redemption set in Paris during the French Revolution. Hugo's father had been a general in Napoleon Bonaparte's army. Hugo supported Napoleon's heir, but when he turned out to be a tyrant, Hugo opposed him and was forced into exile for nineteen years. Over three million people attended Hugo's funeral in Paris. In his Preface to Cromwell, 1827, Victor Hugo wrote: "Lastly, this threefold poetry flows from three great sources-The Bible, Homer, Shakespeare... The Bible before the Iliad, the Iliad before Shakespeare." Victor Hugo stated: "England has two books, the Bible and Shakespeare. England made Shakespeare, but the Bible made England."

American Minute
February 27th

"Listen my children and you shall hear of the midnight ride of Paul Revere... Hang a lantern aloft in the belfry arch... One if by land, two if by sea..." These lines are from the famous poem, Paul Revere's Ride, written by Henry Wadsworth Longfellow, who was born this day, February 27, 1807. He was an American poet and Harvard Professor, and he wrote such American classics as: Evangeline; The Song of Hiawatha; and The Courtship of Miles Standish. Henry Wadsworth Longfellow stated: "Man is unjust, but God is just; and finally justice triumphs."

American Minute
February 28th

The State of New Jersey honored Richard Stockton by placing his statue in the U.S. Capitol Statuary Hall. His grandson, Robert, was the U.S. Naval Commodore who captured California in 1846, and for whom Stockton, California was named. Richard had served as a justice on the New Jersey Supreme Court before becoming a member of the Continental Congress, where he signed the Declaration of Independence. During the Revolutionary War, Richard Stockton was captured by the British and held prisoner for a month. He died shortly after his release, on this day, February 28, 1781, as a result of the harsh treatment he receive while in prison. Richard Stockton wrote in his Will: "As my children will have frequent occasion of perusing this instrument, and may probably be peculiarly impressed with the last words of their father, I think proper here, not only to subscribe to the entire belief of the great leading doctrine of the Christian religion...but also in the heart of a father's affection, to charge and exhort them to remember 'that the fear of the Lord is the beginning of wisdom.'"

American Minute
February 29th

*F*ebruary 29th is Leap Day. In 45BC, Julius Caesar replaced the many calendars used throughout the Roman Empire, based on the moon's cycles, with one calendar based on the sun, having 365 days and an "leap" day every fourth year. An interesting event occurred on this day in 1504. On his last voyage, Christopher Columbus was shipwrecked on the Island of Jamaica. When the Indians became hostile, Columbus correctly predicted a lunar eclipse on this day and the frightened Indians quickly made peace. Columbus wrote: "My hope in the One who created us all sustains me: He is an ever present help in trouble."

American Minute
March 1st

*B*efore the U.S. Constitution was written, the government in the United States was the Articles of Confederation, ratified by the States this day, March 1st, 1781. Signed by such statesmen as Ben Franklin and Roger Sherman, it was an attempt to loosely knit the thirteen States together. The Articles of Confederation declared: "Whereas the delegates of the United States of America in Congress assembled did on the fifteenth day of November in the Year of Our Lord 1777, and in the second year of the independence of America agree on certain Articles of Confederation and perpetual union between the States... The said states hereby severally enter into a firm league of friendship with each other, for their common defense, the security of their liberties, and their mutual and general welfare, binding themselves to assist each other, against all force offered to, or attacks made upon them, or any of them, on account of religion, sovereignty, trade, or any other pretense... And whereas it has pleased the Great Governor of the World to incline the hearts of the Legislatures we respectively represent in Congress, to approve of, and to authorize us to ratify the said Articles of Confederation."

American Minute
March 2nd

March 2, 1836, the people of Texas signed a Declaration of Independence, stating: "The government of General Santa Ana...now offers, as the cruel alternative, either abandon our homes acquired by so many privations, or submit to the most intolerable of all tyranny.... It denies us the right of worshiping the Almighty according to the dictates of our own conscience... It has demanded us to deliver up our arms, which are essential to our defence - the rightful property of freemen - and formidable only to tyrannical governments...It has, through its emissaries, incited the merciless savage, with the tomahawk and scalping knife, to massacre the inhabitants of our defenseless frontiers." The Texas Declaration, signed this day in 1836, concluded: "Conscious of the rectitude of our intentions, we fearlessly and confidently commit the issues to the decision of the Supreme Arbiter of the Destinies of Nations."

American Minute
March 3rd

*H*ow did the phrase "In God We Trust" get on our coins? It was on this day, March 3, 1865, that Congress approved inscribing the motto on all our national coins. Abraham Lincoln signed the bill into law. Less than two months later Lincoln was assassinated. At a Memorial Address for Lincoln, Speaker of the House Schuyler Colfax noted: "Nor should I forget to mention here that the last act of Congress ever signed by President Lincoln was one requiring that the motto, in which he sincerely believed, 'In God We Trust,' should hereafter be inscribed upon all our national coin."

American Minute
March 4th

March 4th was Inauguration Day up until 1937, when it was changed to January 20th. Every President acknowledged a Supreme Being in their address upon assuming office. For example, Thomas Jefferson referred to: "That Infinite Power which rules the destinies of the universe..." Andrew Jackson: "My fervent prayer to that Almighty Being..." Abraham Lincoln: "The Almighty has His own purposes..." FDR: "We humbly ask the blessing of God..." Calvin Coolidge: "America...cherishes no purpose save to merit the favor of Almighty God." Harry S Truman: "We believe that all men are created equal because they are created in the image of God..." John F. Kennedy: "The rights of man come not from the generosity of the state but from the hand of God..." Ronald Reagan: "With God's help, we can and will resolve the problems which now confront us. And after all, why shouldn't we believe that? We are Americans."

American Minute
March 5th

On this day, March 5, in the year 1770, the Boston Massacre took place. The British had been forcing Colonists to house their soldiers. A crowd had gathered to protest and in the confusion British soldiers fired into the mob, killing five of them. On the 4th anniversary of the Massacre, in 1774, John Hancock, who would later become famous for being the first to sign the Declaration of Independence, stated: "Let us play the man for...the cities of our GOD. While we are using the means in our power, let us humbly commit our righteous cause to the great LORD of the Universe."

American Minute
March 6th

On March 6, 1776, General Washington issued the order from his headquarters at Cambridge: "The...Legislature has set apart a day of fasting, prayer and humiliation, 'to implore the Lord and Giver of all victory to pardon our manifold sins and wickedness, and...bless the Continental army with His divine favor and protection,' all officers and soldiers are strictly enjoined to pay...reverence...to...the Lord of hosts for His mercies...and for those blessings which our...uprightness of life can alone encourage us to hope through His mercy obtain." Within eleven days, Washington, using fifty captured cannons, forced the British to evacuate Boston.

American Minute
March 7th

On March 7, 1774, the British passed the Boston Port Act, closing the harbor to all commerce to punish the colonists for the Boston Tea Party. The surrounding towns rallied to their aid by secretly sending food to the inhabitants of Boston. Colonel William Prescott, who commanded the colonial militia at Bunker Hill wrote: "Providence has placed you where you must stand the first shock... If we submit to these regulations, all is gone. Our forefathers passed the vast Atlantic, spent their blood and treasure, that they might enjoy their liberties, both civil and religious, and transmit them to their posterity.... Now if we should give them up, can our children rise up and call us blessed?"

American Minute
March 8th

KKnown as THE GREAT DISSENTER because of his unconventional opinions, he served for thirty years on the Supreme Court. Who was he? Oliver Wendell Holmes, Jr., born this day, March 8, 1841. A Union soldier during the Civil War, he went on to become a Harvard Law School Professor. In 1902, President Theodore Roosevelt appointed him to the U.S. Supreme Court, where he served to a more advanced age than other justice. On his 90th birthday, Oliver Wendell Holmes, Jr., replied to a reporter: "Young man, the secret of my success is that at an early age I discovered I was not God."

American Minute
March 9th

*O*n this date, March 9,1862, the historic Civil War battle took place between the Confederate iron-plated ship Merrimac, which had just destroyed two Union boats, and the Union's iron-clad vessel, the Monitor, designed by Swedish Immigrant John Ericsson. After 4 hours of bombardment, with cannon balls deflecting off their decks, the Confederate ship was crippled and withdrew to Virginia. Naval warfare was forever changed that day. When John Ericsson was offered payment for designing the Monitor, he replied: "Nothing could induce me to accept any remuneration... It is my contribution to the glorious...triumph...which freed 4,000,000 bondsmen..." John Ericsson wrote to President Abraham Lincoln: "Attachment to the Union alone impels me to offer my services at this frightful crisis - my life if need be - in the great cause which Providence has caused you to defend."

American Minute
March 10th

26-year-old William Penn received from King Charles the charter to Pennsylvania on this date, March 10, 1681, as repayment of a debt owed to his deceased father. An Oxford graduate, Penn had previously converted to Quakerism and suffered imprisonment in the Tower of London. His colony became a refuge for the persecuted peoples of Europe. Before his arrival, Penn wrote to the Indians in America, whom he insisted on treating fairly: "My Friends, There is one...God....and He hath made...the king of the country where I live, give...unto me a great province therein, but I desire to enjoy it with your...consent, that we may always live together as...friends." History records that since William Penn insisted on paying the Indians a fair sum for their land and treated them with honesty and respect, Pennsylvania never experienced the Indian problems which some of the other colonies had.

American Minute
March 11th

*H*is outspoken stand against slavery resulted in enraged Congressman Preston S. Brooks from Carolina violently beating him on the head with a cane while he was sitting at his desk on the floor of the United States Senate, the injuries from which he never fully recovered. Who was he? Senator Charles Sumner, who died this day, March 11, 1874. A Senator from Massachusetts for 23 years and a founder of the Republican Party, Charles Sumner declared: "That great story of redemption, when God raised up the slave-born Moses to deliver His chosen people from bondage, and...that sublimer story where our Saviour died a cruel death that all men, without distinction of race, might be saved, makes slavery impossible."

American Minute
March 12th

The Girls Scouts of America was started on this date, March 12, 1912, in Savannah, Georgia, by Mrs. Juliette Low. After meeting Sir Robert Baden-Powell, founder of the Boy Scouts, Juliette formed the Girl Scouts to be a nonsectarian, non-political and interracial organization, for the purpose of building good character and citizenship. By the 1920s the movement had spread across America and grown to a membership of millions world-wide. The original Girl Scout promise, made upon joining, was: "On my honor, I will try: to do my duty to God and my country, to help other people at all times, to obey the Girl Scout laws."

American Minute
March 13th

Susan B. Anthony, whose face is on a U.S. dollar coin, died this day, March 13, 1906. Raised a Quaker, her father owned a cotton mill and refused to buy cotton from farmers who owned slaves. Her religious upbringing instilled in her the concept that every one is equal before God and motivated her to crusade for freedom for slaves and women's right to vote. Opposing liquor, drunkenness and abortion, she encountered mobs, armed threats, things thrown at her and was hung in effigy. After the Civil War, Susan B. Anthony worked hard for the passage of the 13th, 14th and 15th Amendments. She got women admitted to the University of Rochester and was arrested for voting in the 1872 Presidential Election. Fourteen years after her death, women won the right to vote. "I deplore the horrible crime of child-murder," wrote Susan B. Anthony in The Revolution (July 1869), "No matter what the motive, love of ease, or a desire to save from suffering the unborn innocent, the woman is awfully guilty who commits the deed. It will burden her conscience in life, it will burden her soul in death; but oh! Thrice guilty is he who...drove her to the desperation which impels her to the crime."

American Minute
March 14th

Born in Germany this day, March 14, 1879, he began teaching himself calculus at the age of fourteen. He developed the theory of relativity, which was the basis for the application of atomic energy and won the Nobel Prize in 1921. His name was Albert Einstein. While on a lecture tour in America, the Nazis government confiscated his home. Einstein then became a U.S. citizen. In 1952 he was offered the position of President of Israel, but declined. Albert Einstein's statement inscribed in Fine Hall at Princeton University reads: "God is clever, but not dishonest."

American Minute
March 15th

On this day, March 15, 1984, the Senate voted down voluntary silent prayer in public schools. President Ronald Reagan responded: "I am deeply disappointed that, although a majority of the Senate voted for it, the school prayer amendment fell short." President Reagan later remarked: "In 1962, the Supreme Court...banned the...saying of prayers. In 1963, the Court banned the reading of the Bible in our public schools,...a series of assaults were made in one court after another... Without God there is no virtue because there is no prompting of the conscience,...without God democracy will not and cannot long endure."

American Minute
March 16th

He was called the "Chief Architect of the Constitution," and wrote many of the Federalist Papers, which where instrumental in convincing the States to ratify the Constitution. He introduced the First Amendment in the first session of Congress. As President, he and his wife Dolly had to flee the White House when the British set it on fire during the War of 1812. He responded by proclaiming a National Day of Public Humiliation, Fasting and Prayer to Almighty God. Who was he? James Madison, born this day, March 16, 1751. James Madison, in his Memorial and Remonstrance, wrote: "Before any man can be considered as a member of Civil Society, he must be considered as a subject of the Governor of the Universe."

American Minute
March 17th

March 17th, around 461 AD, St. Patrick died. As a teenager, the Roman Legions protecting his community in Britain were withdrawn to defend Rome from invading tribes, like the Huns. Unprotected, Britain was attacked by raiders, who carried away thousands. Patrick was captured and sold as a slave in Ireland, which was ruled by the Druids, who practiced human sacrifice. For six years Patrick herded animals until he escaped. In his forties he had a dream calling him back to Ireland. In his Confession, he wrote: "In the depth of the night, I saw a man named Victoricus coming as if from Ireland, with innumerable letters, and he gave me one and while I was reading I thought I heard the voice of those near the western sea call out: 'Please, holy boy, come and walk among us again.' Their cry pierced my very heart, and I could read no more, and so I awoke." Patrick returned to Ireland, confronted the Druids, converted Chieftains, and used the three-leaf clover to teach the Trinity. Baptizing 120,000 and founding 300 churches, he wrote: "Patrick the sinner, an unlearned man to be sure. None should ever say that it was my ignorance that accomplished any small thing, it was the gift of God."

American Minute
March 18th

On this date, March 18, 1845 missionary John Chapman died, better known as Johnny Appleseed. His father was one of the Minutemen who fought the British at Concord in 1775. Collecting apple seeds from cider presses in western Pennsylvania, he began planting nurseries from the Alleghenies to central Ohio, giving thousands of seedlings to pioneers. Bare foot, wearing a mush pan over his eccentric long hair, and an old coffee sack over his shoulders, Johnny's harmony with the Indians and devotion to the Bible led William Venable to write: "Remember Johnny Appleseed-All ye who love the apple-He served his kind by word and deed-In God's grand greenwood chapel."

American Minute
March 19th

William Bradford was born this day, March 19, 1590. He sailed with the Pilgrims on the Mayflower and was chosen as their governor in 1621, being reelected 30 times until his death. In his History of the Plymouth Plantation, William Bradford wrote of the Pilgrims' plight: "What could now sustaine them but ye spirite of God and His grace? May not and ought not the children of these fathers rightly say: Our fathers...came over this great ocean, and were ready to perish in this wilderness; but they cried unto ye Lord, and He heard their voyce... All great and honourable actions are accompanied with great difficulties...Last and not least, they cherished a great hope and inward zeal of laying good foundations, or at least making some ways toward it, for the propagation and advance of the gospel of the kingdom of Christ in the remote parts of the world, even though they should be but stepping stones to others in the performance of so great a work."

American Minute
March 20th

On this date, March 20, 1727, Sir Isaac Newton, one of the world's greatest scientists, died. With his mother widowed twice, he was raised by his grandmother before being sent off to grammar school and later Cambridge. He discovered calculus, the laws of gravity and built the first reflecting telescope. Using a prism, Newton demonstrated how a beam of sunlight contained of all the colors of the rainbow. In 1704, in his work titled, Optics, Sir Isaac Newton stated: "God in the beginning formed matter." Regarding the Bible, Sir Isaac Newton wrote: "The system of revealed truth which this Book contains is like that of the universe, concealed from common observation yet the labors of the centuries have established its Divine origin."

American Minute
March 21st

March 21, 1685, Johann Sebastian Bach was born. By the age of ten, both his parents had died. At eighteen he was appointed organist at a church, followed by positions in royal courts. Once he was imprisoned because the duke he worked for did not want him seeking employment elsewhere. Widowed with seven children, he remarried and had thirteen more. Bach composed hundreds of pieces, sometimes at the rate of one per week and influenced composers such as Mozart and Beethoven. John Sebastian Bach stated: "The aim...of all music should be none other than the glory of God and the refreshment of the soul." In his Bible Reading Proclamation (1990), President George Bush stated: "The Bible has had a critical impact upon the development of Western civilization.. Western literature, art, and music are filled with images and ideas that can be traced to its pages." Justice Robert Jackson concurred in McCollum v. Board of Education (1948): "It would not seem practical to teach either practice or appreciation of the arts if we are to forbid exposure of youth to any religious influences. Music without sacred music would be incomplete, even from a secular point of view."

American Minute
March 22nd

On this date, March 22, 1758, Princeton University President Jonathan Edwards died as a result of a smallpox inoculation. Himself a Yale graduate, being valedictorian of his class, Jonathan Edwards' preaching began the Great Awakening, a revival of such proportions that history credits it with uniting the colonies prior to the Revolution. Of this awakening, Benjamin Franklin wrote: "It was wonderful to see... From being thoughtless or indifferent...it seemed as if all the world were growing religious, so that one could not walk thro' the town in an evening without hearing psalms sung in...every street."

American Minute
March 23rd

*O*n this date, March 23, 1775, Patrick Henry spoke to the Second Virginia Convention, which, because of British hostilities, was meeting in St. John's Church. He proclaimed: "There is a just God who presides over the destines of nations...who will raise up friends to fight our battle for us. The battle, sir, is not to the strong alone; it is to the vigilant, the active, the brave.... Patrick Henry concluded: "Is life so dear, or peace so sweet, as to be purchased at the price of chains and slavery? Forbid it, Almighty God! I know not what course others may take; but as for me, give me liberty or give me death."

American Minute
March 24th

Rufus King was born this day, March 24, 1755. He was one of the signers of the U.S. Constitution, noted for being one of the youngest delegates at the Constitutional Convention, only 32 years old. A Harvard graduate, Rufus had been an aide to General Sullivan during the Revolutionary War. He later served as U.S. Minister to England and was a Senator from New York. In a speech made before the Senate at the time Missouri was petitioning for statehood, Rufus King stated: "I hold that all laws...imposing...slavery upon any human being are absolutely void because they are contrary to the law of nature, which is the law of God."

American Minute
March 25th

"*O*ld Hickory." During the Revolution, young Andrew Jackson refused to polish the boots of a British officer and was slashed on the arm with a sword and jailed. His mother died of prison fever while caring for captured American soldiers. Jackson carried a bullet in his body from a duel defending his wife's honor. In the War of 1812, General Jackson defeated over 2,000 British in the Battle of New Orleans. In January of 1835, President Andrew Jackson survived an assassination attempt when a bearded man fired two pistols at him at point blank range. On this day, March 25, 1835, Andrew Jackson wrote in a letter: "I was brought up a rigid Presbyterian, to which I have always adhered. Our excellent Constitution guarantees to every one freedom of religion, and charity tells us (and you know Charity is the real basis of all true religion)...judge the tree by its fruit. All who profess Christianity believe in a Saviour, and that by and through Him we must be saved." Jackson concluded: "We ought, therefore, to consider all good Christians whose walks correspond with their professions, be they Presbyterian, Episcopalian, Baptist, Methodist or Roman Catholic."

American Minute
March 26th

Richard Allen was born to slave parents in Philadelphia and sold with his family to a plantation in Dover, Delaware. With the permission of his master, he began attending the Methodist meetings and learned to read and write. Richard Allen was converted at age 16 and is said to have worked harder to prove that Christianity did not make slaves worse servants. He then invited a minister to visit and preach to his master, resulting in his master's conversion after hearing that on the Day of Judgement slaveholders would be "weighed in the balance and found wanting." His repentant master then made arrangements for Richard, now 26, to become free. Richard Allen became a licensed exhorter and founded the African Methodist Episcopal Church, their building being dedicated by Francis Asbury, the circuit-riding preacher who became the Methodists' first American Bishop. By the time of Richard Allen's death, this day, March 26, 1831, the African Methodist Episcopal Church had grown to over 10,000 members.

American Minute
March 27th

*H*e was the grandson of the sixth president, John Quincy Adams, and the great-grandson of John Adams, the second President. His name was Henry Adams, and he died this day, March 27, 1918. An American philosopher and historian, Henry Adams authored a nine volume work titled: History of the United States. With insight from his unique heritage going back to the founding of the United States, Henry Adams wrote: "The Pilgrims of Plymouth, the Puritans of Boston, the Quakers of Pennsylvania, all avowed a moral purpose, and began by making institutions that consciously reflected a moral idea."

American Minute
March 28th

On this date, March 28, 1885, the Salvation Army was officially organized in the United States. It was begun in England by "General" William Booth in 1865, who conducted meetings among the poor in London's East End slums. Originally named the Christian Mission, he designed uniforms and adopted a semi-military system of leadership. Today thousands of officers, both men and women, minister across the globe. In 1965, one hundred years after its founding, President Lyndon Johnson remarked to the Salvation Army in New York: "For a century now, the Salvation Army has offered food to the hungry and shelter to the homeless-in clinics and children's homes, through disaster relief, in prison and welfare work, and a thousand other endeavors...But you have not stopped there... The Salvation Army has reminded men that physical well-being is just not enough; that spiritual rebirth is the most pressing need of our time and of every time; that the world cannot be changed unless men change."

American Minute
March 29th

*T*enth President John Tyler was born this day in March 29, 1790. He was the first Vice-President ever to assume the Presidency when William Henry Harrison died after only one month in office. To mourn his death, President John Tyler's first act in office was to proclaim a National Day of Fasting and Prayer, in which he stated: "When a Christian people feel themselves to be overtaken by a great public calamity, it becomes them to humble themselves under the dispensation of Divine Providence, to recognize His righteous government over the children of men...and to supplicate His merciful protection for the future."

American Minute
March 30th

During the Civil War, after issuing his Emancipation Proclamation, President Abraham Lincoln set a National Day of Humiliation, Fasting and Prayer, March 30, 1863, stating: "It is the duty of nations...to own their dependence upon the overruling power of God, to confess their sins...with assured hope that genuine repentance will lead to mercy...The awful calamity of civil war...may be but a punishment inflicted upon us for our presumptuous sins...We have been the recipients of the choicest bounties of Heaven...We have grown in numbers, wealth and power as no other nation has ever grown. But we have forgotten God. We have forgotten the gracious Hand which preserved us in peace, and multiplied and enriched and strengthened us; and we have vainly imagined, in the deceitfulness of our hearts, that all these blessings were produced by some superior wisdom and virtue of our own. Intoxicated with unbroken success, we have become too self-sufficient to feel the necessity of redeeming and preserving grace, too proud to pray to the God that made us! It behooves us then to humble ourselves before the offended Power, to confess our national sins and to pray for...forgiveness."

American Minute
March 31st

Queen Ka'ahumanu served as regent-prime minister of Hawaii after the death of her husband, King Kamehameha. Together with her son, King Kamehameha II, they ended all idolatry and human sacrifice on the islands. On this date, March 31, 1820, the first missionaries, led by Hiram Bingham, arrived in Hawaii on the ship, Thaddeus. Hiram learned the Hawaiian language, devised a twelve letter alphabet and, with his associates, translated the Bible into Hawaiian. He originated Hawaii's first newspaper and pastored the first church. The Queen received Christ and helped spread the Gospel throughout the islands. Just prior to her death, Queen Ka'ahumanu was presented with the newly completed version of the New Testament in the Hawaiian language. Her last words were: "I am going where the mansions are ready."

American Minute
April 1st

60,000 U.S. troops landed on the Island of Okinawa this day, April 1, 1945, in the largest amphibious attack mounted by the Americans in the Pacific war. One of the bloodiest campaigns, it cost Americans 12,000 dead, 36,000 wounded and 400 ships sunk or damaged. Though Japan's losses exceeded 100,000, their kamikaze suicide attacks grew more intense, not relenting until the bombing of Hiroshima. After receiving Japan's surrender in Tokyo Bay, General Douglas MacArthur stated: "Let us pray that peace be now restored to the world and that God will preserve it always."

American Minute
April 2nd

*T*he world of communication was revolutionized by a man who died this day, April 2, 1872. His name: Samuel Morse. He invented the telegraph and the Morse Code. An outstanding portrait artist in his own right, founding the National Academy of Design, Morse erected the first telegraph lines between Baltimore and the U.S. Supreme Court chamber in Washington, D.C. in 1844. The first message he sent over this new communication system was only four words, a verse from the Bible, Numbers 23:23: "What hath God Wrought! "

American Minute
April 3rd

The story "A Man Without a Country" was partially based on the life of Benedict Arnold, the American patriot turned traitor, yet the British never trusted him so he died a lonely man "without a county." This classic was written by Edward Everett Hale, born this day, April 3, 1822. The son of the editor of the Boston Daily Advertiser and nephew of Revolutionary hero Nathan Hale, Edward entered Harvard College at age 13 and after graduation taught at the prestigious Boston Latin School. He published more than fifty books, spoke out against slavery, served forty-five years as pastor of Boston's South Congregational Church and in 1903 became Chaplain of the United States Senate. Edward Everett Hale wrote: "I am only one, but I am one. I cannot do everything, but I can do something. What I can do, I should do and, with the help of God, I will do."

American Minute
April 4th

Reverend Martin Luther King, Jr., was assassinated this day, April 4th, 1968. He had been pastor of Ebenezer Baptist Church in Atlanta and rose to national prominence through the Southern Christian Leadership Conference. Awarded the Nobel Prize in 1964, Congress set aside his birthday as a National Holiday. Martin Luther King said: "I have a dream...where little black boys and black girls will be able to join hands with little white boys and white girls and walk together as sisters and brothers....I have a dream that one day...the glory of the Lord shall be revealed, and all flesh shall see it....This will be the day when all of God's children will be able to sing...'Let Freedom Ring...' When we let it ring...we will be able to speed up that day when all of God's children, black men and white men, Jews and Gentiles, Protestants and Catholics, will be able to join hands and sing in the words of the old Negro spiritual, "Free at last! Free at last! Thank God Almighty, we are free at last!"

American Minute
April 5th

Born in a slave hut this day, April 5th, 1856, was Booker T. Washington. In dire poverty after the Civil War, he moved to West Virginia to work in a salt furnace and coal mine. At age 16 he walked nearly 500 miles to attend Hampton Institute. After graduation, he taught in West Virginia until he founded Tuskegee Institute in Alabama, where he recruited George Washington Carver as a professor. At his death, the school boasted of 1,500 students, and a faculty of 200 teaching 38 trades. The first African American to have his image on a U.S. coin and postage stamp, Booker T. Washington wrote in his book, Up From Slavery (1907): "If no other consideration had convinced me of the value of the Christian life, the Christlike work which the Church of all denominations in America has done during the last thirty-five years for the elevation of the black man would have made me a Christian."

American Minute
April 6th

Today, April 6, 1917, the United States entered World War I by declaring war on Germany. Within the next two years, America enlisted four million soldiers and spent 35 billion dollars, resulting in an Allied victory. In a National Day of Prayer Proclamation, President Woodrow Wilson stated: "In view of the entrance of our nation into the vast and awful war which now afflicts the greater part of the world...I set apart...a day upon which our people should...offer concerted prayer to Almighty God for His divine aid in the success of our arms."

American Minute
April 7th

The "Greatest Show on Earth" was a gigantic success, owned by American showman P.T. Barnum, who died this day, April 7, 1891. His biggest draw, selling 20 million tickets, was General Tom Thumb, a man only 25 inches tall. They were received by President Lincoln and even gave a command performance before Queen Victoria. The circus not being open Sundays, Barnum let his "Great Roman Hippodrome" in New York be used by Dwight L. Moody for large evangelistic campaigns. P.T. Barnum stated: "Most persons, on the whole, are humbugged by believing too little, than by believing too much."

American Minute
April 8th

*F*ive Star General Omar Bradley died this day, April 8, 1981. During World War II, he commanded the Army in North Africa and in 1944, led the 12th Army Group in France and Germany, which consisted of one million men in four armies. In 1950, he became the first chairman of the Joint Chiefs of Staff. Omar Bradley stated: "We have grasped the mystery of the atom and rejected the Sermon on the Mount.... The world has achieved brilliance without conscience. Ours is a world of nuclear giants and ethical infants."

American Minute
April 9th

The Civil War ended this day, April 9, 1865, as General Robert E. Lee surrendered to General Ulysses S. Grant in the home of Wilmer McLean near Appomattox Court House, Virginia. The War had resulted in approximately 258,000 Confederate deaths and 360,000 Union deaths. General Lee took off his sword and handed it to General Grant, and Grant handed it back. The next day, General Lee issued his final order: "After four years of arduous service, marked by unsurpassed courage and fortitude.... I have determined to avoid the useless sacrifice of those whose past services have endeared them to their countrymen. By the terms of the agreement, officers and men can return to their homes." Robert E. Lee concluded: "I earnestly pray that a merciful God will extend to you His blessing and protection."

American Minute
April 10th

Millions of people in 91 countries are helped by The Salvation Army, founded by William Booth, who was born this day, April 10, 1829. He began by ministering to the poor, drunk and outcast, and fought to end teenage prostitution in England. Awarded an honorary degree from Oxford, he traveled the U.S., met with President Theodore Roosevelt and was given the honor of opening a session of the United States Senate with prayer. Booth wrote: "While there is a drunkard left, while there is a lost girl upon the streets, where there remains one dark soul without the light of God - I'll fight! I'll fight to the very end."

American Minute
April 11th

*"H*ouston, we've had a problem" were the fateful word received from Apollo 13, which was launched for the moon this day, April 11, 1970. Mission control identified that an oxygen tank had exploded, irreparably damaging the craft. Special prayer services were held at the Chicago Board of Trade, at St. Peter's Basilica by the Pope, at the Wailing Wall in Jerusalem and reported in The New York Times. Even the U.S. Senate adopted a resolution urging prayer. In sub-zero temperature, the crew ingeniously pieced together an oxygen filter, jump-charged the command module batteries, and manually steered the ship to land successfully in the ocean near a raging hurricane.

American Minute
April 12th

*L*ess than two months after Lincoln was inaugurated President, the Civil War began this day, April 12, 1861, with Confederate troops in Charleston, South Carolina, firing upon Fort Sumter. The Confederate Army was unstoppable, twice winning battles at Bull Run, Virginia, just twenty miles from Washington, D.C., forcing the Union troops to retreat to the fortifications of the Capitol. It wasn't until the Battle of Gettysburg, over two years into the war, that the tide began to turn. President Lincoln confided: "I have been driven many times upon my knees by the overwhelming conviction that I had nowhere else to go."

American Minute
April 13th

On this day, April 13, 1743, the 3rd U.S. President was born. He approved the Louisiana Purchase and commissioned Lewis and Clark to explore it. Best known for drafting the Declaration of Independence, he was also Governor of Virginia. His name was Thomas Jefferson. Exerpts of Jefferson's various writings are inscribed on the walls of the Jefferson Memorial in Washington, DC: "God who gave us life gave us liberty. Can the liberties of a nation be secure when we have removed a conviction that these liberties are the gift of God? Indeed I tremble for my country when I reflect that God is just, that his justice cannot sleep forever."

American Minute
April 14th

Noah Webster published the first edition of his Dictionary on this day, April 14, 1828. This 26-year project standardized the spelling of the English language. With 30,000 new definitions, it gave American English its first identity. Proving unprofitable, though, the rights to reprint were purchased after Webster's death by George and Charles Merriam. In the preface of his original edition, Noah Webster wrote: "To that great and benevolent Being, who, during the preparation of this work...has borne me and my manuscripts in safety across the Atlantic, and given me strength...to bring the work to a close, ...present...my most grateful acknowledgments."

American Minute
April 15th

April 15, the day income taxes are due to the IRS, is the day the Titanic sank in the North Atlantic in the year 1912. It had struck an iceberg the night before, just five days after departing from England on its maiden voyage. Over 1500 lost their lives. Also on April 15, President Abraham Lincoln died in 1865. He had been shot the night before in Ford's Theater by John Wilkes Booth, just five days after the Civil War ended. Over a half a million lost their lives in that War. President Lincoln, whose last act in office was to sign the bill placing "In God We Trust" on our national coins, declared in a speech at Independence Hall, Philadelphia, 1861: "The Declaration of Independence gave liberty not alone to the people of this country, but hope to all the world, for all future time. It was that which gave promise that in due time the weights would be lifted from the shoulders of all men, and that all should have an equal chance. This is the sentiment embodied in the Declaration of Independence....I would rather be assassinated on this spot than surrender it."

American Minute
April 16th

*I*n 1859, on this day, April 16, French historian Alexis de Tocqueville died. For nine months he had traveled the U.S. to observe its institutions, writing his famous work, Democracy in America, published 1835, which has been described as "the most comprehensive...analysis of... character and society in America...ever...written." In it, de Tocqueville wrote: "Upon my arrival in the United States the religious aspect of the country was the first thing that struck my attention.... In France I had almost always seen the spirit of religion and the spirit of freedom marching in opposite directions. But in America I found they were intimately united."

American Minute
April 17th

On this day, April 17, 1790, the son of a poor candle-maker died. The 15th of 17 children, he apprenticed as a printer, and published a popular almanac. He retired at age 42, then taught himself five languages, invented the rocking chair, bifocal glasses, and the lighting rod, which earned him degrees from Harvard and Yale. He helped found the University of Pennsylvania, a hospital, America's first postal system and fire department. He became the governor of Pennsylvania, signed the Declaration of Independence and called for prayer at the Constitutional Convention. He was also president of America's first anti-slavery society. His name was Ben Franklin. In his Poor Richard's Almanac (May 1757), Ben Franklin wrote: "Work as if you were to live 100 years; pray as if you were to die tomorrow."

American Minute
April 18th

Plymouth Colony founder William Brewster died this day, April 18, 1644. He helped lead the Pilgrim's church in England, allowing them to meet for worship at his home. He was captured, imprisoned, and later fled with them to Holland. He sailed with the Pilgrims to America, signed the Mayflower Compact and was elected a ruling elder. Governor William Bradford wrote of him: "My dear and loving friend, Mr. William Brewster...had...suffered much...for...the gospel's sake and...this poor persecuted church for over thirty-five years in England, Holland, and this wilderness."

American Minute
April 19th

*P*aul Revere was captured along the way, but William Dawes and Samuel Prescott continued the midnight ride from Boston's Old North Church to warn the inhabitants of Concord that British troops were coming to seize their guns. In early dawn, April 19, 1775, American "Minutemen," as poet Emerson wrote, fired the "shot heard round the world" by confronting the British on Lexington Green and at Concord's Old North Bridge. The conflict began that in eight years would end in independence. New England celebrates this as "Patriots' Day." General Douglas MacArthur retired from 48 years of patriotic service this day, April 19, 1951. The most decorated soldier in U.S. history, he served in France in WWI, was Superintendent of West Point and the youngest Army Chief of Staff. Supreme Allied Commander in the Pacific in WWII, he received Japan's surrender. He commanded UN forces against North Korea, but was dismissed by President Truman for not fighting a limited war. Douglas MacArthur said: "Like the old soldier of that ballad, I now close my military career and just fade away, an old soldier who has tried to do his duty as God gave him the light to see that duty."

American Minute
April 20th

The Indians of New York, New Jersey, and Pennsylvania had been ministered to by colonial missionary David Brainerd, born this day, April 20, 1718. With his interpreter, Moses Tinda Tautamy, he rode horseback along the Susquehanna and Delaware Rivers, camping at night. David Brainerd contracted tuberculosis and was nursed at the home of Princeton University president Jonathan Edwards, eventually dying at the age of 29. Though the number of converts during his lifetime were few, his diary has inspired millions around the world, including John Wesley, missionary William Carey and devotional writer Oswald J. Smith. David Brainerd wrote: "Oh, how precious is time, and how it pains me to see it slide away, while I do so little to any good purpose. Oh, that God would make me more fruitful."

American Minute
April 21st

"**M**ark Twain," a river measurement meaning "twelve feet deep," was the pen name of Samuel Langhorne Clemens, who died this day, April 21, 1910. Growing up along the Mississippi, he left school at age twelve when his father died and became a printer's apprentice. He piloted steamboats, but the War between the States suspended all river traffic. Famous for such works as "Adventures of Huckleberry Finn" and "Tom Sawyer," he was responsible for talking Ulysses S. Grant into writing memoirs of the Civil War. In his classic style, Mark Twain remarked: "If the Ten Commandments were not written by Moses, then they were written by another fellow of the same name."

American Minute
April 22nd

A gunshot at high noon on this day, April 22, 1889, began the famous Oklahoma land rush. Within nine hours some two million acres became the private property of settlers who staked their claims. Riding as fast as they could, many found desirable plots already taken by "Sooners," individuals who entered the territory sooner than was permitted. The remaining land was assigned to the various Indian tribes, who joined together in approving the Constitution of the State of Oklahoma in 1907. The Preamble begins: "Invoking the guidance of Almighty God, in order to secure and perpetuate the blessing of liberty; to secure just and rightful government; to promote our mutual welfare and happiness, we, the people of the State of Oklahoma, do ordain and establish this Constitution."

American Minute
April 23rd

William Shakespeare was born this day, April 23, 1564. His 37 plays have impacted world literature. He married Ann Hathaway, had three children, moved to London, and became shareholding director of the Globe Theater, writing such classics as Hamlet, Macbeth, Othello, and A Midsummer Night's Dream. Four years before the Pilgrims landed in America at Plymouth Rock, William Shakespeare died on this same day, April 23, in the year 1616. Shakespeare wrote in his Will: "I commend my soul into the hands of God, my Creator, hoping and assuredly believing, through the only merits of Jesus Christ, my Saviour, to be made partaker of life everlasting." Carved on William Shakespeare's Tombstone in the Holy Trinity Church, Stratford-on-Avon, England, are the lines: "Good Friend For Jesus Sake Forbeare, To Digg The Dust Enclosed Heare. Blese Be Ye Man Spares Thes Stones, And Curst Be He Moves My Bones."

American Minute
April 24th

*O*riginally for legislators to do research, it was begun this day, April 24, 1800, with a five thousand dollar allocation from Congress. The British set fire to it during the War of 1812, burning hundreds books, but the Library of Congress was restocked by Thomas Jefferson, who provided over six thousand volumes. It has since grown to be one of the largest libraries in the world. Relocated to its present site in 1897, the Library of Congress is inscribed with the verse: "What does the Lord require of thee, but to do justly, love mercy and walk humbly with thy God."

American Minute
April 25th

The U.S. Senate, starting this day, April 25, 1789, decided to open every session with prayer. This continued the practice of the Continental Congress during the Revolution, as Ben Franklin remarked "In the beginning of the Contest with Great Britain, when we were sensible of danger, we had daily prayer in this room for Divine protection." The first Senate Chaplain was Bishop Samuel Provoost, who conducted George Washington's Inaugural Service at St. Paul's Chapel. All 62 Senate Chaplains have been Christian, though leaders of other faiths have periodically been invited to offer prayer. The U.S. Senate Chaplain after World War II was Peter Marshall, who prayed: "Our liberty is under God and can be found nowhere else. May our faith be...not merely stamped upon our coins, but expressed in our lives."

American Minute
April 26th

*E*nglish settlers landed in North America on this day, April 26, 1607, at the site of Cape Henry, named for Prince Henry of Wales. Their first act was to erect a wooden cross and commence a prayer meeting. They ascended the James River, named for King James, and settled Jamestown, Virginia, the first permanent English settlement in America. Virginia, so named for the "Virgin Queen" Elizabeth, stated in its Charter: "For the Furtherance of so noble a Work...in propagating of Christian Religion to such People, as yet live in Darkness and miserable Ignorance of the true Knowledge and Worship of God."

American Minute
April 27th

*F*orced to resign from the Army for excessive drinking, he failed as a farmer and a businessman. Not until he volunteered for the Civil War did things changed. He was promoted to brigadier general, captured Fort Henry and Vicksburg, and established Union control of the Mississippi. Lincoln then placed him over the entire Army and within a year he forced Lee to surrender. His name: Ulysses S. Grant, who was born this day, April 27, 1822. As the 18th President, Grant stated: "It seems fitting that on the occurrence of the hundredth anniversary of our existence as a nation a grateful acknowledgment should be made to Almighty God for the protection and the bounties which He has vouchsafed to our beloved country."

American Minute
April 28th

Leading the charge at the Battle of Trenton, a musket ball struck his shoulder, hitting an artery. He recovered and continued to fight for General Washington, becoming friends with French officer Lafayette. After the Revolution, he studied law under Thomas Jefferson, was elected Senator, Governor of Virginia, and Secretary of State. He negotiated the Louisiana Purchase and set the Monroe Doctrine. Who was he? James Monroe, the fifth President of the United States, born this day, April 28, 1758. In his First Annual Message to Congress, 1817, President James Monroe stated: "For advantages so numerous and highly important it is our duty to unite in grateful acknowledgments to that Omnipotent Being from whom they are derived, and in unceasing prayer that He will endow us with virtue and strength to maintain and hand them down in their utmost purity to our latest posterity."

American Minute
April 29th

"*D*amn the torpedoes! Full steam ahead!" were the words of Admiral David Farragut, who first captured Mobile, Alabama, and then on this day, April 29, 1862, captured New Orleans. Under tremendous fire, he breached the heavy chain cable that was stretched across the Mississippi, and courageously led his ships up the channel filled with mines, called "torpedoes." The loss of New Orleans was a major disaster for the South, as it was the Confederacy's largest city. During his last illness, David Farragut, the Navy's first four star Admiral, asked for a clergyman to pray to the Lord for him, saying: "He must be my pilot now!"

American Minute
April 30th

The size of the U.S. doubled this day, April 30, 1803, with the Louisiana Purchase. Nearly a million square miles, at less than three cents an acre - it was the greatest land bargain in history! How did it happen? Napoleon Bonaparte needed money quickly for his military campaigns, therefore he sold all the French controlled land west of the Mississippi for just fifteen million dollars. Napoleon fought in Europe, Egypt and Russia, yet in the end he was banished to the tiny island of St. Helena in the South Atlantic, where he commented to General Count de Montholon: "Alexander, Caesar, Charlemagne, and myself founded empires; but upon what foundation did we rest the creations of our genius? Upon force! But Jesus Christ founded His upon love; and at this hour millions of men would die for Him."

American Minute
May 1st

May 1st, 305 AD, the most powerful man in the world, Emperor Diocletian, stepped down from ruling Rome. Two years prior he began a systematic persecution of Christians, intending to exterminate them. He forbade worship, burned books, arrested clergy, and demanded pagan sacrifices. From Europe to North Africa, hundreds were martyred. Suddenly Diocletian was struck with a painful intestinal disease and resigned. Eight years later Emperor Constantine ended persecution of Christians. In 1984, President Reagan said: "In the fourth century, a monk thought he heard God telling him to go to Rome...He followed a crowd into the Coliseum and saw the gladiators. He realized they were going to fight to the death. He cried out, 'In the Name of Christ, stop!'...made his way through the crowd and climbed the wall into the arena.... As he was pleading with the gladiators...one of them plunged his sword into his body...his last words were, 'In the Name of Christ, stop!' Suddenly the gladiators stood looking at this tiny form...In dead silence, everyone left. That was the last battle in the Coliseum. One tiny voice...'In the Name of Christ, stop!' We could be saying that today."

American Minute
May 2nd

The director of the FBI, J. Edgar Hoover, died this day, May 2, 1972. For forty-eight years, under eight U.S. Presidents, he oversaw the Federal Bureau of Investigation, becoming famous for his dramatic campaigns to stop gangsters and organized crime. He established the use of the fingerprint in law enforcement, and successfully tracked down well-known criminals. FDR gave him the task of investigating foreign espionage and left-wing activist groups. J. Edgar Hoover stated: "The criminal is the product of spiritual starvation. Someone failed miserably to bring him to know God, love Him and serve Him."

American Minute
May 3rd

*H*e was a physician in the Revolutionary War, a member of the Continental Congress and signed the Constitution. He was Secretary of War under Washington and Adams, and helped plan the Military Academy at West Point. The Star-Spangled Banner was written while the British bombed the fort which was named for him. Who was he: James McHenry, who died this day, May 3, 1816. As president of the Baltimore Bible society, James McHenry stated: "Neither...let it be overlooked that public utility pleads most forcibly for the general distribution of the Holy Scriptures. The doctrines they preach...can alone secure to society order and peace."

American Minute
May 4th

Selling one million copies a year for over one hundred years, McGuffey's Readers were the mainstay of public education in America. Millions of school children read them, making them some of the most influential textbooks of all time. They were written by William McGuffey, who died this day, May 4, 1873. He was a professor at the University of Virginia, president of Ohio University, and formed one of nation's first teachers' associations. A lesson in McGuffey's Fifth Eclectic Reader stated: "How powerless conscience would become without the belief of a God."

American Minute
May 5th

President Washington declared a National Day of Prayer, as did President John Adams when France threatened war, President Madison during the War of 1812, , President Tyler when the previous president died, and President Taylor during a cholera epidemic. President Buchanan proclaimed a Day of Prayer to avert civil strife, as did President Lincoln during the Civil War, President Johnson when Lincoln was shot and President Woodrow Wilson during World War I. In 1952, President Truman made it an annual event, stating: "In times of national crisis when we are striving to strengthen the foundations of peace...we stand in special need of Divine support." President Reagan signed the Act making it the first Thursday in May, stating: "Americans in every generation have turned to their Maker in prayer...We have acknowledged both our dependence on Almighty God and the help He offers us as individuals and as a Nation...Now, Therefore, I, Ronald Reagan, President of the United States of America, do hereby proclaim May 5, 1988, as a National Day of Prayer. I call upon the citizens of our great Nation to gather together on that day in homes and places of worship to pray.

American Minute
May 6th

*I*n exchange for some brass buttons, and scarlet cloth worth about twenty-four dollars, Manhattan Island was purchased from the Manhattan Indian tribe on this day, May 6, 1626, by the Peter Minuit, Dutch Governor of the New Netherlands Province. Naming the Island New Amsterdam, it was later taken over by the British and renamed New York City. The original Charter of Freedoms for the colony stated: "The...colonists shall...in the speediest manner, endeavor to find out ways...whereby they may support a Minister and Schoolmaster, that thus the service of God and zeal for religion may not grow cool and be neglected."

American Minute
May 7th

World War II ended in Europe on this day, May 7, 1945, when German emissaries entered a schoolhouse in Reims, France, where General Dwight Eisenhower had his headquarters, and signed an unconditional surrender. The War in Europe had lasted five and half years and cost tens of millions of lives. After the war Eisenhower was elected the 34th President by the largest number of votes in history. In a nationally broadcast address from an American Legion event, 1955, President Eisenhower stated: "Without God there could be no American form of government nor an American way of life. Recognition of the Supreme Being is the first - the most basic - expression of Americanism."

American Minute
May 8th

The 33rd U.S. President was born this day, May 8, 1884. He was captain of a field artillery battery in France during World War I, judge in Jackson County, Missouri; a U.S. Senator; and Vice-President under Franklin D. Roosevelt. As President, he ended World War II by dropping the atomic bomb. His name: Harry S. Truman, who stated at the Attorney General's Conference on Law Enforcement, 1950: "The fundamental basis of this nation's laws was given to Moses on the Mount. The fundamental basis of our Bill of Rights comes from the teachings...of Isaiah and St. Paul. I don't think we emphasize that enough these days."

American Minute
May 9th

Mothers' Day was held in Boston in 1872 at the suggestion of Julia Ward Howe, writer of "The Battle Hymn of the Republic." But it was Anna Jarvis, daughter of a Methodist minister in Grafton, West Virginia, who made it a national event. During the Civil War, Anna's mother organized Mothers' Day Work Clubs to care for wounded soldiers, both Union and Confederate, raised money for medicine, inspected bottled milk, improved sanitation and hired women to care for families where mothers suffered from tuberculosis. In her honor, Anna Jarvis persuaded her church to set aside the 2nd Sunday in May, the anniversary of her mother's death, as a day to appreciate all mothers. Encouraged by the reception, Anna organized it in Philadelphia, then began a letter-writing campaign to ministers, businessmen and politicians to establish a national Mothers' Day. In response, on May 9, 1914, President Woodrow Wilson proclaimed the first National Mothers' Day as a "public expression of...love and reverence for the mothers of our country." In his Mother's Day Proclamation, 1986, President Ronald Reagan said: "A Jewish saying sums it up: 'God could not be everywhere-so He created mothers.'"

American Minute
May 10th

A surprise attack before dawn, on this day May 10, 1775, gave America one of its first great victories of the Revolutionary War. Ethan Allen, who commanded the Green Mountain Boys of Vermont, captured Fort Ticonderoga on Lake Champlain without the loss of a man, by overrunning the stronghold in the early morning while the British were still sleeping. Allen demanded immediate surrendered, whereupon the bewildered British captain asked in whose name such a request was being made. Ethan Allen responded: "In the Name of the Great Jehovah and the Continental Congress."

American Minute
May 11th

The son of a rabbi, he was born this day, May 11, 1888. When he was four-years old, he immigrated with his family from Russia to New York. Falling in love with America, he served in the U.S. infantry during World War I and wrote some of the country's most popular songs, including: "Alexander's Ragtime Band," "White Christmas" and "God Bless America," the royalties from which he gave to the Boy Scouts and Girl Scouts. Who was he? Irving Berlin, who in 1945 received the Army's Medal of Merit from President Truman, in 1955 received the Congressional Gold Medal from President Eisenhower, and in 1977 received the Freedom Medal from President Ford. "God Bless America, Land that I Love, Stand Beside Her, and Guide Her, Through the Night, with the Light From Above."

American Minute
May 12th

"*T*he Battle Hymn of the Republic" was performed for the first time this day, May 12, 1861, for Union recruits during the Civil War. Said to have been Lincoln's favorite song, it was written by Julia Ward Howe when she visited Washington and saw the city teeming with military horses and campfires burning. Sleeping unsoundly one night, Julia Ward Howe wrote her poem, which ends: "In the beauty of the lilies Christ was born across the sea; With a glory in his bosom that transfigures you and me: As he died to make men holy, let us die to make men free, While God is marching on."

American Minute
May 13th

The first settlers to establish a permanent English settlement in the New World landed in Jamestown, Virginia, this day, May 13, 1607. Many of the one hundred colonists sent out by the London Company died of hunger, malaria, exposure or were killed by Indians. When their minister died, they wrote: "In memory of the Reverend Robert Hunt...During his life our factions were ofte healed, and our greatest extremities so comforted that they seemed easy in comparison with what we endured after his...death. We all received from him...Holy Communion...as a pledge of reconciliation."

American Minute
May 14th

Midnight, May 14, 1948, the State of Israel came into being and was immediately recognized by the United States and the Soviet Union. A homeland for the thousands of Jews who were persecuted and displaced during World War II, it was attacked the next day by the Transjordanian Army, the Arab Legion, Egypt, Syria, Lebanon and Iraq. Against all odds, Israel survived. In November of 1948, President Harry S. Truman wrote to Dr. Chaim Weizmann, the first president of Israel: "I want to tell you how happy and impressed I have been at the remarkable progress made by the new State of Israel." In 1968, President Johnson stated: "America and Israel have a common love of human freedom and a democratic way of life....Through the centuries, through dispersion and through very grievous trials, your forefathers clung to their Jewish identity and their ties with the land of Israel. The prophet Isaiah foretold - 'And He shall set up an ensign for the nations and He shall assemble the outcasts of Israel and gather together the dispersed of Judah from all the four corners of the earth.' History knows no more moving example of persistence against the cruelest odds."

American Minute
May 15th

Army Day, Navy Day and Air Force Day were combined in 1949 to become Armed Forces Day, celebrated the third Saturday of May. This day honors the men and women of all armed forces, now serving under one Department of Defense. Army Day formerly was the date the US entered World War I, Navy Day was on President Theodore Roosevelt's birthday and Air Force Day was on the day the War Department established a division of aeronautics. . On Armed Forces Day, May 1995, Secretary of Defense William Perry stated: "In World War II, the United States Armed Forces helped defeat the forces of aggression and oppression on two sides of the globe....In the Cold War, we faced down the global Soviet threat. Today, our forces stand guard, at home and abroad, against a range of potential threats....On Armed Forces Day, the nation says thank you to our men and women in uniform, their families, and the communities that support them....Daniel Webster said, 'God grants liberty only to those who love it and are always ready to guard and defend it.'"

American Minute
May 16th

*S*eward's Folly is what Alaska was called when it was first purchase from the Russians, as it was thought to be of no value. Only when it was discovered to be rich in natural resources was appreciation shown to Secretary of State William Seward, who was born this day, May 16, 1801. Serving under Abraham Lincoln, he was wounded by an accomplice of John Wilkes Booth the same night Lincoln was shot. As the vice-president of the American Bible Society, 1836, William Seward stated: "I know not how long a republican government can flourish among a great people who have not the Bible; the experiment has never been tried."

American Minute
May 17th

Amazing! The first Chief Justice of the U.S. Supreme Court was also the president of the American Bible Society. Who was he? John Jay, who died this day, May 17, 1829. A member of the Continental Congress, even serving as its president, John Jay signed the Treaty of Paris with Benjamin Franklin and John Adams, officially ending the Revolutionary War. He helped ratify the Constitution by writing the Federalist Papers with Madison and Hamilton. In December of 1776, John Jay addressed the New York Convention, stating: "We have the highest reason to believe that the Almighty will not suffer slavery and the Gospel to go hand in hand. It cannot, it will not be."

American Minute
May 18th

On May 18, 1920, in a small town in Poland, Karol Wojtyla was born. A chemical worker during World War II, he risked punishment by Communists for being ordained a priest. In 1967, he became Archbishop of Krakow, and in 1978, Pope John Paul II, the first non-Italian pope since 1522. Leader of one billion Catholics, he spoke eight languages and traveled a million miles in 170 countries, more than any pope. In 1981, he survived an assassination attempt by a Muslim Turk, whom he forgave during a prison visit. The most recognized person in the world, Pope John Paul met with Presidents Carter, Reagan, Bush, Clinton and Bush. He helped end communism in Europe. The third longest papal term, he died April 2, 2005. President Bush ordered flags flown half staff. In 1993, greeted by President Clinton in Denver, Pope John Paul said: "The inalienable dignity of every human being and the rights which flow from that dignity-in the first place the right to life and the defense of life-are at the heart of the church's message." Pope John Paul ended: "In spite of divisions among Christians, 'all those justified by faith through baptism are incorporated into Christ...brothers and sisters in the Lord.'"

American Minute
May 19th

The invincible Spanish Armada sailed off this day, May 19, 1588, to conquer England. Queen Elizabeth relied on Sir Francis Drake, who used smaller, faster vessels and ingeniously sent burning ships at midnight downwind where the Spaniards were anchored, dispersing them in a panic. Aided by gale force winds half the Spanish fleet was wrecked. Had England lost, there would have been no Pilgrims, no New England, and no United States. A coin minted after the event in the Netherlands, 1588, showed on one side the ships of the Spanish Armada sinking and on the other side men kneeling under the inscription "Man Proposeth, God Disposeth."

American Minute
May 20th

*T*his day, May 20, 1927, at 7:52 am, one of the greatest feats in aviation began, as Charles Lindbergh departed Roosevelt Field in New York, in his silver monoplane named "The Spirit of St. Louis." Thirty-three and a half hours later he landed in France, completing the first solo flight across the Atlantic. At twenty-five years old, he was decorated by the president of France, the King of England, and President Calvin Coolidge. At the Institute of Aeronautical Sciences, February of 1954, Charles Lindbergh stated: "It was not the outer granduer of the Roman but the inner simplicity of the Christian that lived through the ages."

American Minute
May 21st

The American Red Cross was organized this day, May 21, 1881, by Clara Barton, a schoolteacher who had moved to Washington at the outbreak of the Civil War. She distributed relief supplies to wounded soldiers and, at the request of President Lincoln, aided in searching for missing men. She helped in hospitals in Cuba during the Spanish-American War and in Europe during the Franco-German war, working with Henri Dunant, founder of the International Red Cross. In May of 1918, at the opening of the Second Red Cross Drive in New York City, President Woodrow Wilson recognized those in this great service, stating: "Being members of the American Red Cross...a great fraternity and fellowship which extends all over the world...this cross which these ladies bore here today is an emblem of Christianity itself....When you think of this, you realize how the people of the United States are being drawn together into a great intimate family whose heart is being used for the service of the soldiers not only, but for the long night of suffering and terror, in order that they and men everywhere may see the dawn of a day of righteousness and justice and peace."

American Minute
May 22nd

A Signer of the Constitution who was licensed to preach? That was Hugh Williamson, delegate from North Carolina, who died this day, May 22, 1819 and was buried at Trinity Church. At age 24 he studied theology in Connecticut and was admitted in the Presbytery of Philadelphia. He preached two years, visiting and praying for the sick, but a chronic chest weakness would not permit him to continue a career of public speaking. He traveled to London to study medicine, but not before witnessing the Boston Tea Party, of which he testified before a Privy Counsel that if Britain did not change its policy, the Colonies would rebel. Dr. Hugh Williamson distinguished himself as a Surgeon General, caring for wounded soldiers during the Revolutionary War. He also helped his friend Dr. Benjamin Franklin conduct electrical experiments. In 1784, during the Congress of the Confederation, Williamson helped write the laws for the Northwest Territory, voting to forbid slavery and recommending the Territory "reserve the central section of every township for the maintenance of public schools and the section immediately to the northward for the support of religion."

American Minute
May 23rd

*F*ur trapper, Indian agent, and soldier; this was Kit Carson, who died this day, May 23, 1868. Carson's exploits west of the Mississippi were as famous as Daniel Boone's east. In January of 1868, Kit was appointed superintendent of Indian Affairs in Colorado. Though suffering severe breathing pain, he brought the Ute Indian Chiefs to Washington to arrange a treaty. As they toured northern cities, meeting crowds and posing for pictures with dignitaries such as John C. Fremont and General James Carleton, Kit became wearied. He almost died while staying with the Indian Chiefs at New York City's Metropolitan Hotel. Kit wrote: "I felt my head swell and my breath leaving me. Then, I woke...my face and head all wet. I was on the floor and the chief was holding my head on his arm and putting water on me. He was crying. He said, 'I thought you were dead. You called on your Lord Jesus, then shut your eyes and couldn't speak.' I did not know that I spoke...I do not know that I called on the Lord Jesus, but I might - it's only Him that can help me where I now stand...My wife must see me. If I was to write about this, or died out here, it would kill her. I must get home."

American Minute
May 24th

Abolitionist leader William Lloyd Garrison, died this day, May 24, 1879. He published the anti-slavery paper in Boston called "The Liberator," and founded the American Anti-Slavery Society in 1833. Suffering hundreds of death threats for his politically incorrect stand for the value of all human life, William Lloyd Garrison wrote: "I desire to thank God, that He enables me to disregard 'the fear of man which bringeth a snare,' and to speak His truth...and...while life-blood warms my throbbing veins...to oppose...the brutalizing sway - till Afric's chains are burst, and freedom rules the rescued land."

American Minute
May 25th

"The shot heard around the world " was a line in the famous poem "The Concord Hymn," recounting the Revolutionary War battle between the Minutemen and the British troops by a bridge in Concord, Massachusetts. It was written by poet Ralph Waldo Emerson, who was born this day, May 25, 1803. Being friends with such notable writers as Nathaniel Hawthorne and Louisa May Alcott, Emerson composed some of the best poems in American literature. Ralph Waldo Emerson stated: "America is another name for opportunity. Our whole history appears like a last effort of divine Providence in behalf of the human race."

American Minute
May 26th

On this day, May 26, 1907, a movie legend was born named Marion Michael Morrison, better known as John Wayne. He played football at USC and held some behind-the-scenes jobs at Fox Studios, before being discovered by director John Ford, who cast "The Duke" in many epic western and war films. Exemplifying courage, respect and patriotism, John Wayne stated in the album America-Why I Love Her: "If we want to keep these freedoms, we may have to fight again. God forbid, but if we do, let's always fight to win... Face the flag, son...and thank God it's still there."

American Minute
May 27th

*T*wentieth-Century Fox made a motion picture in 1955 titled "A Man Called Peter," about the life of U.S. Senate Chaplain Peter Marshall, who was born this day, May 27, 1902. He emigrated from Scotland, was ordained a Presbyterian minister, and became a U.S. citizen in 1938. A novel titled "Christy," written by his wife, Catherine, was made into a CBS television series. His son, Peter Marshall, Jr., is the nationally renown author of such best-selling books as: "The Light and the Glory," "From Sea to Shining Sea" and "Sounding Forth The Trumpet," which chronicle the Providential expansion of liberty throughout American history. In July of 1947, U.S. Senate Chaplain Peter Marshall opened a session of the 80th Congress with the prayer: "God of our Fathers, whose Almighty hand hath made and preserved our Nation... May it be ever understood that our Liberty is under God and...to the extent that America honors Thee, wilt Thou bless America."

American Minute
May 28th

*H*e left Yale for four years to fight in the Revolutionary War. After graduation, he became a lawyer and taught school in New York. Dissatisfied with the children's spelling books, he wrote the famous "Blue-Backed Speller," which sold over one hundred million copies. After twenty-six years of work, he published the first American Dictionary of the English Language. His name was Noah Webster, and he died this day, May 28, 1843. In his book, "The History of the United States," published in 1832, Noah Webster wrote: "All the miseries and evils which men suffer from vice, crime, ambition, injustice, oppression, slavery and war, proceed from their despising or neglecting the precepts contained in the Bible."

American Minute
May 29th

The 35th U.S. President was born this day, May 29, 1917. He was awarded the Navy's medal for heroism for his service during World War II, and the Pulitzer Prize for his book Profiles in Courage. The youngest man ever elected President, he served three years before being assassinated. His name: John F. Kennedy. In his Inaugural Address, January of 1961, President Kennedy stated: "The same revolutionary beliefs for which our forebears fought are still at issue around the globe - The belief that the rights of man come not from the generosity of the state but from the hand of God."

American Minute
May 30th

Southern women scattered spring flowers on the graves of both the Northern and Southern soldiers who died during the Civil War. This was the origin of Memorial Day, which in 1868 was set on May 30th. In 1968 it was moved to the last Monday in May. From the Spanish-American War, to World Wars I and II, Korea, Vietnam, Desert Storm, up through the present, all who gave their lives to preserve America's freedom are honored. Beginning in 1921, every President placed a wreath on the Tomb of the Unknown Soldier, which is guarded 24 hours a day, 365 days a year. The number 21 being the highest salute, the sentry takes 21 steps, faces the tomb for 21 seconds, turns and pauses 21 seconds, then retraces his steps. Inscribed on the Tomb is the phrase: "HERE RESTS IN HONORED GLORY AN AMERICAN SOLDIER KNOW BUT TO GOD." In his 1923 Memorial Address, Calvin Coolidge stated: "There can be no peace with the forces of evil. Peace comes only through the establishment of the supremacy of the forces of good. That way lies through sacrifice....'Greater love hath no man than this, that a man lay down his life for his friends.'"

American Minute
May 31st

At a Memorial Day event, May 31, 1923, Calvin Coolidge, the 30th President, gave a message titled "The Destiny of America," saying: "Settlers came here from mixed motives, some for...adventure, some for trade and refuge, but...generally defined.... They were intent upon establishing a Christian commonwealth in accordance to the principle of self-government.... It has been said that God sifted the nations that He might send choice grain into the wilderness." President Coolidge concluded: "Who can fail to see in it the hand of destiny? Who can doubt that it has been guided by a Divine Providence?"

American Minute
June 1st

"**D**on't Give Up The Ship!" were the dying words uttered this day, June 1, 1813 by Captain James Lawrence, as he lay on the deck of the U.S. Frigate Chesapeake. The British had bombarded them as they sailed out of Boston during the War of 1812. Captain Oliver Hazard Perry was so taken by his courage that he named his flagship on Lake Erie "Lawrence" and put Captain Lawrence's dying words on his battle flag. It later became the slogan of the U.S. Navy. After a great victory on Lake Erie, Captain Perry stated: "The prayers of my wife are answered."

American Minute
June 2nd

There was a marriage in the White House this day, June 2nd, 1886. One of three Presidents to marry while in office and the only President to wed on White House grounds, Grover Cleveland married Frances Folsom, and together they had five children. Cleveland was both the 22nd and 24th President, being the only person to serve a second term after being defeated following his first. President Grover Cleveland stated in his Second Inaugural Address, March of 1893: "Above all, I know there is a Supreme Being who rules the affairs of men and whose goodness and mercy have always followed the American people, and I know He will not turn from us now if we humbly and reverently seek His powerful aid."

American Minute
June 3rd

*T*he Dutch hoped there existed a water route across America to the Pacific, and they sent Henry Hudson to find it. Although he was unsuccessful, he did lay claim to the land along the Hudson River, so named for him. There the Dutch West India Company founded the colony of New Netherlands, receiving their charter this day, June 3, 1621. New Netherlands later became New York. The Dutch leader, called the "Staten Generaal," after which Staten Island was named, gave the regulation: "Colonists shall...by their Christian life and conduct, lead Indians...to the knowledge of God and His Word, without, however, persecuting anyone because of his faith."

American Minute
June 4th

The turning point in the Pacific War began today, June 4, 1942. American intelligence intercepted Japan's plans to capture Midway Island and from there Hawaii. The outnumbered U.S. Fleet ambushed the Japanese armada, but was losing badly. It was not until American dive bombers, navigating by guess and by God, sighted the Japanese aircraft carriers far below through a break in the clouds at the precise moment the Japanese planes had left to attack the U.S.S. Yorktown. In just five minutes, the screeching American dive bombers sank three Japanese carriers, and a fourth shortly after. This providential event turned the War and Japan was never again able to go on the offensive.

American Minute
June 5th

Today, June 5, 1967, the Six-Day War began. Egypt had 80,000 troops and 900 tanks advancing on Israel. Jordan and Syria, with Soviet weapons, violently shelled Jerusalem and Israeli villages. Cairo radio announced: "The hour has come in which we shall destroy Israel." The hot line between Washington and Moscow was used for the first time. In a surprise move, Israeli air force destroyed 400 Egyptian planes, courageously drove Syria from the Golan Heights and captured all of Jerusalem. In a CBS-TV interview, Prime Minister David Ben-Gurion stated: "In Israel, in order to be a realist you must believe in miracles." Seven months later, at a dinner at the LBJ Ranch in Texas, President Lyndon B. Johnson toasted Israeli Prime Minister Eshkol, saying: "That is our intention in the Middle East and throughout our world. To pursue peace. To find peace. To keep peace forever among men. If we are wise, if we are fortunate, if we work together-perhaps our Nation and all nations may know the joys of that promise God once made about the children of Israel: 'I will make a covenant of peace with them...it shall be an everlasting covenant.'"

American Minute
June 6th

"D-Day" June 6, 1944, one hundred and fifty-six thousand men landed on the Normandy coast of France. It was the largest invasion force in history. General Dwight Eisenhower, the Supreme Allied Commander, had issued the order: "You are about to embark upon the Great Crusade.... The hopes and prayers of liberty-loving people everywhere march with you.... Your task will not be an easy one. Your enemy is well trained, well equipped and battle-hardened. He will fight savagely." General Eisenhower concluded: "Let us all beseech the blessing of Almighty God upon this great and noble undertaking."

American Minute
June 7th

Daniel Boone began to explore Kentucky on this day, June 7, 1769. Six years later he brought the first settlers to Kentucky and founded the fort of Boonesboro. He was captured by the Shawnee Indians and taken to Detroit. There learned the British had incited an Indian attack on the Kentucky settlement. He escaped and his warning saved the town. As to his faith, Boone wrote to his wife in October of 1816: "The religion I have is to love and fear God, believe in Jesus Christ, do all the good to my neighbor, and myself that I can, do as little harm as I can help, and trust on God's mercy for the rest."

American Minute
June 8th

On June 8, 1845, "Old Hickory" died. Wounded by a sword during the Revolutionary War, he later fought the Seminole Indians, and in the War of 1812 defeated the British at New Orleans. He was governor of the Florida Territory, and is credited with having proposed the name "Tennessee" at that State's first convention. His beloved wife Rachel died just three months before he took office as the seventh President of the United States. His name? Andrew Jackson. In reference to the Bible, President Jackson stated: "That book, Sir, is the Rock upon which our republic rests."

American Minute
June 9th

Withholding taxes from people's paychecks began this day, June 9, 1943. Congress passed it as an emergency measure to get money to fight Hitler. The idea came from Beardsley Ruml, treasurer of Macy's and chairman of New York's Federal Reserve Bank. He called it the "pay-as-you-go" tax. So much money came in with so few complaints that it was continued after the war. President John F. Kennedy, in April of 1961, stated to Congress: "Introduced during the war when the income tax was extended to millions of new taxpayers, the wage-withholding system has been one of the most important and successful advances in our tax system in recent times. Initial difficulties were quickly overcome, and the new system helped the taxpayer no less than the tax collector." But Americans weren't always taxed. In a Veto Message to Congress, May of 1830, President Andrew Jackson stated: "Through the favor of an overruling and indulgent Providence our country is blessed with general prosperity and our citizens exempted from the pressure of taxation, which other less favored portions of the human family are obliged to bear."

American Minute
June 10th

The U.S. Naval Academy at Annapolis, Maryland, graduated its first class on this day, June 10, 1854. The Academy was established under the direction of George Bancroft, Secretary of the Navy for President James Polk. Bancroft was also known as the "father of American history," having written the first comprehensive history of the United States. In an address titled, "The Progress of Mankind," published in his work "Literary and Historical Miscellanies," George Bancroft stated: "The Divine Being should...be known, not as a distant Providence...but as God present in the flesh... The consciousness of an incarnate God carried peace into the bosom of humanity.... The idea of GOD WITH US dwelt and dwells in every system of thought that can pretend to vitality; in every oppressed people, whose struggles to be free have the promise of success; in every soul that sighs for redemption."

American Minute
June 11th

*H*e sent Paul Revere on his midnight ride to warn Lexington that the British were coming. A Harvard graduate, he was a successful doctor in Boston, but left his comfortable career when the British passed the hated "Stamp Act." With Samuel Adams, he organized the Provincial Congress to protest. Courageously fighting in the Battle of Bunker Hill, a monument marks the spot where he died. His name was Joseph Warren, born this day, June 11, 1741. On the second anniversary of the Boston Massacre, March of 1772, Joseph Warren stated: "If you perform your part, you must have the strongest confidence that the same Almighty Being who protected your pious and venerable forefathers...will still be mindful of you."

American Minute
June 12th

*H*e received the Distinguished Flying Cross for his service in the Pacific during World War II. He studied at Yale, was a congressman, ambassador to the U.N., CIA director and Vice-President under Ronald Reagan before becoming America's forty-first President. His name: George Bush, born this day, June 12, 1924. In his Inaugural Address, January of 1989, President Bush stated: "I have just repeated word for word the oath taken by George Washington 200 years ago, and the Bible on which I place my hand is the Bible on which he placed his.... And my first act as President is a prayer. I ask you to bow your heads."

American Minute
June 13th

Nineteen-year-old Marquis de Lafayette purchased a ship and sailed to America, arriving this day, June 13, 1777. Trained in the French Military, he was appointed a major general. He endured the freezing winter at Valley Forge, and fought at Brandywine, Barren Hill and Monmouth. He led troops against the traitor Benedict Arnold and commanded at Yorktown, pressuring Cornwallis to surrender. In July of 1791, George Washington wrote to Lafayette: "We must, however, place a confidence in that Providence who rules great events, trusting that out of confusion He will produce order, and, notwithstanding the dark clouds which may threaten at present, that right will ultimately be established."

American Minute
June 14th

Thirteen Stars and Thirteen Stripes. It was on this day, June 14, 1777, that the Second Continental Congress selected the Flag of the United States. In 1916, President Woodrow Wilson signed a Proclamation making this day "National Flag Day." On this day in 1954, President Dwight Eisenhower signed the Joint Resolution of Congress (Public Law 396) adding the phrase "One Nation Under God" to the Pledge of Allegiance. Eisenhower stated: "From this day forward, the millions of our school children will daily proclaim in every city and town, every village and rural school house, the dedication of our nation and our people to the Almighty. To anyone who truly loves America, nothing could be more inspiring than to contemplate this rededication of our youth, on each school morning, to our country's true meaning." Eisenhower concluded: "In this way we are reaffirming the transcendence of religious faith in America's heritage and future; in this way we shall constantly strengthen those spiritual weapons which forever will be our country's most powerful resource, in peace or in war."

American Minute
June 15th

The Legend of Robinhood speaks of Richard the Lionheart. The real King Richard the Lionheart, so named for his courage in battle, joined the Third Crusade in 1190AD to win back Jerusalem from the Muslims, who had taken it away from the Byzantine Christian and Jewish inhabitants in a bloody siege in 636AD. Though he did not retake Jerusalem, Richard made a truce with Saladin to open the region to religious pilgrims. On his return trip to England, Richard was captured by a rival king in Austria and spent three years in prison. He was eventually found and purchased back with an enormous "king's ransom." He returned to England and took back the throne from his brother John. Just five years later Richard died and John again ruled oppressively in England. The angry barons responded by capturing London and, on this date, June 15, 1215, surrounded King John on the plains of Runnymeade, forcing him to sign the Magna Carta. This was the first time in history that the arbitrary powers of a king were limited. The Magna Carta ends with the words: "for the salvation of our souls, and the souls of all our...heirs, and unto the honor of God."

American Minute
June 16th

The father of the American space program died this day, June 16, 1977. He developed the famed V-2 rocket for Germany before emigrating to the US, where in 1958, he launched America's first satellite. He became the director of NASA, the U.S. guided missile program and founded the National Space Institute. His name was Wernher von Braun, who stated: "The laws of nature that enable us to fly to the Moon also enable us to destroy our home planet with the atom bomb. Science itself does not address the question whether we should use the power at our disposal for good or for evil. The guidelines of what we ought to do are furnished in the moral law of God. It is no longer enough that we pray that God may be with us on our side. We must learn to pray that we may be on God's side."

American Minute
June 17th

"Don't Shoot Until You See the Whites of Their Eyes!" was the order given this day, June 17, 1775, by Colonel William Prescott to colonial troops defending Bunker Hill. They were aiming at the wall of twenty-three hundred British soldiers marching toward them from the Boston Harbor in their bright red uniforms with bayonets fixed. Twice the Americans repelled them until they ran out of gunpowder. Over one thousand British died and five hundred Americans. Colonel William Prescott had written to the citizens of Boston: "Let us all be of one heart, and stand fast in the liberty wherewith Christ has made us free."

American Minute
June 18th

The War of 1812 began on this day, June 18th. The British had captured American ships and enslaved sailors. They incited Indians to capture Fort Mims, massacring 500 men, women and children. They captured the Capitol, burnt the White House, bombarded Fort McHenry and attacked New Orleans. Outraged, many volunteered for the Army, including Davy Crockett. In his Proclamation of War, President James Madison stated: "I do moreover exhort all the good people of the United States...as they feel the wrongs which have forced on them the last resort of injured nations...to consult the best means under the blessing of Divine Providence of abridging its calamities." In the three years of the War, President Madison, who had introduced the First Amendment in the First Session of Congress, issued two separate Proclamations of Public Humiliation and Prayer, followed by a Proclamation of Public Fasting: "in the present time of public calamity and war a day may be...observed by the people of the United States as a day of public humiliation and fasting and of prayer to Almighty God." After the War, Madison proclaimed a National Day of Thanksgiving to Almighty God.

American Minute
June 19th

*T*he first formal "Father's Day" was celebrated on this day, June 19, 1910. It began in Spokane, Washington, when a woman named Sonora Louise Smart Dodd heard a Mother's Day sermon at church. She wanted to honor her father, who had raised all six children by himself after his wife died. Sonora drew up a petition, which was immediately supported by the Young Men's Christian Association and the ministers of Spokane. In 1972, President Richard M. Nixon established Father's Day as a permanent national observance of on the third Sunday of June.

American Minute
June 20th

Today, June 20, in the year 1632, King Charles of England granted a charter for the Colony of Maryland, named for Queen Henrietta Maria. Lord Baltimore sent two ships, the Ark and the Dove, to settle the colony. Buying land from the Indians, they founded the city of St. Mary's, as a refuge for persecuted Catholics, but soon extended religious toleration to all faiths. The Charter reads: "Whereas our...right trusty subject...Baron of Baltimore...being animated with a...pious Zeal for extending the Christian Religion, and also the Territories of our Empire, hath humbly besought Leave."

American Minute
June 21st

The U.S. Constitution went into effect this day, June 21, 1788, when the ninth state ratified it. Of those who wrote the Constitution, twenty-nine were Episcopalians, nine Presbyterians, seven Congregationalists, two Lutherans, two Dutch Reformed, two Methodists, two Roman Catholics, one Quaker and one Deist - Dr. Benjamin Franklin, who stated during the debates at the Constitutional Convention, June of 1787: "We have been assured, Sir, in the Sacred Writings, that 'except the Lord build the House, they labor in vain that build it.' I firmly believe this; and I also believe that without his concurring aid we shall succeed in this political building no better than the Builders of Babel."

American Minute
June 22nd

As of this date, June 22, 1970, eighteen-year-olds could begin voting in elections, thanks to President Richard M. Nixon signing the Voting Rights Act. The Supreme Court limited this right, so the following year the 26th Amendment was passed to confirm it. This was spurred by the protests during the Vietnam War, where students declared "If we're old enough to fight, we're old enough to vote." A proponent of Civil Rights, President Nixon stated in his Inaugural Address: "The laws have caught up with our conscience. What remains is to give life to what is in the law: to insure at last that as all are born equal in dignity before God, all are born equal in dignity before man."

American Minute
June 23rd

William Penn signed a treaty with the Delaware Indians this day, June 23, 1683, under an elm tree in what was to become the city of Philadelphia. A Quaker who took his faith seriously, Penn insisted on dealing fairly with the Indians, buying the land rather than taking it by force. As a result his colony was spared the Indian problems experienced by other colonies. William Penn addressed the tribe: "My Friends: There is one great God...that hath made the world and all things therein, to whom you and I and all people owe their being... This great God hath written His law in our hearts...to love and help and do good to one another and not to do harm."

American Minute
June 24th

$H$is travels were exceeded only by Lewis and Clark. He led expeditions up the Missouri River, discovered the South Pass through the Rockies and the first land route to California. He led settlers across the Santa Fe Trail, the Mojave Desert and up the Oregon Coast. His name was Jedediah Smith, born this day, June 24, 1798. In a letter to his brother, Ralph, dated December of 1829, Jedediah Smith wrote: "Many Hostile tribes of Indians inhabit this Space.... In August 1827, ten Men who were in company with me lost their lives by the Amuchabas Indians,..in July 1828, fifteen men who were in company with me lost their lives by the Umpquah Indians...Many others have lost their lives in different parts... My Brother...I have need of your Prayers...to bear me up before the Throne of Grace."

American Minute
June 25th

The Korean War started this day, June 25, 1950, when communist North Korea invaded South Korea, killing tens of thousands within the first weeks. General Douglas MacArthur was placed in command of the U.N. Forces and quickly turned the war by a daring landing of troops at Inchon and recapturing the city of Seoul. Politicians limited the military from pursuing victory and the war dragged on three years with millions of casualties. General MacArthur once stated: "History fails to record a single precedent in which nations subject to moral decay have not passed into political and economic decline. There has been either a spiritual awakening to overcome the moral lapse, or a progressive deterioration leading to ultimate national disaster"

American Minute
June 26th

The United Nations Charter was signed this day, June 26, 1945, by 51 member nations. Two months earlier, President Truman addressed the delegates: "At no time in history has there been a more important Conference than this one in San Francisco which you are opening today...As we are about to undertake our heavy duties, we beseech our Almighty God to guide us in the building of a permanent monument to those who gave their lives that this moment might come." In 1953, President Eisenhower addressed the UN: "The whole book of history reveals mankind's never-ending quest for peace and mankind's God-given capacity to build." As UN actions began opposing the U.S., former President Herbert Hoover told the American Newspaper Publishers Association, 1959: "I suggest that the United Nations be reorganized...with those peoples who disavow communism, who stand for morals and religion, and who love freedom...What the world needs today is a definite, spiritual mobilization of the nations who believe in God against this tide of Red agnosticism...It is a proposal for moral and spiritual cooperation of God-fearing free nations...rejecting an atheistic other world."

American Minute
June 27th

*H*elen Keller was born this day, June 27, 1880. At the age of two she suffered an illness that left her both blind and deaf. Her parents took her to Dr. Alexander Graham Bell who recommended the Perkins Institute for the Blind in Boston. There, at the age of seven, Anne Sullivan began tutoring her through the sense of touch, eventually teaching her to read Braille. She attended Radcliffe College, wrote several books and was recognized for her efforts to help the blind. Helen Keller wrote: "I thank God for my handicaps, for, through them, I have found myself, my work, and my God."

American Minute
June 28th

The Constitutional Convention was in a heated deadlock over how both large and small states could be represented equally. Some delegates even left, giving up hope. Then, on this day, June 28, 1787, the 81 year-old Benjamin Franklin spoke, and shortly after the U.S. Constitution became a reality. As recorded by James Madison, Franklin stated: "In the...Contest with Great Britain...we had daily prayer in this room for Divine protection. - Our prayers, Sir, were heard, &...graciously answered.... And have we now forgotten that powerful Friend? or do we imagine we no longer need His assistance?"

American Minute
June 29th

"I would rather be right than President," was the famous phrase uttered by Henry Clay, who died this day, June 29, 1852. Elected Speaker of the House six times, he served in Congress over 40 years with Daniel Webster and John Calhoun. Struggling to hold the Union together prior to the Civil War, Henry Clay stated to the Kentucky Colonization Society, in Frankfort, 1829: "Eighteen hundred years have rolled away since the Son of God...offered Himself...for the salvation of our species.... When we shall...be translated from this into another form of existence...we shall behold the common Father of the whites and blacks, the great Ruler of the Universe."

American Minute
June 30th

What was the first settlement in North America? Was it Jamestown or Plymouth? Actually, it was Fort Caroline at Saint John's River in Florida. It was founded this day, June 30, 1564, by the French Christians known as Huguenots, and was the first attempt at religious toleration in America. A settler recorded: "We sang a psalm of Thanksgiving unto God, beseeching Him that it would please Him to continue His accustomed goodness towards us." Unfortunately, this French colony was short-lived. The Spanish, whose treasure ships passed that route, destroyed it, butchering hundreds of men, and taking captive the women and children. In September of 1950, a bill sponsored by Rep. Charles E. Bennett, was passed in the U.S. Congress establishing Fort Caroline National Memorial on St. John's River to commemorate the first people who came to North America seeking freedom.

American Minute
July 1st

*T*eddy Roosevelt and Rough Riders charged up Cuba's San Juan Hill and captured it this day, July 1, 1898. After eight hours of heavy fighting over fifteen hundred Americans lay dead or wounded. Just four months prior the U.S. ship Maine was blown up in Havana's Harbor. Roosevelt resigned as Assistant Secretary of the Navy and organized the first volunteer cavalry, made up of polo riders, cowboys and even Indians. After the battle, President McKinley wrote in July of 1898: "At a time...of the...glorious achievements of the naval and military arms of our beloved country at Santiago de Cuba, it is fitting that we should pause and... reverently bow before the throne of divine grace and give devout praise to God, who holdeth the nations in the hollow of His Hands."

American Minute
July 2nd

One bullet grazed his elbow, but a second lodged in the back of President James Garfield, who was shot this day, July 2, 1881, as he waited in the Washington train station. He had been in office four months. Though not wounded seriously, unsterile medical practices caused him to die two months later. A distinguished Civil War major general, James Garfield was also a college president and a preacher for the Disciples of Christ. As a Congressman, Chairing the Committee on Appropriations, James Garfield stated in July of 1876: "If the next century does not find us a great nation...it will be because those who represent the...morality of the nation do not aid in controlling the political forces."

American Minute
July 3rd

Washington, D.C., was in a panic as 70,000 Confederate troops were marching toward it just sixty miles away. The furious fighting lasted three days. As General Lee found his ammunition running low, he ordered General Pickett to make a direct attack. After an hour of murderous fire and bloody hand-to-hand combat, the Confederates were pushed back and the Battle of Gettysburg ended this day, July 3, 1863, with over 50,000 casualties. President Lincoln confided: "When everyone seemed panic-stricken...I went to my room...and got down on my knees before Almighty God and prayed."

American Minute
July 4th

The Declaration of Independence was approved this day, July 4, 1776. John Hancock, the first to sign, said: "the price on my head has just doubled." Benjamin Franklin signed saying "We must hang together or most assuredly we shall hang separately." Of the fifty-six signers: 17 lost their fortunes, 12 had their homes destroyed, 9 fought and died, 5 were arrested as traitors, and 2 lost sons in the War. As Samuel Adams signed, he said: "We have this day restored the Sovereign to whom all men ought to be obedient. He reigns in heaven and from the rising to the setting of the sun, let His kingdom come." At the 150th anniversary of the Declaration, 1926, President Calvin Coolidge stated: "It is but natural that the first paragraph of the Declaration of Independence should open with a reference to Nature's God and should close in the final paragraphs with an appeal to the Supreme Judge of the world and an assertion of reliance on Divine Providence...No one can examine this record and escape the conclusion that in the great outline of its principles the Declaration was the result of the religious teachings of the preceding period...The Declaration is a great spiritual document."

American Minute
July 5th

Once political enemies they became close friends, and died yesterday, July 4th in the year 1826. An awe swept America as these two men, at distance of 700 hundred miles from each other, died on the same day exactly 50 years since they both signed the Declaration of Independence. Their names: John Adams and Thomas Jefferson. President John Quincy Adams, in an Executive Order, stated: "A coincidence...so wonderful gives confidence...that the patriotic efforts of these...men were Heaven directed, and furnishes a new...hope that the prosperity of these States is under the special protection of a kind Providence." In his Second Annual Message to Congress, 1826, President John Quincy Adams stated: "Since your last meeting at this place, the fiftieth anniversary of the day when our independence was declared...two of the principal actors in that solemn scene - the hand that penned the ever-memorable Declaration and the voice that sustained it in debate - were by one summons, at the distance of 700 miles from each other, called before the Judge of All to account for their deeds done upon earth."

American Minute
July 6th

Prior to the Civil War there were two major political parties in the United States: the Democrats, who believed Americans should have the freedom of choice to own slaves; and the Whigs, who wanted to be the big tent party embracing free and slave states. The Whigs diminished in power and in Ripon, Wisconsin, an anti-slavery group met in February of 1854 to discuss a new party. Later that year, on this day, July 6, 1854, anti-slavery activists came from all over the North to a State Convention in Jackson, Michigan, where they named their new party the Republican Party. They demanded the Fugitive Slave Law be repealed, and that polygamy, the having of more than one wife, which was growing in western territories, be stopped by supporting the traditional definition of marriage as one man and one woman. The chief plank in the Republican Party's original National Platform, 1856, was "to prohibit...those twin relics of barbarism: polygamy and slavery."

American Minute
July 7th

*H*awaii became a U.S. Territory this day, July 7, 1898, as President McKinley signed the Treaty of Annexation. Discovered by Captain James Cook in 1778, the islands were soon united by King Kamehamaha. After his death in 1819, his son, with his mother as prime minister, abolished their pagan religion which included human sacrifice. The next year the first missionaries, led by Hiram Bingham, arrived from New England, creating a written language and translating the Bible. Hawaii's Motto, "The Life of the Land is Perpetuated in Righteousness," was first uttered by Queen Ke'opuolani in 1825 as she was baptized into the Christian faith.

American Minute
July 8th

The Liberty Bell got its name from being rung this day, July 8, 1776, to call the citizens of Philadelphia together to hear the Declaration of Independence read out loud for the first time. Made in England, this massive bell, weighing over 2000 pounds, was rung on each successive anniversary, until 1835, when it cracked on July 8th while tolling at the funeral of the famous Supreme Court Justice John Marshall. Inscribed on the Liberty Bell is a verse from Old Testament Book of Leviticus, Chapter 25: "Proclaim Liberty throughout the land unto all the inhabitants thereof." At the 150th anniversary of the Declaration, 1926, President Calvin Coolidge stated: "People at home and abroad consider Independence Hall as hallowed ground and revere the Liberty Bell as a sacred relic. That pile of bricks and mortar, that mass of metal, might appear as only the outgrown meeting place and the shattered bell...but to those who know, they have become consecrated. They are the framework of a spiritual event. The world looks upon them because of their associations of one hundred and fifty years ago, as it looks upon the Holy Land because of what took place there nineteen hundred years ago."

American Minute
July 9th

"*O*ld Rough and Ready" died this day, July 9, 1850. He fought the British in the War of 1812, the Indians in the Black Hawk War, and defeated the Seminole Indians in Florida. But it was his courageous victories in the Mexican War, being greatly outnumbered by Santa Anna's forces, that made him a national hero. His popularity spread like fire and he was elected America's twelfth President. Refusing to be sworn in on the Sabbath, President Zachary Taylor stated: "The only ground of hope for the continuance of our free institutions is in the proper moral and religious training of the children."

American Minute
July 10th

Millard Fillmore became the 13th President this day, July 10, 1850, when President Zachary Taylor died unexpectedly. He was remembered for sending Commodore Perry to open trade with Japan, admitting California, which had just begun the Gold Rush, into the Union as a free state, and when the Library of Congress caught on fire, he and his Cabinet formed a bucket brigade to help extinguish the flames. After being sworn into office, President Millard Fillmore addressed Congress: "I dare not shrink...I rely upon Him who holds in His hands the destinies of nations to endow me with...strength for the task."

American Minute
July 11th

*H*e intentionally fired into the air, but his political rival, Aaron Burr, took deadly aim and fatally shot him in a duel this day, July 11, 1804. Born in the West Indies, he fought in the Revolution and served as aide-de-camp to General Washington. He helped write the Constitution and convinced the states to ratify it by writing The Federalist Papers. His name was Alexander Hamilton, the first Secretary of the Treasury. In April of 1802, Hamilton wrote to his friend, James Bayard: "Let an association be formed to be denominated 'The Christian Constitutional Society,' its object to be first: The support of Christian religion; second: The support of the United States."

American Minute
July 12th

Born a slave around this date, July 12, 1864, George Washington Carver became a scientist of international renown. In 1921, the U.S. House Ways and Means Committee invited him to speak on uses of the peanut to improve Southern economy. After two captivating hours, the chairman asked: "Dr. Carver, how did you learn all of these things?" Carver answered: "From an old book" "What book?" asked the Chairman. Carver replied, "The Bible." The Chairman inquired, "Does the Bible tell about peanuts?" "No, Sir" Dr. Carver replied, "But it tells about the God who made the peanut. I asked Him to show me what to do with it and He did."

American Minute
July 13th

Did you know that after Washington retired from being President, he again became the Commander-in-Chief of the Army? It was just a year and a half before he died that he received an urgent plea from President John Adams to put on his general's uniform again. France, in the midst of revolution, was demanding payment not to harass American ships. The cry went out "Millions for defense, but not a cent for tribute." Washington agreed and replied this day, July 13, 1798: "We can, with pure hearts, appeal to Heaven for the justice of our cause and may confidently trust the final result to that kind Providence who has heretofore, and so often, signally favored the people of these United States."

American Minute
July 14th

The 38th President was born this day, July 14, 1913. His given name was Leslie Lynch King, Jr., but his stepfather renamed him. The only Eagle Scout to become President, he attended the University of Michigan on a football scholarship, graduated from Yale Law School, served in the Navy during World War II. He was House Minority Leader and when Richard Nixon resigned, he became the only person to become President without being elected. His name...? Gerald Rudolph Ford, who said: "I ask you to confirm me as your President with your prayers. And I hope that such prayers will also be the first of many."

American Minute
July 15th

Robert Aitken, the publisher of The Pennsylvania Magazine, died this day, July 15, 1802. During the Colonial Era, the Bible most used in America was the King's authorized version, printed on the King's official presses in Britain. But since the Revolutionary War interrupted trade with England, and since the Bible was commonly used in education, the Continental Congress, in 1782, responded to the shortage by approving and recommending that Robert Aitken of Philadelphia print the first Bibles in America. They were to be "A neat edition of the Holy Scriptures for the use of schools."

American Minute
July 16th

Apollo 11 blasted off from Cape Kennedy this day, July 16, 1969, on the first mission to walk on the moon. Commenting on the Apollo program, President Richard M. Nixon stated in his Inaugural Address: "Only a few short weeks ago we shared the glory of man's first sight of the world as God sees it, as a single sphere reflecting light in the darkness. As the Apollo astronauts flew over the moon's gray surface...they spoke to us the beauty of earth - and in that voice so clear across the lunar distance, we heard them invoke God's blessing on its goodness."

American Minute
July 17th

Bartolome' de Las Casas, the "Apostle of the Indies," died this day, July 17, 1566. He was one of the first Christian missionaries known for his devotion to the oppressed and enslaved natives of Latin America. His work Apologetic History of the Indies, published in 1530, exposed the oppression of the Indians in the forced labor and influenced Madrid to enact New Laws to protect them. Bartolome' de Las Casas stated: "The main goal of divine Providence in the discovery of these tribes...is...the conversion and well-being of souls, and to this goal everything temporal must necessarily be directed."

American Minute
July 18th

Prior to the Revolution, Americans and British fought the French. As British troops were marching toward Fort Duquesne they were ambushed by the French and Indians. Not accustomed to fighting unless in an open field, the British were being annihilated. Colonel George Washington rode back and forth across the battlefield delivering orders for General Braddock. Eventually, General Braddock was mortally wounded, and every other officer on horseback was shot down, except Washington. Writing of the Battle of Monongahela to his brother John, this day, July 18, 1755, Washington stated: "As I have heard, since my arrival at this place, a circumstantial account of my death and dying speech, I take this early opportunity of contradicting the first, and of assuring you, that I have not as yet composed the latter. But by the All-Powerful Dispensations of Providence, I have been protected beyond all human probability or expectation; for I had four bullets through my coat, and two horses shot under me, yet escaped unhurt, although death was leveling my companions on every side of me!"

AMERICAN MINUTE - WILLIAM J. FEDERER

American Minute
July 19th

"V" for Victory! It was on this day, July 19, 1941, that British Prime Minister Winston Churchill held up two fingers as a sign of victory. It became a symbol for all Western European resistance during WWII, with V signs painted on walls and over Nazi posters. Over a year earlier, Churchill stated before the House of Commons, June of 1940: "I expect that the Battle of Britain is about to begin. Upon this battle depends the survival of Christian civilization....The whole fury and might of the enemy must very soon be turned on us. Hitler knows that he will have to break us in this Island or lose the war. If we can stand up to him, all Europe may be free and the life of the world may move forward into broad, sunlit uplands. But if we fail, then the whole world, including the United States, including all that we have known and cared for, will sink into the abyss of a new Dark Age made more sinister, and perhaps more protracted, by the lights of perverted science. Let us therefore brace ourselves to our duties, and so bear ourselves that, if the British Empire and its Commonwealth last for a thousand years, men will still say, 'This was their finest hour.'"

American Minute
July 20th

"*O*ne small step for a man, one giant leap for mankind," were the words uttered this day, July 20, 1969, by Neil Armstrong, as he became the first man to walk on the moon. He, along with Colonel Aldrin, had landed their lunar module, the "Eagle," and spent a total of 21 hours and 37 minutes on the moon's surface, before redocking with the command ship "Columbia." Addressing a joint session of Congress, September of 1969, Commander Neil Armstrong stated: "To those of you who have advocated looking high we owe our sincere gratitude, for you have granted us the opportunity to see some of the grandest views of the Creator."

American Minute
July 21st

The famous Monkey Trial ended this day, July 21, 1925, as John Scopes, a High school biology teacher in Tennessee was fined for teaching a theory of origins called evolution. Williams Jennings Bryan, three time Democratic Presidential candidate, was the prosecuting attorney. He objected to a tooth being presented as proof of humans evolving from apes. Later the tooth was admitted to be that of a pig. William Jennings Bryan, who died five days after the trial, once stated: "I am interested in the science of government, but I am more interested in religion...and I shall be in the church even after I am out of politics."

American Minute
July 22nd

"**A** baby is God's opinion that the world should go on," wrote poet Carl Sandburg, who died this day, July 22, 1967. Sandburg received the Pulitzer Prize and the Presidential Medal of Freedom. His two volume history of Abraham Lincoln received such acclaim that he was asked to address a joint session of Congress on the 150th anniversary of Lincoln's birthday. Carl Sandburg wrote: "I see America not in the setting sun of a black night of despair.... I see America in the crimson light of a rising sun fresh from the burning, creative hand of God."

American Minute
July 23rd

*H*e was the only person to sign all four of America's founding documents: the Declaration of Independence, Articles of Confederation, Articles of Association and the U.S. Constitution. A shoe cobbler by trade, he was also a surveyor and merchant prior to his political career. As a Congressman, he help write the First Amendment, and at age 70 was elected U.S. Senator. Who was he?... Roger Sherman, who died this day, July 23, 1793. Upon hearing the British had surrendered over 5000 troops to the Americans at Saratoga, Roger Sherman exclaimed: "This is the Lord's doing and marvelous in our eyes!"

American Minute
July 24th

*T*ennessee became the first State to be readmitted back into the Union after the Civil War on this day, July 24, 1866. In a proclamation of Amnesty and Pardon, President Andrew Johnson declared: "Every person who shall seek to avail himself of this proclamation shall take...the following oath...namely: 'I, ____ ____, do solemnly swear, in presence of Almighty God, that I will henceforth faithfully support, protect, and defend the Constitution of the United States...and...abide by...all laws and proclamations which have been made during the late rebellion with reference to the emancipation of slaves. So help me God.'"

American Minute
July 25th

*U*lysses S. Grant was commissioned this day, July 25, 1866, as General of the Army, being the first officer to hold that rank. His courageous victories during the Civil War catapulted him into national prominence and, in 1868, he was elected America's eighteenth President. To the Editor of the Sunday School Times in Philadelphia, President Ulysses S. Grant wrote: "Your favor of yesterday asking a message from me to the children and youth of the United States to accompany your Centennial number, is this morning received. My advice to Sunday schools, no matter what their denomination, is: Hold fast to the Bible as the sheet anchor of your liberties; write its precepts in your hearts, and practice them in your lives. To the influence of this Book are we indebted for all the progress made in true civilization, and to this must we look as our guide in the future. 'Righteousness exalteth a nation; but sin is a reproach to any people.' Yours respectfully, U.S. Grant."

American Minute
July 26th

On this day, July 26, 1775, Benjamin Franklin became the first Postmaster General of the United States. Before the Revolution he served in that position under the British Crown. Franklin also established the first volunteer fire department, a circulating public library and the lighting of city streets. He helped found the University of Pennsylvania, a hospital, an insurance company, a city police force, a night watch and the first militia. He was a printer, scientist, philosopher and statesmen. In 1787, as the President (Governor) of Pennsylvania, Benjamin Franklin hosted the Constitutional Convention in Philadelphia, where he made the motion: "I therefore beg leave to move - that henceforth prayers imploring the assistance of Heaven, and its blessing on our deliberations, be held in this Assembly every morning before we proceed to business." Benjamin Franklin wrote in 1787: "Only a virtuous people are capable of freedom. As nations become corrupt and vicious, they have more need of masters."

American Minute
July 27th

"*F*REEDOM IS NOT FREE" is the inscription on the Washington, D.C., Memorial, to those who fought in the Korean War, which ended this day, July 27, 1953, with the armistice signed at Panmunjom. Begun three years earlier as a UN "police" action, the outnumber U.S. troops fought courageously against the Communist Chinese and North Korean troops, who were supplied with arms and MIG fighters from the Soviet Union. With temperatures sometimes forty degrees below zero, and Washington politicians limiting the use of air power against the Communist Chinese, there were nearly 140,000 American casualties in the defense of the Pusan Perimeter and Taego; landing at Inchon and freeing of Seoul; capture of Pyongyang; Yalu River invasion by nearly a million Communist Chinese soldiers, Battles of Changjin Reservoir, Old Baldy, White Horse Mountain, Heartbreak Ridge, Pork Chop Hill, T-Bone Hill, and Siberia Hill. Of her son who was serving in Korea, Mrs. Dwight Eisenhower said: "He has a mission to fulfill and God will see to it that nothing will happen to him till he fulfills it."

American Minute
July 28th

German composer Johann Sebastian Bach died this day, July 28, 1750. He was considered the "master of masters," combining the tradition of Baroque music with harmonic innovations. The majority of his works are religious, including "Passion According to St. Matthew," and "Jesus, Meine Freude" (Jesus, My Joy!). In commenting on his music, Bach stated: "The aim and final end of all music should be none other than the glory of God and the refreshment of the soul. If heed is not paid to this, it is not true music but a diabolical bawling and twanging." In the U.S. Supreme Court case McCollum v. Board of Education (1948), Justice Robert H. Jackson wrote: "It would not seem practical to teach...appreciation of the arts if we are to forbid exposure of youth to any religious influences. Music without sacred music, architecture minus the cathedral, or painting without the Scriptural themes would be eccentric and incomplete, even from a secular point of view....One can hardly respect a system of education that would leave a student wholly ignorant of the currents of religious thought that moved the world."

American Minute
July 29th

Alexis de Tocqueville was born this day, July 29, 1805. He was a French social philosopher who traveled the United States in 1831. His work, "Democracy in America," has been described as "the most comprehensive...analysis...between character and society in America that has ever been written." In it, de Tocqueville wrote: "In France I had almost always seen the spirit of religion and the spirit of freedom marching in opposite directions. But in America I found they were intimately united and that they reigned in common over the same country.... Religion in America...must be regarded as the foremost of the political institutions of that country; for if it does not impart a taste for freedom, it facilitates the use of it....There is no country in the whole world where the Christian religion retains a greater influence over the souls of men than in America, and there can be no greater proof of its utility...than that its influence is powerfully felt over the most enlightened and free nation of the earth."

American Minute
July 30th

King Charles gave him a land grant in America in payment of a great debt owed to his father. He then invited all the persecuted peoples of Europe to join him in establishing a colony of religious toleration, as he himself had been imprisoned in the Tower of London for converting to the Quaker faith. Calling it a "holy experiment," he admonished the settlers to work together, naming the first city Philadelphia, meaning "Brotherly Love." It was there, nearly a hundred years later, that the Declaration and Constitution were written. He died this day, July 30, 1718. His name was William Penn. The Charter granted to William Penn by King Charles in 1681, stated: "Whereas our trusty and well beloved subject, William Penn, Esquire, son and heir of Sir William Penn, deceased, out of a commendable desire to enlarge our English Empire...and also to reduce the savage natives by gentle and just manners to the Love of Civil Societe and Christian religion, hath humbly besought leave of us to transport an ample colony unto a certain country hereinafter describe in the parts of America not yet cultivated and planted."

American Minute
July 31st

*O*n his third voyage, Columbus sailed south along the west coast of Africa and was caught in the doldrums, a notorious condition of no winds and intense heat. After drifting aimlessly for eight days, the winds returned, but now they were running low on water. Columbus promised to name the first new land he discovered in honor of the Trinity. Sighting an island off the coast of Venezuela this day, July 31, 1498, which coincidentally had three peaks, he gave it the name Trinidad. There they obtained fresh water and in the process were the first Europeans to see South America.

American Minute
August 1st

"*T*here she blows!" was the cry as the lookout sighted Moby Dick. Captain Ahab, with his chief mate Starbuck, sailed the oceans of the world to capture this great white whale. But as fate would have it, when the harpoon struck, the rope flew out so fast it entangled Captain Ahab, pulling him under. This American classic was written by Herman Melville, who was born this day, August 1, 1819. In the opening chapters Mehlville warned: "With this sin of disobedience...Jonah flouts at God... He thinks that a ship made by men will carry him into countries where God does not reign."

American Minute
August 2nd

The Navy torpedo boat PT 109 was rammed this day, August 2, 1943, by a Japanese destroyer and sunk. The commander, who sustained permanent back injury, helped the survivors swim miles to shore, only to find that they far behind enemy lines in the Solomon Islands. After a daring rescue, he was awarded the Medal of heroism. Though his brother was killed in the war, this commander went on to become a Congressman, Senator, and America's 35th President. His name was John F. Kennedy, who stated in his Inaugural Address: "Let us go forth to lead the land we love, asking His blessing and His help, but knowing that here on earth God's work must truly be our own."

American Minute
August 3rd

"*T*here are but 155 years left...at which time...the world will come to an end," wrote Christopher Columbus in his book Libro de Las Profecias. "The sign which convinces me that our Lord is hastening the end...is the preaching of the Gospel...in so many lands." Though his predictions were off, Columbus described in detail his motivation for setting sail this day, August 3, 1492, with the Nina, Pinta and the Santa Maria. He carried a letter from King Ferdinand and Queen Isabella to the Gran Khan of India, with the instructions "to see the said princes and peoples...and the manner which should be used to bring about their conversion to our Holy Faith."

American Minute
August 4th

"*T*o sink the foe or save the maimed, Our mission and our pride, We'll carry on 'til Kingdom Come, Ideals for which we've died." Thus went the anthem of the US Coast Guard, which was established this day, August 4, 1790, when Congress authorized ten boats to be built for the Revenue Marine. Four years later they were charged with stopping slave-traders from bringing new slaves from Africa. They freed almost 500 slaves. At a US Coast Guard commencement, President Reagan stated: "It's our prayer to serve America in peace. It's our commitment to defend her in war."

American Minute
August 5th

The very first book printed in America was the Bay Psalm Book, written by John Eliot, who was born around this date, August 5, 1604. Called the "Apostle to the Indians," Eliot translated the Old and New Testaments into the Algonquian language. He organized thousands of "Praying Indians" into self-ruling villages, with their own leaders and ministers. They built houses, streets, bridges, and were very prosperous until King Phillip's War, where thousands tragically died. In his plan of government, Eliot wrote: "The Word of God is the perfect System of Laws to guide all moral actions of man."

American Minute
August 6th

Camelot and King Arthur's Court, Knights of the Round Table and the quest for the Holy Grail... our imaginations soar with history and legend immortalized by poet Alfred Lord Tennyson, whose birth was celebrated this day, August 6, 1809. The son of a clergyman, he not only brought to life Guinevere and Sir Lancelot, but wrote The Charge of the Light Brigade, recording the courage of the British Cavalry as they rode to their deaths fighting the Russians. Honored by Queen Victoria as Poet-Laureat, Alfred Lord Tennyson wrote: "Cast all your cares on God; that anchor holds."

American Minute
August 7th

The largest town in Kentucky had less than 2000 people, yet 25,000 arrived at Cane Ridge, Kentucky, this day, August 7, 1801, from as far away as Ohio and Tennessee, to hear the preaching of Methodist, Baptist and Presbyterian ministers. Called "camp meetings," Reverend Moses Hodge described: "Nothing that imagination can paint can make a stronger impression... Sinners dropping down on every hand, professors praying, others in raptures of joy!... There can be no question but it is of God, as the subjects...can give a clear and rational account of their conversion."

American Minute
August 8th

August 8, 1974, President Richard Nixon chose to resign, the first ever to do so, rather than put the country through the ordeal of an impeachment. In a televised address, he said: "To continue to fight...for my personal vindication would...totally absorb the time and attention of...the President and the Congress." In a private farewell to his Cabinet, President Nixon stated: "Mistakes, yes...for personal gain, never... I can only say to each...one of you...we come from many faiths...but really the same God... You will be in our hearts and...in our prayers."

American Minute
August 9th

The groans of a dying man kept him awake in the little inn outside New York. He was hardened to the cries because a college friend had persuaded him to be an atheist. The next morning he learned the man who died in the night was none other than his college friend. His faith renewed, he became America's first foreign missionary. His name was Adonirum Judson, born this day, August 9, 1788. Adonirum and his wife sailed for India, but were forced by the British East India Tea Company to flee to Burma. There they translated Scriptures, started schools, and their work grew to over a half-million people.

American Minute
August 10th

*H*erbert Hoover was born this day, August 10, 1874. The son of a Quaker blacksmith, he studied at Stanford and became a world renowned engineer. Trapped in China when the Boxer Rebellion broke out in 1900, he directed the building of barricades under heavy fire while his wife worked in hospitals. In World War I, at the request of the American Consul, he helped 120,000 Americans stranded in Europe return to the U.S. He directed the feeding of Belgium after the Germans had overran it, feeding of the Allies, while avoiding rationing at home, and after the war feeding the starving millions in Central Europe and Russia. Secretary of Commerce for Presidents Harding and Coolidge, he became the 31st U.S. President in 1929. Seven months later the Stock Market crashed. Though implementing a plan of aid through the States, political opponents sabotaged his efforts and blamed him. After World War II, Presidents Truman and Eisenhower appointed him to commissions. Hoover, based on a suggestion of FDR's for peace in the Middle East, recommended in November of 1945: "that Iraq might be financed...be made the scene of resettlement of the Arabs from Palestine."

American Minute
August 11th

On this day, August 11, 1984, Congress voted the Equal Access Act into law, allowing students who wish to conduct religious meetings the same access to schools as other groups. President Ronald Reagan stated: "In 1962, the Supreme Court banned prayers. In 1963, the Court banned the reading of the Bible... We had to pass a special law to allow student prayer groups the same access to school rooms that a Young Marxist Society enjoys... Without God there is a coarsening of the society... If we ever forget that we are One Nation Under God, then we will be a Nation gone under."

American Minute
August 12th

"O Beautiful, For Spacious Skies, For Amber Waves of Grain..." Did you know this song, "America the Beautiful," was so popular in the 1920's that it almost became our National Anthem? It was written by Katherine Lee Bates, who was born this day, August 12, 1859. An American poet and educator, she was the daughter of a Congregational minister, taught high school and then became professor of English literature at Wellesley College. In 1892, she journeyed to the top of Pike's Peak in Colorado, and was so inspired by the view she penned the verse: "America, America, God shed His grace on thee."

American Minute
August 13th

New Jersey is being invaded by Martians! This was the script of a 1938 radio drama based on the novel War of the Worlds, written by H.G. Wells, who died this day, August 13, 1946. Wells' novel inspired a boy named Robert Goddard that space flight was possible and he grew up to be the father of modern rocketry. H.G. Wells also wrote the best sellers The Time Machine, The Invisible Man, and The First Men in the Moon. Though a skeptic, in his Outlines of History (1920), H.G. Wells described the U.S. Constitution, saying: "Its spirit is indubitably Christian."

American Minute
August 14th

Over 3,000 American troops were killed or wounded when the Japanese attacked Pearl Harbor. 20,000 American and Filipino troops died on the infamous Bataan Death March and imprisonment, when Japanese forced starving prisoners to march 65 miles without food or water through searing heat and jungles to a disease infested camp. Over 100,000 died retaking Okinawa and other Pacific islands. Though devastating, President Truman's decision to drop the Atomic Bomb prevented an estimated one million casualties on both sides and Emperor Hirohito surrendered Japan on this day, August 14, 1945. U.S. Army Chaplain Father William Thomas Cummings was among those captured at Bataan and died when the prisoner "hell ship" he was on sank from a torpedo explosion. In a battlefield sermon, Chaplain Fr. Cummings made the now-famous remark: "There are no atheists in the fox-holes."

American Minute
August 15th

He conquered from Austria to Palestine, Holland to Egypt. He uncovered the Pyramid treasures and the Rosetta Stone. He sold a million square miles of land to United States to raise money for his army. His name was Napoleon Bonaparte, born this day, August 15, 1769. Though emperor for life, disasters in Russia and Waterloo led to his banishment on the Island of Saint Helena. There, in reflection, Napoleon wrote: "The Bible is no mere book, but a Living Creature, with a power that conquers all that oppose it."

American Minute
August 16th

Charles Finney died this day, August 16, 1875. An attorney, he saw so many references to Scriptures in Blackstone's Law Commentaries that he purchased a Bible and found faith in Christ. He became a convincing speaker influencing George Williams to found the YMCA - Young Men's Christian Association. Finney's Lectures on Revival inspired William Booth to found the Salvation Army. Finney was President of Oberlin College, which graduated the first Black woman in America. Concerning the Kingdom of God, Charles Finney wrote: "Every member must work or quit. No honorary members."

American Minute
August 17th

On this day, August 17, 1955, President Dwight Eisenhower authorized the code of conduct for American soldiers captured in war. Revealing the high level of commitment made by those in the armed services, the code states: "I serve in the forces which guard my country and our way of life. I am prepared to give my life in their defense... If captured...I will accept neither parole nor special favors from the enemy... I will never forget I am an American fighting man, responsible for my actions and dedicated to the principles which made my country free. I will trust in my God and in the United States of America."

American Minute
August 18th

*H*is legal decisions were so respected they were referenced in U.S. Supreme Court Cases. For forty years he served on the New York District Court and the U.S. Court of Appeals before dying this day, August 18, 1961. His name was Learned Hand. During World War II in New York's Central Park, Judge Learned Hand stated: "The spirit of liberty is the spirit of Him who, nearly two thousand years ago, taught mankind the lesson it has never learned, but has never quite forgotten-that there may be a kingdom where the least shall be...side by side with the greatest."

American Minute
August 19th

A graduate of Georgetown University, he was a Fulbright Scholar before becoming the Governor of Arkansas and then America's 42nd President. In 1998, he became the 2nd president ever to be impeached. His original name was William Jefferson Blythe IV, born this day, August 19, 1946. At age 15, he took his stepfather's name Clinton. Also on this day, August 19, 1785, Thomas Jefferson wrote to his nephew, Peter Carr: "He who permits himself to tell a lie once, finds it much easier to do it a second and third time, till at length it becomes habitual... This falsehood of the tongue leads to that of the heart."

American Minute
August 20th

$3$00,000 miles on horseback, from the Atlantic to the Appalachians, from Maine to the Gulf of Mexico, for forty-five years, he spread the gospel. This was Francis Asbury, Methodist Circuit riding preacher who was born this day, August 20, 1745. When the Revolution started, he refused to return to England: "I can by no means agree to leave such a field for gathering souls to Christ as we have in America." He befriended Richard Bassett, a signer of the Constitution, who converted, freed his slaves and paid them as hired labor. Francis Asbury dedicated the first African Methodist Episcopal Church and met personally with George Washington, congratulating him on his election. By the time he died, the Methodist Church in America had grown from 300 members to over 200,000. Unveiling the Equestrian Statue of Francis Asbury in Washington, D.C., 1924, President Calvin Coolidge stated: "Our government rests upon religion It is from that source that we derive our reverence for truth and justice, for equality and liberty...This circuit rider spent his life making stronger the foundation on which our government rests...Francis Asbury is entitled to rank as one of the builders of our nation."

American Minute
August 21st

Born in Scotland, he was one of only six founding fathers to sign both the Declaration of Independence and the Constitution. President George Washington appointed him a Justice on the Supreme Court. One of the most active members at the Constitutional Convention, he spoke 168 times. His name was James Wilson and he died this day, August 21, 1798. The first law professor of the University of Pennsylvania, James Wilson wrote: "It should always be remembered, that this law, natural or revealed, flows from the same divine source; it is the law of God.... Human law must rest its authority, ultimately, upon the authority of that law, which is divine."

American Minute
August 22nd

*H*e served in Vietnam and commanded the U.S. invasion of Grenada. A four star general, he was commander in Desert Storm. After the war, he was awarded the Congressional Gold Medal and knighted by the Queen of England. His name: General Norman Schwarzkopf, born this day, August 22, 1934. In an interview, he described an extreme flanking maneuver to cut off the Iraqi retreat: "When my forward commander radioed that they had reached the Euphrates River... I waited... 'General,' he said, 'I've got to tell you about the casualties.' I braced myself. 'One man was slightly wounded.' That's when I knew God was with us."

American Minute
August 23rd

"We have met the enemy and they are ours," wrote Navy Captain Oliver Hazard Perry, who died this day, August 23, 1819. Captain Perry was renown for his encounter with six powerful British warships in the Battle of Lake Erie during the War of 1812. With no long range firepower, the winds prevented him from getting in a safe position and the British cannons crippled his flagship. In a courageous move, he switched to the ship "Niagara," sailed directly into the British line, firing broadside, and won the battle in fifteen minutes. To the sailors on deck he remarked: "The prayers of my wife are answered."

American Minute
August 24th

*G*utenberg means "Beautiful mountain." An appropriate name for Johannes Gutenberg, who invented the first moveable type printing press. His masterpiece was the printing of the Gutenberg Bible around this day, August 24, 1455. No longer were Bibles painstakingly copied by hand and chained to pulpits. They were mass produced and accessible to the multitudes. Though millions were grateful, his business partner sued him and took his rights. Of his press, Gutenberg wrote: "Let us break the seal which seals up holy things and give wings to Truth in order that she may win every soul that comes into the world." In August of 1993, Pope John Paul II spoke at Regis University in Denver, Colorado, regarding the nation's current moral crisis and then presented an original Gutenberg Bible to President Bill Clinton, who was in attendance.

American Minute
August 25th

An English astronomer, he became world renown for the discovery of the planet Uranus. He was noted for his recognition of double stars. Using the technology of the late eighteenth century, he constructed the greatest reflecting telescopes of his time. He cataloged and studied the nebulae and galaxies as had never been done before. For his accomplishments, he was knighted by the Royalty. His name was Sir William Herschel, and he died this day, August 25, 1822. Commenting on the grandeur of the heavens, Sir William Herschel stated: "The undevout astronomer must be mad."

American Minute
August 26th

Women can vote! That was the monumental news this day, August 26th, 1920, as the nineteenth amendment became law. It reads: "The right of citizens of the U.S. to vote shall not be denied or abridged by the United States or by any State on account of sex." This culminated fifty years effort by many of the women leaders who fought to abolish slavery, one of whom was Julia Ward Howe, author of The Battle Hymn of the Republic. She wrote in the third verse: "Let the Hero, born of woman, crush the serpent with his heel, Since God is marching on."

American Minute
August 27th

August 27, 1776, British General Howe had trapped 8,000 American troops on Brooklyn Heights, intending to crush them the next morning. Desperate, Washington spent all night ferrying his army across the East River. Morning came yet half his troops were still in danger. Surprisingly a fog arose, allowing the entire army to evacuated! Never again did the British have such a chance to trap the American army. Major Ben Tallmadge, Washington's Chief of Intelligence, wrote: "As the dawn of the next day approached, those of us who remained in the trenches became very anxious for our own safety, and when the dawn appeared there were several regiments still on duty. At this time a very dense fog began to rise off the river, and it seemed to settle in a peculiar manner over both encampments. I recollect this peculiar providential occurrence perfectly well, and so very dense was the atmosphere that I could scarcely discern a man at six yards distance....We tarried until the sun had risen, but the fog remained as dense as ever.."

American Minute
August 28th

August 28, 1963. The event: the Civil Rights March on Washington, D.C. Reverend Martin Luther King, Jr., declared: "I have a dream that my four little children will one day live in a nation where they will not be judged by the color of their skin, but by the content of their character....where little black boys and black girls will be able to join hands with little white boys and white girls and walk together... I have a dream that one day...the glory of the Lord shall be revealed...when all of God's children, black and white, Jews and Gentiles, Protestants and Catholics, will be able to join hands and sing... 'Free at Last! Thank God Almighty, we are free at last!'"

American Minute
August 29th

*"B*eloved Cherokees," wrote President Washington on this day, August 29, 1796, "The wise men of the United States meet once a year, to consider what will be for the good of their people.... I have thought that a meeting of your wise men...would be alike useful to you.... I now send my best wishes to the Cherokees and pray the Great Spirit to preserve them." On another occasion, May 12, 1779, the Delaware Indian Chiefs brought to the Middle Brook military encampment three of their sons to be trained in American schools. Washington replied: "You do well to wish to learn our arts and ways of life, and above all, the religion of Jesus Christ... I pray God He may make your Nation wise and strong."

American Minute
August 30th

*H*e was once one of America's greatest generals. During the Revolution, he captured Fort Ticonderoga with Ethan Allen, and defeated the British at Saratoga. But it was on this date, August 30, 1780, that General Benedict Arnold conspired with General Clinton of Britain to surrender West Point for twenty thousand pounds. When discovered, George Washington wrote: "Treason of the blackest dye was yesterday discovered! General Arnold who commanded at West Point, was about to... give the American cause a deadly wound if not fatal stab.... Its discovery affords the most convincing proof that the Liberties of America are the object of divine Protection."

American Minute
August 31st

Imprisoned 12 years - his crime: preaching without a license from the King. But injustice turned to good for during this time the classic book Pilgrim's Progress was penned by prisoner John Bunyan, who died this day, August 31, 1688. It is an allegory of a man named Christian who flees the City of Destruction, and is directed by Evangelist to follow a narrow path to the City of Zion. The friends and dangers he meets along the way inspired the modern story of the Wizard of Oz. Translated into over one hundred languages, John Bunyan's Pilgrim's Progress was found in nearly every home in colonial America, along with the Bible. John Bunyan wrote: "I saw in my dream that he made haste....looking very narrowly before him as he went, he espied two lions in the way....Then he was afraid...for he thought nothing but death was before him. But the porter at the lodge, whose name is Watchful, perceiving...he would go back, cried: 'Is thy strength so small? Fear not the lions, for they are chained, and are placed there for trial of faith, and for discovery of those that had none. Keep in the midst of the path, and no hurt shall come unto thee.'"

American Minute
September 1st

*T*he British invaded Washington, D.C. The Capitol was burned. President James and Dolly Madison fled the White House. On this day, September 1, 1814, President Madison wrote: "The enemy by a sudden incursion has succeeded in invading the capitol of the nation... During their possession...though for a single day only, they wantonly destroyed the public edifices.... An occasion which appeals so forcibly to the...patriotic devotion of the American people, none will forget... Independence...is now to be maintained...with the strength and resources which...Heaven has blessed." Less than 3 months later, November 1814, President Madison wrote: "The two Houses of the National Legislature having by a joint resolution expressed their desire that in the present time of public calamity and war a day may be recommended to be observed by the people of the United States as a day of public humiliation and fasting and of prayer to Almighty God for the safety and welfare of these States, His blessing on their arms, and a speedy restoration of peace, I have deemed it proper...to recommend...a day of...humble adoration to the Great Sovereign of the Universe."

American Minute
September 2nd

*T*he torpedo-bomber he flew was hit by anti-aircraft fire while making a run over Bonin Island, 600 miles south of Japan. He headed out to sea and ejected from his burning plane this day, September 2, 1944, and was rescued by a submarine. Receiving the Distinguished Flying Cross, he graduated from Yale, became successful in the Texas oil industry and entered politics, eventually becoming America's 41st President. His name: George Bush, who began his Inaugural Address with a prayer: "Heavenly Father, we bow our heads and thank You for Your love... Make us strong to do Your work, willing to heed and hear Your will."

American Minute
September 3rd

"*I*n the name of the most holy and undivided Trinity." This is how the Treaty of Paris began, which ended the eight-year long American Revolutionary War. The Treaty continued: "It having pleased the Divine Providence to dispose the heart of...Prince George the Third...to forget all past misunderstandings...between the two countries..." The Treaty was signed this day by the American leaders Benjamin Franklin, John Adams, the second President, and John Jay, the first Chief Justice, and ends with the phrase: "Done at Paris, this third day of September in the year of our Lord, one thousand seven hundred and eighty-three."

American Minute
September 4th

*I*n the dead of winter, 1842, clad in buckskin breeches, fur leggings and moccasins, he trekked 4000 miles, in a race against time, from his mission in the Oregon wilderness to Washington, D.C., to plead with President Tyler not to give the land to Britain. He then led the first wagon trains across the Oregon Trail. This was Dr. Marcus Whitman, born this day, September 4, 1802. In dedicating the Oregon Trail Monument, President Warren G. Harding stated: "Such was Marcus Whitman, the missionary hero of the vast, unsettled, unexplored Oregon country, who had come out of the West to plead that the state should acquire for civilization the empire that the churches were gaining for Christianity...Never in the history of the world has there been a finer example of civilization following Christianity. The missionaries led under the banner of the cross, and the settlers moved close behind under the star-spangled symbol of the nation."

American Minute
September 5th

The world was shocked as just five days after Princess Diana was killed, Mother Teresa died this day, September 5, 1997. The daughter of an Albanian grocer, she joined an order at age 18 and began working in the slums of Calcutta. She started the Missionaries of Charity, caring for the blind, aged, lepers, crippled, and the dying. A Nobel Prize recipient, 83-year-old Mother Teresa spoke at the National Prayer Breakfast, February 1994, which was attended by over 3,000 individuals, including the President and Mrs. Clinton and Vice-President Al Gore. Mother Teresa stated: "I feel that the greatest destroyer of peace today is abortion, because it is a war against the child, a direct killing of the innocent child, murder by the mother herself, and if we accept that a mother can kill even her own child, how can we tell other people not to kill one another?...Please don't kill the child. I want the child. Please give me the child. I am willing to accept any child who would be aborted and to give that child to a married couple who will love the child and be loved by the child."

American Minute
September 6th

Born this day, September 6, 1757, his father died before he was two-years-old and his mother died when he was twelve. He inherited their fortune. At fourteen-years-old, he joined the French Military and, at age 16, became a captain and married Marie Adrienne Francoise de Noailles, whose family was related to the King. At 19, against the King's wishes, he purchased a ship and persuaded several French officers to accompany him to fight in the American Revolution. Washington appointed him a major general. His name was Marquis de Lafayette. He fought at Brandywine, endured the freezing winter at Valley Forge, saw action at Barren Hill and Rhode Island. He returned to France and, along with Franklin's efforts, secured troops and supplies for the American cause which helped force Cornwallis to surrender at Yorktown. Nearly fifty years later, Lafayette was guest at a ceremony at Bunker Hill, along with 200 Revolutionary Veterans. Secretary of State Daniel Webster spoke: "God...has allowed you to behold the reward of your patriotic toils; and He has allowed to us...in the name of the present generation...in the name of liberty to thank you!"

American Minute
September 7th

As recorded in the Journals of the Continental Congress, at nine o'clock in the morning, on this day, September 7, 1774, in Carpenter's Hall, Philadelphia, the very first act of Congress was to open with prayer. John Adams wrote: "Reverend Duche'... read several prayers in the established form, and...the thirty-fifth Psalm... I never saw a greater effect upon an audience. It seemed as if heaven had ordained that Psalm to be read on that morning. After this, Mr. Duche', unexpectedly to every body, struck out into an extemporary prayer, which filled the bosom of every man present. I must confess, I never heard a better prayer."

American Minute
September 8th

Near this day, September 8, 70 AD, the city of Jerusalem fell. Historian Josephus recorded that Roman General Titus finally smashed through the defenses of Jerusalem, destroying the city and the Temple. Over a million perished in the siege. Through the centuries, people of faith have desired to pilgrimage there, including Abraham Lincoln. Mrs. Lincoln recalled his last words as they sat in Ford's Theater: "He said he wanted to visit the Holy Land and see those places hallowed by the footprints of the Saviour. He was saying there was no city he so much desired to see as Jerusalem."

American Minute
September 9th

The same year the United States won California from Mexico, some workers constructing a sawmill for John Sutter on the south fork of the American River, discovered gold. News spread like fire and soon "Forty-Niners," as the prospectors were called, poured in from all parts of the world. Quickly populated, California became the thirty-first State on this day, September 9, 1850. The Constitution, which prohibited slavery, stated in its Preamble: "We, the People of the State of California, grateful to Almighty God for our freedom, in order to secure and perpetuate its blessings, do establish this Constitution."

American Minute
September 10th

The son of one of the Boston Tea Party "Indians," he graduated from Harvard and eventually became Massachusetts Speaker of the House. At age 32, President James Madison appointed him the youngest Justice on the U.S. Supreme Court. He served 34 years, and helped establish the illegality of the slave trade in the Amistad case. His name was Joseph Story, and he died this day, September 10, 1845. A founder of the Harvard Law School, Justice Joseph Story stated in Vidal v. Girard's Executors (1844): "Where can the purest principles of morality be learned so clearly or so perfectly as from the New Testament?" Justice Joseph Story, having been appointed to the Supreme Court by the person who introduced the First Amendment in Congress, James Madison, commented on the First Amendment in his "Familiar Exposition of the Constitution of the United States" (1840): "The real object of the First Amendment was not to countenance, much less to advance Mohammedanism, or Judaism, or infidelity, by prostrating Christianity, but to exclude all rivalry among Christian sects."

American Minute
September 11th

"*F*reedom itself was attacked this morning by a faceless coward, and freedom will be defended," spoke President Bush on September 11, 2001, after the most devastating terrorist attack upon America. Islamic radicals hijacked three passenger jets, flying two into New York's World Trade Center and one into the Pentagon. Another crashed in Pennsylvania. That evening President Bush addressed the nation: "Thousands of lives were suddenly ended by evil, despicable acts of terror. Pictures of planes flying into buildings, fires burning, huge structures collapsing have filled us with disbelief, terrible sadness and a quiet, unyielding anger... America was targeted...because we're the brightest beacon for freedom and opportunity in the world. ... I ask for your prayers for all those who grieve... And I pray they will be comforted by a power greater than any of us spoken through the ages in Psalm 23: "Even though I walk through the valley of the shadow of death, I fear no evil for you are with me.""

American Minute
September 12th

He had been Chief Justice of the Michigan Supreme Court, dean of the University of Michigan Law School and President of the American Bar Association. His name was Thomas Cooley, and he died this day, September 12, 1898. The first chairman of the Interstate Commerce Commission, Thomas Cooley's legal commentaries have had a major impact on law in America. In his General Principles of Constitutional Law (1890), Thomas Cooley wrote: "It was never intended by the Constitution that the government should be prohibited from recognizing religion, or that religious worship should never be provided for in cases where a proper recognition of Divine Providence in the working of government might seem to require it....The Christian religion was always recognized in the administration of the common law of the land, the fundamental principles of that religion must continue to be recognized in the same cases and to the same extent as formerly."

American Minute
September 13th

Sent to negotiate the release of an American doctor, the enemy detained him all night on a ship. It was September 13, 1814. He watched the British fleet mercilessly bombard Fort McHenry from a distance, as Chesapeake Bay had been blocked by sunken ships. This was just two weeks after the British burned the Capitol. The next morning, "through the dawn's early light," this young lawyer, Francis Scott Key, saw the American flag still flying. Elated, he penned the Star-Spangled Banner, which states in its fourth verse: "O! thus be it ever when free men shall stand, Between their loved home and the war's desolation; Blest with vict'ry and peace, may the Heav'n-rescued land, Praise the Pow'r that hath made and preserved us a nation! Then conquer we must, when our cause it is just; And this be our motto, "In God is our trust!" And the star spangled banner in triumph shall wave O'er the land of the free and the home of the brave!"

American Minute
September 14th

The son of a butcher, most of his family died in a plague that swept England, leaving him with a fair estate. He attended Emmanuel College and became a minister. He married, sailed for America, and served as assistant pastor of the First Church of Charlestown, before dying of tuberculosis on this day, September 14, 1638. His name was John Harvard. The founders of Harvard College wrote: "After God had carried us safe to New-England...it pleased God to stir up the heart of one Mr. Harvard, a godly gentleman...to give...one half of his estate...towards the erecting of a college."

American Minute
September 15th

*H*e was the only U.S. President to also serve as Chief Justice of the Supreme Court. He was appointed by President McKinley as the first governor of the Philippines after the Spanish-American War and by President Theodore Roosevelt as Secretary of War. The largest President, weighing over 300 lbs, a bathtub was installed for him in the White House, big enough to hold four men. His name was William Howard Taft, and he was born this day September 15, 1857. President Taft stated: "A God-fearing nation, like ours, owes it to its inborn...sense of moral duty to testify...devout gratitude to the All-Giver for...countless benefits."

American Minute
September 16th

September 16, 1620, using the Gregorian Calendar, one hundred and two Pilgrims set sail on the Mayflower. The two-month journey was beset with storms. At one point the beam under the main mast cracked, being propped back in place using the screw of a printer's press. One youth was rescued after being swept overboard by a freezing wave. A boy died, and a mother gave birth. Intending to land in Virginia, they were blown off-course. In that first bitter winter half died. Governor Bradford wrote: "Last and not least, they cherished a great hope and inward zeal of laying good foundations...for the propagation and advance of the gospel of the kingdom of Christ in the remote parts of the world."

American Minute
September 17th

"**D**one...the seventeenth day of September, in the year of our LORD one thousand seven hundred and eighty seven." This was the last line of U.S. Constitution, which was approved this day. A study done by Professors Donald Lutz and Charles Hyneman, examining nearly 15,000 writings of the fifty-five men that wrote the Constitution, including newspaper articles, pamphlets, books and monographs, reported that the Bible, especially the book of Deuteronomy, contributed 34% of all direct quotations. When indirect citations were included, they found the majority of all quotations referenced by the Founders were derived from the Bible.

American Minute
September 18th

A member of the Continental Congress, he not only led military expeditions during the Revolutionary War, but paid for them out of his own pocket. He built ships with which to raid the British, signed the Constitution, and was the first President pro tem of the Senate. His name was John Langdon, and he died this day, September 18, 1819. As Governor of New Hampshire, John Langdon proclaimed: "It...becomes our...Duty, not only to acknowledge, in general with the rest of Mankind, our dependence on the Supreme Ruler of the Universe, but as a People peculiarly favoured, to testify our Gratitude to the Author of all our Mercies."

American Minute
September 19th

*L*ike the Roman leader Cincinnatus, who twice led the Roman Republic to victory in battle and twice gave up his power to return to a life of farming, George Washington led the American Republic to victory over the British, resigned, then served two terms as President, and returned to a life of farming at Mount Vernon. The world stood in awe as Washington gave up his powerful position and delivered his Farewell Address on this day, September 19, 1796. He stated: "Of all the dispositions and habits which lead to political prosperity, Religion and Morality are indispensable supports. In vain would that man claim the tribute of Patriotism, who should labor to subvert these great Pillars."

American Minute
September 20th

*H*e helped write the Bill of Rights in the first session of Congress. He was a Representative of Massachusetts and participated in ratification of the Constitution. He was offered the presidency of Harvard, but declined due to ill health. His name was Fisher Ames. In an article published this day, September 20, 1789, in the Palladium magazine, Fisher Ames wrote: "We have a dangerous trend beginning to take place in our education...putting...books into the hands of children containing fables....and spending less time in the classroom on the Bible... The Bible states the great moral lessons better than any other manmade book."

American Minute
September 21st

On this day, September 21, 1924, America's 30th President, Calvin Coolidge, addressed the Holy Name Society in Washington, D.C. He stated: "The worst evil that could be inflicted upon the youth...would be to leave them without restraint...at the mercy of their own uncontrolled inclinations. Under such conditions education would be impossible, and all orderly development...hopeless. I do not need to picture the result." President Coolidge concluded: "It seems...perfectly plain that...the right to equality, liberty and property...have for their foundation reverence for God. If we could imagine that swept away...our American government could not long survive."

American Minute
September 22nd

"**I** only regret that I have but one life to lose for my country." These were the last words of American patriot Nathan Hale, who was hanged by the British, without a trial, this day, September 22, 1776. A Yale graduate and school teacher, he fought in the siege of Boston. He captured a boat full of provisions from under the gun of a British man-of-war. On Long Island, he penetrated the British line to spy for information, but was captured as he returned. His nephew, Edward Everett Hale, a well-known author, wrote: "We are God's children...you and I, and we have our duties... Thank God I come from men who are not afraid in battle."

American Minute
September 23rd

*I*magine writing a book which would sell a million copies a year for over one hundred years! Well, one man did. His name was William Holmes McGuffey, born this day, September 23, 1800. Considered the "Schoolmaster of the Nation," McGuffey's Readers were the mainstay of America's public school system from 1836 till the 1920's. McGuffey was the president of Ohio University and formed the first teachers' association in that part of the nation. In his Fifth Eclectic Reader, William McGuffey wrote: "Erase all thought and fear of God from a community, and selfishness and sensuality would absorb the whole man."

American Minute
September 24th

"The power to tax is the power to destroy," wrote John Marshall, the fourth Chief Justice of the Supreme Court, who was born this day, September 24, 1755. No one had a greater impact on Constitutional Law in America, as he served on the bench 34 years and helped write over 1000 decisions. He fought in the Revolution under Washington, enduring the terrible winter at Valley Forge. The nation felt a profound loss at his death. The Liberty Bell cracked while tolling at his funeral in July of 1835. Chief Justice John Marshall wrote in a letter to Jasper Adams, May 9, 1833: "The American population is entirely Christian, and with us Christianity and Religion are identified. It would be strange indeed, if with such a people, our institutions did not presuppose Christianity, and did not often refer to it, and exhibit relations with it."

American Minute
September 25th

"*C*ongress shall make no law respecting the establishment of religion, or prohibiting the free exercise thereof." Thus began the Ten Amendments, or Bill of Rights, which were approved this day, September 25, 1789. George Mason, known as "The Father of the Bill of Rights," wrote the Virginia Declaration of Rights from which Jefferson drew to write the Declaration of Independence. Mason was one of fifty-five who wrote the U.S. Constitution, but was also one of sixteen who refused to sign it because it did not abolish slavery and did not limit the power of the Federal Government. He worked with Patrick Henry and Samuel Adams to prevent the Constitution from being ratified, as the abuses of King George's concentrated power were still fresh. It was through Mason's insistence that in the first session of Congress ten limitations were put on the Federal Government. George Mason had suggested the wording of the First Amendment be: "All men have an equal, natural and unalienable right to the free exercise of religion, according to the dictates of conscience; and that no particular sect or society of Christians ought to be favored or established by law in preference to others."

American Minute
September 26th

Harvard, the oldest institution of higher learning in America, located in Cambridge, Massachusetts, declared its purpose was to "train a literate clergy." Ten of its twelve presidents prior to the Revolution were ministers and over fifty percent of the 17th-century graduates became ministers. The *Rules and Precepts* for the students, adopted September, 26, 1642, stated: "Seeing the Lord only giveth wisedome, Let every one seriously set himself by prayer in secret to seeke it of him Proverbs 2,3." In 1790, it stated: "All the scholars shall, at sunset in the evening preceding the Lord's Day, lay aside all their diversions and...apply himself to the duties of religion." The dedication inscribed near the old iron gate at the main entrance to the campus, as well as the catalog of the Harvard Divinity School, reads: "After God had carried us safe to New England and we had builded our houses, provided necessaries for our livelihood, reared convenient places for God's worship and settled the civil government, one of the next things we longed for and looked after was to advance learning and perpetuate it to posterity, dreading to leave an illiterate ministry to the churches when our present ministers lie in the dust."

American Minute
September 27th

Crying "no taxation without representation," he instigated the Stamp Act riots and the Boston Tea Party. After the "Boston Massacre," he spread Revolutionary sentiment throughout the Colonies with his Committees of Correspondence. He called for a Continental Congress and signed the Declaration. Known as "The Father of the American Revolution," Samuel Adams was born this day, September 27, 1722. Samuel Adams wrote in 1750: "He therefore is the truest friend to the liberty of his country who tries most to promote its virtue, and who, so far as his power and influence extend, will not suffer a man to be chosen into any office of power and trust who is not a wise and virtuous man....The sum of all is, if we would most truly enjoy this gift of Heaven, let us become a virtuous people."

American Minute
September 28th

*H*e developed the vaccines for rabies and anthrax. He revolutionized the medical field by establishing the germ theory of disease, laying the foundation for the control of tuberculosis, cholera, diphtheria, and tetanus. He was appointed dean of the faculty of sciences at Lille University in France. He developed the process of "Pasteurization" of milk. His name: Louis Pasteur, and he died this day, September 28, 1895. Louis Pasteur stated: "Science brings man nearer to God... There is something in the depths of our souls which tells us that the world may be more than a mere combination of events."

American Minute
September 29th

*L*ate September, in the year 1622, Squanto died. He had helped the Pilgrims' survive in the new world, as "A special instrument sent of God." Governor Bradford wrote: "The winds drove their boat in; Captain Standish fell ill with fever... they could not get round the shoals of Cape Cod, for flats and breakers...so they put into Manamoick Bay... Here Squanto fell ill of Indian fever, bleeding much at the nose, - which the Indians take for a symptom of death... He begged the Governor to pray for him, that he might go to the Englishmen's God in Heaven, and bequeathed several of his things to...his English friends... His death was a great loss."

American Minute
September 30th

Seven times he came to America, preaching across the Colonies, sometimes to crowds of over 30,000 people. This Great Awakening spread like fire. Benjamin Franklin not only attended his meetings and printed his sermons, but built an auditorium for him to speak in, afterwards donating it as the first building of the University of Pennsylvania. Who was he: George Whitefield, who died this day, September 30, 1770. To Whitefield, Franklin wrote: "I sometimes wish that you and I were jointly employed by the Crown to settle a colony on the Ohio...to settle in that fine country a strong body of religious and industrious people!..Might it not greatly facilitate the introduction of pure religion among the heathen, if we could, by such a colony, show them a better sample of Christians than they commonly see in our Indian traders?"

American Minute
October 1st

"*I*n the language of the Holy Writ, there is a time for all things. There is a time to preach and a time to fight." Thus ended the sermon of Lutheran pastor John Peter Muhlenburg, as he removed his clerical robes to reveal the uniform in the Continental Army. After church service, 300 men of his congregation rode off with him to join General Washington's troops. Born this day, October 1, 1746, and he died this same day in 1807. John Peter Muhlenburg was promoted to Major-General, and later elected U.S. Congressman and Senator. In 1889, Pennsylvania presented a statue of John Peter Muhlenburg to represent the State in the U.S. Capitol Statuary Hall.

American Minute
October 2nd

Oxford historian Arnold Joseph Toynbee died this day, October 2, 1975. He had worked for the British government doing foreign intelligence and research and was a delegate to the Paris Peace Conferences following World Wars I and II. Gaining international acclaim for his history books, Arnold Joseph Toynbee wrote: "The course of human history consists of a series of encounters...in which each man or woman or child...is challenged by God to make the free choice between doing God's will and refusing to do it. When Man refuses, he is free to make his refusal and to take the consequences."

American Minute
October 3rd

On October 3, 1789, from the capital of New York City, President George Washington issued the first Proclamation of a National Day of Thanksgiving and Prayer. There was reason to rejoice as just one week earlier, the first session of the United States Congress approved the First Ten Amendments, better known as the Bill of Rights, thereby limiting the power and scope of the Federal Government. Washington wrote: "Now, therefore, I do recommend...the People of these United States to the service of that great and glorious Being, who is the beneficent Author of all the good that was, that is, or that will be."

American Minute
October 4th

A Joint Resolution of the 97th Congress, signed by Speaker of the House Tip O'Neil and President of the Senate Strom Thurmond, declared "A Year of the Bible." President Reagan signed the Proclamation on this day October 4, 1982, stating: "Now, therefore, I, Ronald Reagan, President of the United States of America, in recognition of the contributions and influence of the Bible on our Republic and our people, do hereby proclaim 1983 the Year of the Bible in the United States. I encourage all citizens, each in his or her own way, to reexamine and rediscover its priceless and timeless message."

American Minute
October 5th

*H*e entered Yale College at age 13 and graduated with honors. He became a pastor, and his sermon, "Sinners in the Hands of An Angry God," started the Great Awakening, a revival that swept America, uniting the colonies prior to the Revolution. He became President of Princeton College. His name was Jonathan Edwards, born October 5, 1703. Jonathan married Sarah Pierrepont, and, according to "A Study in Education and Heredity" by A.E. Winship (1900), their descendants included a U.S. Vice-President, 3 U.S. Senators, 3 governors, 3 mayors, 13 college presidents, 30 judges, 65 professors, 80 public office holders, 100 lawyers, and 100 missionaries. This same study examined a family known as "Jukes." In 1877, after visiting New York's prisons, Richard Dugdale found inmates with 42 different last names all descended from one man, called "Max," born 1720 of Dutch stock. Max was idle, ignorant and vulgar His descendants included only 20 with a trade, 310 paupers, who, combined spent 2,300 years in poorhouses, 50 women of debauchery, 400 physically wrecked by indulgent living, 7 murderers, 60 thieves, and 130 other convicts. The "Jukes" cost the state more than $1,250,000.

American Minute
October 6th

On October 6, 1862, just three weeks after the Battle of Antietam, the single bloodiest day in the Civil War where the North and the South lost 10,000 men each, President Lincoln met with Eliza Gurney and three other Quakers. He said: "We are indeed going through a great trial - a fiery trial...Being a humble instrument in the hands of our Heavenly Father...I have sought His aid; but if, after endeavoring to do my best in the light which He affords me, my efforts fail, I must believe that for some purpose unknown to me, He wills it." Lincoln concluded: "We cannot but believe, that He who made the world still governs it."

American Minute
October 7th

*H*enry Muhlenberg died this day, October 7, 1787. He was one of the founders of the Lutheran Church in America. His son, John Peter, became a U.S. Senator, and son, Frederick, became the first Speaker of the House. Henry Muhlenberg pastored near Valley Forge during the Revolutionary War. He commented: "I heard a fine example today, namely that His Excellency General Washington rode around among his army yesterday and admonished each and every one to fear God, to put away wickedness...and to practice Christian virtues... The Lord God has also singularly, yea, marvelously preserved him from harm in the midst of countless perils."

American Minute
October 8th

A race car driver, he served in France during World War I as chauffeur for General Pershing. With Germany's Red Baron dominating the skies, he transferred to the 94th Aero Squadron, which shot down 69 enemy aircraft and earned him the Congressional Medal of Honor. His name was "Eddie" Rickenbacker, born this day, October 8, 1890. After becoming owner of Indianapolis Speedway and Eastern Airlines, he was asked by the Secretary of War in 1942 to inspect bases in the Pacific. With inadequate navigational equipment, their pilot flew hundreds of miles off-course, ran out of fuel, and ditched in the ocean. The oldest among them, 52 years old, Rickenbacker encouraged the other six for 24 days as they drifted. He once caught a sea gull that landed on his head, which he caught for food and bait, using a bent key ring as a fishing hook. Fighting off sharks and ocean swells two-feet high, they drank water wrung from their clothes from infrequent drizzles. In his book, "The Flying Circus," Eddie Rickenbacker recounted: "I am not such an egotist as to believe that God has spared me because I am I. I believe there is work for me to do and that I am spared to do it, just as you are."

American Minute
October 9th

*L*ewis Cass was born this day, October 9, 1782. He fought in the War of 1812, and later became the Governor of the Michigan Territory. Cass made treaties with the Indians, organized townships and built roads. He was a U.S. Senator, Secretary of State under President Buchanan and the Democratic Presidential candidate in 1848. Lewis Cass stated: "The fate of republican government is indissolubly bound up with the fate of the Christian religion, and a people who reject its holy faith will find themselves the slaves of their own evil passions and of arbitrary power."

American Minute
October 10th

*J*ust two days before Columbus sighted land, his men were on the verge of mutiny. They had sailed the longest voyage ever out of the sight of land and wanted to turn back. The entry in Columbus' Journal, October 10, 1492, stated: "Here the people could stand it no longer and complained of the long voyage; but the Admiral cheered them as best he could, holding out good hope of the advantages they would have. He added that it was useless to complain. He had come to the Indies, and so had to continue until he found them, with the help of Our Lord."

American Minute
October 11th

On October 11, 1798, President John Adams addressed the officers of the First Brigade of the Third Division of the Militia of Massachusetts in a letter: "We have no government armed with power capable of contending with human passions unbridled by morality and religion. Avarice, ambition, revenge, or gallantry, would break the strongest cords of our Constitution as a whale goes through a net. Our Constitution was made only for a moral and religious people. It is wholly inadequate to the government of any other."

American Minute
October 12th

October 12, 1492, two hours after midnight, Columbus sighted land. He named the first island San Salvador, meaning "Holy Saviour." After meeting the natives, Columbus wrote: "So that they might be well-disposed towards us, for I knew that they were a people to be...converted to our Holy Faith rather by love than by force, I gave to some red caps and to others glass beads... They were greatly pleased and became so entirely our friends that it was a wonder to see.... I believe that they would easily be made Christians, for it seemed to me that they had no religion of their own."

American Minute
October 13th

Margaret Thatcher was born this day, October 13, 1925. She was the first woman Prime Minister of the United Kingdom. While traveling through New York City in 1996, Margaret Thatcher had an interview with Joseph A. Cannon, which was printed in Human Events. She stated: "The Decalogue Ten Commandments are addressed to each and every person. This is the origin of our common humanity and of the sanctity of the individual. Each one has a duty to try to carry out those commandments. You don't get that in any other political creed....It is personal liberty with personal responsibility. Responsibility to your parents, to your children, to your God. This really binds us together in a way that nothing else does. If you accept freedom, you've got to have principles about the responsibility. You can't do this without a biblical foundation. Your Founding Fathers came over with that. They came over with the doctrines of the New Testament as well as the Old. They looked after one another, not only as a matter of necessity, but as a matter of duty to their God. There is no other country in the world which started that way"

American Minute
October 14th

*H*e was the son of a British Navy Admiral who discovered Bermuda. He attended Oxford University and studied law. At the age of 22, he heard a sermon titled "The Sandy Foundation Shaken" and converted to the Society of Friends, or Quakers. As a result, he suffered imprisonment over three times for his faith, once imprisoned in the Tower of London for eight months. His name was William Penn, born this day, October 14, 1644. King Charles II repaid a debt owed to his father by giving William Penn a land grant in America, named Pennsylvania. While imprisoned in the Tower of London, 1668, William Penn wrote his classic book, "No Cross, No Crown," in which he stated: "Christ's cross is Christ's way to Christ's crown....The unmortified Christian and the heathen are of the same religion, and the deity they truly worship is the god of this world....The false notion that they may be children of God while in a state of disobedience to his holy commandments, and disciples of Jesus though they revolt from his cross."

American Minute
October 15th

On this day, October 15, 1788, James Madison, who was called the Father of the Constitution, commented on the role of the Supreme Court: "As the courts are generally the last in making the decision, it results to them, by refusing or not refusing to execute a law, to stamp it with its final character. This makes the Judiciary department paramount in fact to the Legislature, which was never intended, and can never be proper." Also on this day, October 15, 1991, the United States Senate, by a vote 52-48, confirmed Clarence Thomas as a Justice on the Supreme Court. During the confirmation hearings, Senator Thurmond asked him a question on judicial activism. Clarence Thomas answered: "The role of a judge is a limited one. It is to...interpret the Constitution, where called upon, but at no point to impose his or her will or his or her opinion in that process."

American Minute
October 16th

$H$is barn in Pennsylvania was a station on the Underground Railway, helping slaves escape to freedom. But on this day, October 16, 1859, John Brown and 21 men raided Harper's Ferry, Virginia, and seized the armory. He was captured, sentenced, and hanged. Labeled insane by some, Louisa May Alcott, author of Little Women, called him Saint John the Just. Years before, after hearing the story of how abolitionist publisher Elijah Lovejoy was murdered, John Brown stood up in the back of church and declared: "Here, before God, in the presence of these witnesses, I consecrate my life to the destruction of slavery."

American Minute
October 17th

*F*ive thousand seven hundred British troops, under the command of General Burgoyne, surrendered this day, October 17, 1777, at Saratoga, New York, to the revolutionary forces led by General Gates. After swearing never to fight against America again, the British troops were boarded on ships at Boston and sent back to England. When this news reached Europe, it encouraged further support of the Revolution. In a letter to his brother, John Augustine Washington, General George Washington wrote of this victory, saying: "I most devoutly congratulate my country, and every well-wisher to the cause, on this signal stroke of Providence."

American Minute
October 18th

Pilgrim leader Edward Winslow was born this day, October 18, 1595. He was English agent for the Plymouth Colony and served as their Governor three separate terms, successfully making friendship with Indian chief, Massasoit. He later returned to England and served Oliver Cromwell in the English Civil War. In writing of the Pilgrims' experiences, Edward Winslow recounted: "Drought and the like...moved not only every good man privately to enter into examination with his own estate between God and his conscience, and so to humiliation before Him, but also to humble ourselves together before the Lord by fasting and prayer."

American Minute
October 19th

The British power in America was broken this day, October 19, 1781, as 8000 British troops under Lord Cornwallis surrendered at Yorktown, Virginia. The following day, General George Washington called for a service to render thanksgiving to God: "In order to diffuse the general Joy through every Breast the General orders that...Divine Service be performed tomorrow in the several Brigades or Divisions. The Commander-in-Chief earnestly recommends that the troops not on duty should universally attend, with...gratitude of heart which the recognition of such...astonishing Interposition of Providence demands of us."

American Minute
October 20th

*H*erbert Hoover died this day, October 20, 1964. He was America's 31st President, guiding the country during the first part of the Great Depression. During World War II, in a joint statement signed by such individuals as the widows of Presidents Coolidge, T. Roosevelt, Taft, Harrison, Cleveland, Herbert Hoover stated: "Menaced by collectivist trends, we must seek revival of our strength in the spiritual foundations which are the bedrock of our republic. Democracy is the outgrowth of the religious conviction of the sacredness of every human life. On the religious side, its highest embodiment is The Bible; on the political side, the Constitution."

American Minute
October 21st

On this day, October 21, 1805, in one of the greatest naval battles in history, British Admiral Horatio Nelson defeated the combined Spanish and French fleets - 33 ships with 2,640 guns - in the Battle of Trafalgar off the coast of Spain. The fifteen million dollars Napoleon received two years earlier from selling 600 million acres to the United States was not enough to assure him victory. Though 90,000 French troops were assembled on the coast of France ready to invade Britain, this defeat abruptly ended Napoleon's power on the sea, and with it, his dreams of world conquest. During the battle, cannonades and musket shot ripped apart ships at point blank range, killing or wounding nearly ten thousand men. In the fighting, Admiral Nelson was fatally shot in the spine. He was carried below deck to the ship's surgeon where he died. Admiral Horatio Nelson's last words were: "Thank God I have done my duty."

American Minute
October 22nd

October 22, 1836, General Sam Houston was sworn in as the first President of the Republic of Texas. As a teenager, after his father died, he ran off to live with the Cherokee Indians on the Tennessee River, being adopted by the Chief and given the name "Raven." Three years later, he returned to town, opened a school, joined the army and fought in the War of 1812, being noticed by General Andrew Jackson. In 1818, wearing Indian dress, Houston led a delegation of Cherokee to Washington, D.C., to meet with President Monroe. Elected to U.S. Congress in 1823, he became Governor of Tennessee in 1827. After a failed marriage, he moved to Texas, where he was made Commander to fight Santa Ana. The Texas Declaration of Independence stated: "When a government has ceased to protect the lives, liberty, and property of the people... and...becomes an instrument in the hands of evil rulers for their oppression....it is a...sacred obligation to their posterity to abolish such government, and create another in its stead...Conscious of the rectitude of our intentions, we fearlessly and confidently commit the issue to the decision of the Supreme Arbiter of the Destinies of Nations."

American Minute
October 23rd

On October 23, 1913, President Woodrow Wilson issued a Proclamation of a National Day of Thanksgiving and Prayer. He wrote: "The season is at hand... to turn in praise and thanksgiving to Almighty God for His manifold... blessings to us as a nation. The year that has just passed has been marked...by...His gracious and beneficent providence.... We have seen the practical completion of a great work at the Isthmus of Panama.... 'Righteousness exalteth a nation' and 'peace on earth, good will towards men' furnish the only foundation upon which can be built the lasting achievements of the human spirit."

American Minute
October 24th

The United Nations was established by charter on this day, October 24, 1945, with the promise of preventing future wars. The first Secretary General was Alger Hiss, who in 1948 became the subject of a highly publicized trial - having been accused of being a Communist agent by former Soviet spy Whittaker Chambers. One of the first Presidents of the U.N. General Assembly (1949) and chairman of the U.N. Security Council (1957) was Philippine General Carlos Romulo. He had served with General Douglas MacArthur in the Pacific, was Ambassador to the U.S. and won the Pulitzer Prize. General Carlos Romulo stated: "Never forget, Americans, that yours is a spiritual country. Yes, I know you're a practical people. Like others, I've marveled at your factories, your skyscrapers, and your arsenals. But underlying everything else is the fact that America began as a God-loving, God-fearing, God-worshiping people."

American Minute
October 25th

*O*n October 25, 1887, President Grover Cleveland issued a Proclamation of a National Day of Thanksgiving and Prayer: "The goodness and the mercy of God, which have followed the American people during all the days of the past year, claim their grateful recognition.... I, Grover Cleveland, President of the United States, do hereby designate...a day of thanksgiving and prayer, to be observed by all the people of the land.... Let all secular work and employment be suspended, and let our people assemble in...worship and with prayer and songs of praise give thanks to our Heavenly Father for all that He has done."

American Minute
October 26th

On this day October 26, 1774, the Provincial Congress of Massachusetts reorganized their defense with one-third of their regiments being "Minutemen." They were known as such because they would be ready to fight at a minute's notice. The Provincial Congress gave the charge to the Minutemen: "You...are placed by Providence in the post of honor, because it is the post of danger.... The eyes not only of North America and the whole British Empire, but of all Europe, are upon you. Let us be, therefore, altogether solicitous that no disorderly behavior, nothing unbecoming our characters as Americans, as citizens and Christians, be justly chargeable to us."

American Minute
October 27th

*H*is wife and mother both tragically died on Valentine's Day, 1884. Depressed, he left New York to ranch cattle in the Dakotas. Several years later, he returned to New York and entered politics. Rising to the position of Assistant Secretary of the Navy, he resigned during the Spanish-American War to organized the first Voluntary Cavalry, known as the "Rough Riders," which captured Cuba's San Juan Hill. He was Vice-President under William McKinley and in 1901 became America's youngest President. His name was Teddy Roosevelt, born this day, October 27, 1858. President Roosevelt warned in 1909: "The thought of modern industry in the hands of Christian charity is a dream worth dreaming. The thought of industry in the hands of paganism is a nightmare beyond imagining. The choice between the two is upon us."

American Minute
October 28th

The Statue of Liberty was dedicated this day, October 28, 1886, by President Grover Cleveland. It was presented to the U.S. by France as a symbol of friendship. This four hundred and fifty thousand pound statue is supported by a steel structure built by Gustave Eiffel, who also built the Eiffel Tower. The Statue of Liberty was designed by sculptor Auguste Bartholdi, who wrote: "The statue was born for this place which inspired its conception. May God be pleased to bless my efforts and my work, and to crown it with success, the duration and the moral influence which it ought to have."

American Minute
October 29th

October 29, 1929, the New York Stock Exchange crashed. Panic selling ensued and America plunged into the Great Depression. President Herbert Hoover, in a nation-wide drive to aid the private relief agencies, stated: "Time and time again the American people have demonstrated a spiritual quality...of generosity... This is the occasion when we must arouse that idealism... This civilization...which we call American life, is builded and can alone survive upon the translation into individual action of that fundamental philosophy announced by the Savior nineteen centuries ago... Modern society can not survive with the defense of Cain, 'Am I my brother's keeper?'"

American Minute
October 30th

John Adams was born this day, October 30, 1735. He signed the Declaration of Independence, was Vice-President under George Washington and was elected the second President of the United States. Later in life, John Adams wrote to Thomas Jefferson: "Have you ever found in history, one single example of a Nation thoroughly corrupted that was afterwards restored to virtue?... And without virtue, there can be no political liberty.... Will you tell me how to prevent luxury from producing effeminacy, intoxication, extravagance, vice and folly?... I believe no effort in favour of virtue is lost."

American Minute
October 31st

*U*pon signing the Declaration of Independence, Samuel Adams stated: "This day, I trust, the reign of political protestantism will commence." Of the 56 signers, the majority were Protestant, with the notable exception of Charles Carroll of Carrollton, a Catholic, who was the longest living of the Signers, the wealthiest man in America, and his cousin started Georgetown. British Statesman Edmund Burke addressed Parliament in 1775: "All Protestantism...is a sort of dissent. But the religion most prevalent in our Northern Colonies is a refinement on the principle of resistance; it is the dissidence of dissent, and the protestantism of the Protestant religion." Protestantism began this day, October 31, 1517, as Martin Luther posted his ninety-five theses on the door of Wittenberg Church. Summoned to stand trial before the twenty-one year old Emperor Charles V, he was declared an outlaw. Frederick of Saxony hid him in the Wartburg castle where he translated the New Testament into German. Luther later wrote: "I am much afraid that schools will prove to be the great gates of hell unless they diligently labor in explaining the Holy Scriptures, engraving them in the hearts of youth."

American Minute
November 1st

On this day, November 1, 1800, John Adams became the first U.S. President to move into the White House. The following day he wrote a letter to his wife, Abigail, in which he composed a beautiful prayer. A portion of that prayer was inscribed on the mantlepiece in the State Dining Room by President Franklin D. Roosevelt. It reads: "I pray Heaven to bestow the best of blessings on this house and all that shall hereafter inhabit it." President Adams ended his prayer with the words: "May none but honest and wise men ever rule under this roof."

American Minute
November 2nd

After defeating the British, General George Washington resigned and returned to farming at Mount Vernon. On this day, November 2, 1783, he issued his Farewell Orders to his troops. "Before the Comdr in Chief takes his final leave," he wrote, "he wishes...a slight review of the past.... The singular interpositions of Providence in our feeble condition were such, as could scarcely escape the attention of the most unobserving; while the...perseverance of the Armies of the U. States, through almost every possible suffering...for the space of eight long years, was little short of a standing miracle."

American Minute
November 3rd

On November 3, 1924, in a Radio Address to the nation from the White House, President Calvin Coolidge stated: "I urge all the voters of our country, without reference to party, that they assemble tomorrow at their respective voting places in the exercise of the high office of American citizenship, that they approach the ballot box in the spirit that they would approach a sacrament." President Coolidge continued: "Make choice of public officers solely in the light of conscience. When an election is so held... it sustains the belief that the voice of the people is the voice of God."

American Minute
November 4th

*C*harles Carroll was unique. He was the only Roman Catholic to sign the Declaration of Independence and he outlived all the other signers. At his death, he was considered the wealthiest citizen in America. His cousin, John Carroll, founded Georgetown University, and another cousin, Daniel Carroll, signed the U.S. Constitution. On this day, November 4, 1800, Charles Carroll penned a letter to James McHenry, the signer of the Constitution for whom Fort McHenry was named. Charles Carroll wrote: "Without morals a republic cannot subsist any length of time; they therefore who are decrying the Christian religion, whose morality is so sublime and pure,... are undermining the solid foundation of morals, the best security for the duration of free governments."

American Minute
November 5th

She was the wife of the second President and the mother of the sixth President. Her letters provide some of the most valuable insights of the Revolutionary period. Her name was Abigail Adams. On this day, November 5, 1775, in a letter to Mercy Warren, Abigail wrote: "Is it possible that he whom no moral obligations bind, can have any real Good Will towards Men? Can he be a patriot who, by an openly vicious conduct, is... corrupting the Morals of Youth, and by his bad example injuring the very Country he professes to patronize...Scriptures tell us 'righteousness exalteth a Nation.'"

American Minute
November 6th

Did you know both basketball and volleyball were invented by instructors at the YMCA? The YMCA, or Young Men's Christian Association, was founded in 1844 by George Williams and has grown to a membership of over four million in seventy-six countries. Founder George Williams, who died this day, November 6, 1905, wrote: "My life-long experience as a business man and a... worker among young men, has taught me that the only power... that can effectually keep one from evil... is that which comes from an intimate knowledge of the Lord.... and... the safe Guide-Book by which one may be led to Christ is the Bible."

American Minute
November 7th

*H*e originally wanted to be a baseball player, but after attending a revival meeting at age 16, his life changed. He has since addressed crowds around the world and is unprecedented in having had friendships with U.S. Presidents Truman, Eisenhower, Kennedy, Johnson, Nixon, Ford, Carter, Reagan, Bush, Clinton and Bush. His name is Billy Graham, and he was born this day, November 7, 1918. Upon receiving the Congressional Gold Medal in 1996, Billy Graham stated: "As we face a new millennium, I believe America has gone a long way down the wrong road. We must turn around... If ever we needed God's help, it is now."

American Minute
November 8th

"**O**cian in view! O! the joy," was the wording William Clark entered in his Journal, yesterday, November 7, 1805, but actually Lewis and Clark were only at Gray's Bay, still 20 miles from the Pacific. Fierce storms pinned them down for three weeks. As cold weather set in, the captains decided to let the expedition vote on where to build winter camp, even allowing Clark's slave York and the woman Indian guide Sacagawea to vote. A humble Christmas was celebrated in their new Fort Clatsop, near present-day Astoria, Oregon. By Clark's estimate, their journey, commissioned by President Thomas Jefferson, had taken them 4,162 miles from the mouth of the Missouri River. Three months earlier, Meriwether Lewis, along with three companions, George Drouillard, Private John Shields and Private Hugh McNeal, reached the headwaters of the Missouri. Lewis recorded: "The road took us to the most distant fountain of the waters of the Mighty Missouri...Private McNeal had exultingly stood with a foot on each side of this little rivulet and thanked his God that he had lived to bestride the mighty and heretofore deemed endless Missouri."

American Minute
November 9th

On this day, November 9, 1954, President Eisenhower spoke at the National Conference on the Spiritual Foundation of American Democracy at the Sheraton-Carlton Hotel in Washington DC. He stated: "Now Dr. Lowry said something about my having certain convictions as to a God in Heaven and an Almighty power. Well, I don't think anyone needs a great deal of credit for believing in what seems to me to be obvious." Eisenhower concluded: "And no matter what Democracy tries to do in terms of individual liberty... when you come back to it, there is just one thing... man is worthwhile because he was born in the image of God."

American Minute
November 10th

"**D**octor Livingstone, I presume," was the greeting made this day, November 10, 1871, by New York Herald newspaper reporter Henry Stanley as he met Dr. David Livingstone on the banks of Lake Tanganyika. Dr. Livingstone, an internationally known missionary in Africa, had not been heard from in years and the rumor spread he had died. Stanley, a skeptic, set out to find him and write a story. He described Dr. Livingstone as: "A man who is... sustained as well as guided by influences from Heaven... The heroism, nobility, pure and stainless enthusiasm... come, beyond question, from Christ. There must, therefore, be a Christ."

American Minute
November 11th

At the eleventh hour of the eleventh day of the eleventh month, in the year 1918, World War I ended. Celebrated as Armistice Day, it was changed to Veterans Day after World War II. In 1921, President Warren Harding had the remains of an unknown soldier killed in France buried in Arlington Cemetery. He requested that: "All devout and patriotic citizens of the United States indulge in a period of silent thanks to God for these valuable valorous lives and of supplication for His Divine mercy and for His blessings upon our beloved country." Inscribed on the Tomb of the Unknown Soldier are the words: "Here lies in honored glory an American soldier know but to God."

American Minute
November 12th

*T*his day, November 12, 1620, was the
Pilgrims' first full day in America. It took over
two months for the one hundred and three of
them, cramped between decks on the tiny Mayflower, to cross the freezing North Atlantic. They
had intended to sail to Jamestown, but were blown
off course by violent storms and landed at Plymouth Rock. Governor William Bradford wrote:
"Being thus arrived in a good harbor, and brought
safe to land, they fell upon their knees and blessed
the God of Heaven who had brought them over
the vast and furious ocean, and delivered them
from all the perils and miseries thereof, again to
set their feet on the firm and stable earth."

American Minute
November 13th

*T*he Vietnam War Memorial was dedicated this day, November 13, 1982, honoring the 58,000 American troops who died. In 1966, Marine Sergeant George Hutchings of 1st Battalion, 5th Marine Division, Charlie Company, had over two hundred men killed around him during an ambush by the Viet Cong. Months later, after numerous battles, he was shot three times, bayoneted and left for dead, for which he received the Purple Heart. Of the Vietnam Memorial, George Hutchings said: "On that wall is the name of Corporal Quinton Bice, who was hit in the chest with a rocket running a patrol in my place. A Christian, he had shared the Gospel with me, but I didn't understand it till he gave his life in my place."

American Minute
November 14th

*B*orn a slave, he taught himself to read, and attended school after working all day. At age 25 he founded Tuskegee Institute and recruited George W. Carver. By his death, on this day, November 14, 1915, the school had over 1,500 students. His name was Booker T. Washington, and he was the first Black to have his picture on a U.S. postage stamp, coin, and elected to the Hall of Fame. In his book, Up From Slavery, Booker T. Washington wrote: "While a great deal of stress is laid upon the industrial side of the work at Tuskegee, we do not neglect... the...spiritual side. The school is strictly undenominational, but it is thoroughly Christian... Our preaching service, prayer-meetings, Sunday-school, Christian Endeavour Society, Young Men's Christian Association, and various missionary organizations, testify to this."

American Minute
November 15th

A member of the Continental Congress, he was the only clergyman to sign the Declaration of Independence, and he lost two sons in the Revolutionary War. He was President of Princeton and taught nine of the men that wrote the Constitution, including James Madison. He served on over one hundred and twenty Congressional Committees. His name was Reverend John Witherspoon, and he died this day, November 15, 1794. Rev. Witherspoon wrote: "A Republic must either preserve its virtue or lose its liberty.... Whoever is an avowed enemy of God, I scruple not to call him an enemy of his country."

American Minute
November 16th

"My Country 'tis of Thee, Sweet land of liberty..." This patriotic hymn was written by Samuel Francis Smith, who died this day, November 16, 1895. A classmate at Harvard with the poet Oliver Wendell Holmes, he became a Baptist minister and professor. While in seminary, Samuel heard the national anthems for England, Sweden and Russia. He sat down and within a half hour wrote My Country 'tis of Thee. The fourth verse reads: "Our fathers' God, to thee, Author of liberty, To Thee we sing; Long may our land be bright With freedom's holy light: Protect us by Thy might, Great God, our King."

American Minute
November 17th

*"B*loody Mary" got her nickname from sentencing over 300 people to death. She had been Queen of England for five years following the reign of her father, Henry VIII. Upon her death, this day, November 17, 1558, her half-sister Elizabeth became Queen and ruled forty-five years. During her reign, Elizabeth beheaded her cousin Mary Queen of Scots, Shakespeare wrote theater, Sir Francis Drake defeated the Spanish Armada and Sir Walter Raleigh sailed to America in an attempt to settle an area he named "Virginia" after Elizabeth, the "Virgin Queen." Regarding her epitaph, Queen Elizabeth stated: "I am no lover of pompous title, but only desire that my name may be recorded in a line or two, which shall express my name, my virginity, the years of my reign, and the reformation of religion under it."

American Minute
November 18th

Julius Caesar Watts, Jr., better know as J.C., was born this day, November 18, 1957. A college and pro football player, he was a youth minister and, in 1994, was elected to the U.S. Congress, where he was chosen House Conference Chairman. In response to the President's 1997 State of the Union Address, Congressman J.C. Watts stated: "I was taught to respect everyone for the simple reason that we're all God's children. I was taught, in the words of Martin Luther King, to judge a man not by the color of his skin, but by the content of his character. And I was taught that character is simply doing what's right when nobody's looking." Also on this day, in 1886, President Chester Arthur died. The son of a Baptist minister from Ireland, Arthur became an abolitionist lawyer, defending the rights of African Americans, and, during the Civil War, was Inspector General. When James Garfield was assassinated, President Arthur wrote: "The deep grief which fills all hearts should manifest itself with one accord toward the Throne of Infinite Grace...We should bow before the Almighty and seek from Him consolation in our affliction."

American Minute
November 19th

*"F*ourscore and seven years ago our fathers brought forth upon this continent a new
nation, conceived in liberty, and dedicated to the
proposition that all men are created equal." Thus
began the Gettysburg Address, delivered this day,
November 19, 1863, by President Abraham Lincoln on the battlefield where 50,000 soldiers were
killed or wounded in a three day battle. This ten-
sentence speech ends with the words: "We here
highly resolve that these dead shall not have died
in vain - that this nation, under God, shall have a
new birth of freedom - and that government of
the people, by the people, for the people, shall
not perish from the earth."

American Minute
November 20th

When the Supreme Court declared prayer in schools unconstitutional in 1962, Democratic Senate Majority Leader Robert Byrd from West Virginia, who was born this day, November 20, 1917, gave a moving address to Congress. He stated: "On the south banks of Washington's Tidal Basin, Thomas Jefferson still speaks: 'God who gave us life gave us liberty. Can the liberties of a nation be secure when we have removed a conviction that these liberties are the gift of God?'" Senator Byrd concluded: " Jefferson's words are a forceful and explicit warning that to remove God from this country will destroy it."

American Minute
November 21st

The French author Voltaire was born this day, November 21, 1694. The President of Yale College, Timothy Dwight, referred to Voltaire in an address given on the Fourth of July, 1798, titled, "The Duty of Americans at the Present Crisis": "About the year 1728, Voltaire, so celebrated for his wit and brilliancy and not less distinguished for his hatred of Christianity and his abandonment of principle, formed a systematical design to destroy Christianity and to introduce in its stead a general diffusion of irreligion and atheism. For this purpose he associated with himself Frederick the II, king of Prussia, and Mess. D'Alembert and Diderot, the principal compilers of the Encyclopedie, all men of talents, atheists, and in the like manner abandoned." Bruce Barton, an American advertising executive, wrote: "Voltaire spoke of the Bible as a short-lived book. He said that within a hundred years it would pass from common use. Not many people read Voltaire today, but his house has been packed with Bibles as a depot of a Bible society."

American Minute
November 22nd

Shots rang out as President John F. Kennedy was assassinated this day, November 22, 1963, in Dallas, Texas. The youngest President ever elected, he was also the youngest to die, barely serving one thousand days. The 46-year-old Kennedy was on his way to deliver an address at the Dallas Trade Mart. The speech he prepared, but never gave, stated: "We in this country, in this generation, are - by destiny rather than choice - the watchmen on the walls of world freedom. We ask, therefore, that we may be worthy of our power and responsibility, that we may exercise our strength with wisdom and restraint, and that we may achieve in our time and for all time the ancient vision of peace on earth, goodwill toward men. That must always be our goal - and the righteousness of our cause must always underlie our strength. For as was written long ago, 'Except the Lord keep the city, the watchman waketh but in vain.'"

American Minute
November 23rd

*T*wo months before being elected America's fourteenth President, his eleven year only son, Bennie, was killed as their campaign train rolled off the tracks. This happened to Franklin Pierce, who was born this day, November 23, 1804. Elected to Congress at age 29, he was a U.S. Senator at 33. After one term, he resigned and enlisted in the army as a private. Promoted to brigadier general, he served in General Winfield Scott's campaign against Mexico City. President Franklin Peirce stated: "It must be felt that there is no national security but in the nation's humble, acknowledged dependence upon God and His overruling providence."

American Minute
November 24th

*H*e was sentenced to be a galley slave on a French ship, but after several grueling years he escaped and came back to Scotland to preach. He confronted Mary, Queen of Scots, and so convincingly evangelized that by year 1560 the Scottish Parliament established Presbyterianism as the national faith. His name was John Knox, and he died this day, November 24, 1572. One of his descendants was the Reverend John Witherspoon, who signed the Declaration of Independence and was President of Princeton, teaching many of America's founders - including James Madison. John Knox stated: "A man with God is always in the majority."

American Minute
November 25th

*F*reed from slavery, Sojourner Truth heard "A voice from Heaven" and began traveling the North preaching emancipation for the slaves. During the Civil War she came to Washington, D.C. and helped resettle ex-slaves. This day, November 25, 1883, was her last full day on earth. Sojourner Truth had stated: "When I left the house of bondage, I left everything behind. I wanted to keep nothing of Egypt on me, and so I went to the Lord and asked him to give me a new name.... I set up my banner, and... sing, and then folks always comes up 'round me, and... I tells them about Jesus."

American Minute
November 26th

*I*n 1789, President George Washington proclaimed the first National Day of Thanksgiving. He wrote: "Whereas it is the duty of all nations to acknowledge the Providence of Almighty God, to obey His will... I do recommend... Thursday, the twenty-sixth day of November... to be devoted by the People of these United States to the service of that great and glorious Being, who is the beneficent Author of all the good that was, that is, or that will be." Washington continued: "that we may... humbly offer our prayers... to the great Lord and Ruler of Nations, and beseech Him to pardon our national... transgressions."

American Minute
November 27th

During World War I, Britain was at a great disadvantage in manufacturing explosives, that is, until there was a breakthrough in synthesizing acetone by a Jewish chemist named Dr. Chaim Weizmann, who was born this day, November 27, 1874. The British were so grateful that they issued the Balfour Declaration, establishing a national homeland for the Jewish people. Dr. Weizmann received the support of the President of the United States, Harry S Truman, who wrote to him in November of 1948: "I want to tell you how happy and impressed I have been at the remarkable progress made by the new State of Israel." Dr. Weizmann wrote: "I think that the God of Israel is with us."

American Minute
November 28th

*T*he Revolutionary War started in Massachusetts. Following the hated Stamp Act, the British committed the infamous Boston Massacre, firing into a crowd, killing five. The colonists responded with the Boston Tea Party. The British then blocked the Boston Harbor to starve them into submission. The President of the Massachusetts Provincial Congress, James Warren, who died this day, November 28, 1808, stated: "As it has pleased Almighty GOD in his Providence to suffer the Calamities of an unnatural War to take Place among us...the most effectual Way to escape those desolating Judgements, which so evidently hang over us, and if it may be obtain the Restoration of our former Tranquility, will be - That we repent and return every one from his Iniquities."

American Minute
November 29th

*H*is death went unnoticed, as he died the same day John F. Kennedy was shot, but his works are some of the most widely read in English literature. Originally an agnostic, he served in World War I and became a professor at Oxford and Cambridge. He credits his Catholic friend and fellow writer, J.R.R. Tolkien, author of "Lord of the Rings," as being instrumental in bringing him to faith in Christ. Among his most notable books are: The Screwtape Letters; Miracles; The Problem of Pain; Abolition of Man; and The Chronicles of Narnia, which include The Lion, Witch and Wardrobe. His name was C.S. Lewis, born this day, November 29, 1898. Over 200 million copies of his books have been sold worldwide and continue to sell at a rate of a million copies a year, even forty years after his death. In his book "Mere Christianity," C.S. Lewis wrote: "The Eternal Being, who knows everything and who created the whole universe, became not only a man but a baby, and before that a fetus in a woman's body."

American Minute
November 30th

"*T*he Celebrated Jumping Frog of Calaveras Country" was his first popular story, written while in San Francisco. He then sailed to the Holy Land and wrote Innocents Abroad. While on this trip, he saw the picture of his friend's sister, Olivia, and fell in love. Immediately upon his return, he met and married her, and, under her encouragement, his writing greatly improved. His name was Mark Twain, born this day, November 30, 1835. Regarding the Holy Land, Mark Twain wrote: "Our Saviour... spent His life, preaching His Gospel, and performing His miracles, within a compass no larger than an ordinary county of the United States."

American Minute
December 1st

The Confederates won the Second Battle of Bull Run, crossed the Potomac River into Maryland and captured Harper's Ferry. But the Confederate drive was halted at the Battle of Antietam, the bloodiest day of fighting in American History. Abraham Lincoln responded by issuing his Emancipation Proclamation. On this day, December 1, 1862, President Lincoln stated in his Second Annual Message to Congress: "In giving freedom to the slave, we assure freedom to the free... We shall nobly save - or meanly lose - the last, best hope of earth. Other means may succeed; this could not fail. The way is plain, peaceful, generous, just - a way which if followed the world will forever applaud and God must forever bless."

American Minute
December 2nd

A thirty-three year old conquistador landed in Mexico with five hundred men. He was shocked to find the Aztecs taking prisoners of the weaker tribes, ripping their hearts out atop temples, and in a frenzy eating their bodies. The conquistador freed the prisoners, knocked down idols, and erected crosses. His name was Hernando Cortez, and he died this day, December 2, 1547. His personal secretary, Francisco Lopez de Gomara, recorded how Cortez spoke to the Tabascan tribe through his interpreter, Jeronimo de Aguilar, a Catholic priest who had been shipwrecked on the Yucatan eight years earlier: "Cortez told them of their blindness and great vanity in worshipping many gods and making sacrifices of human blood to them, and in thinking that those images, being mute and soulless, made by the Indians with their own hands, were capable of doing good or harm. He then told them of a single God, Creator of Heaven and earth and men, whom the Christians worshiped and served, and whom all men should worship and serve. In short, after he had explained the Mysteries to them, and how the Son of God had suffered on the Cross, they accepted it and broke up their idols."

American Minute
December 3rd

President Thomas Jefferson, author of the phrase "Separation of church and state," asked Congress to ratify a treaty with the Kaskaskia Indians, which they did this day, December 3, 1803. It stated: "And whereas the greater part of the said tribe have been baptized and received into the Catholic Church, to which they are much attached, the United States will give annually, for seven years, one hundred dollars toward the support of a priest of that religion, who will engage to perform for said tribe the duties of his office, and also to instruct as many of their children as possible, in the rudiments of literature." The treaty, signed by Jefferson, concluded: "The United States will further give the sum of three hundred dollars to assist the said tribe in the erection of a church."

American Minute
December 4th

*F*ather Jacques Marquette arrived in Quebec from France to be a missionary among the Indians. Governor Frontenac commissioned him to explore the unknown Mississippi River. He traveled by canoe from Lake Michigan, across Green Bay, up Fox River to the Wisconsin River and down to the Mississippi, where they floated as far as the Arkansas River, deciding not to go further for fear of Spaniards. On their return trip up the Illinois River, Father Marquette founded a mission among the Illinois Indians. Caught by the winter on this day, December 4, 1674, Father Marquette and two companions erected a rough log cabin near the shore of Lake Michigan. The settlement would afterwards grow into the city of Chicago. In an account written by Father Dablon of the Society of Jesus, 1678, Marquette met with over 500 chiefs and "explained to them the principal mysteries of our religion, and the end for which he had come to their country; and especially he preached to them Christ crucified, for it was the very eve of the great day on which he died on the cross for them." In 1895, the State of Wisconsin placed a statue of Father Jacques Marquette in the U.S. Capitol Statuary Hall.

American Minute
December 5th

A signer of the U.S. Constitution who was licensed to preach? This was Hugh Williamson, born this day, December 5, 1735. He studied divinity in Connecticut and was admitted to the Presbytery of Philadelphia, where he preached nearly two years, till a chronic chest weakness convinced him to pursue a career which did not involve public speaking. Williamson then entered medical school and during the Revolution served as Surgeon General to the North Carolina troops. As a scientist, Hugh Williamson joined Dr. Benjamin Franklin in many electrical experiments and in 1811 wrote a book titled "Observations of the Climate in Different Parts of America," in which he gave scientific explanations for the credibility of Noah's flood and the events of Moses' exodus.

American Minute
December 6th

*H*is name was Nicholas and he was born to a wealthy, elderly couple in what is now Turkey in the 3rd century AD. When his parents died, he inherited great wealth and gained a reputation for helping the poor. Reportedly, one night he threw gold in the window of a bankrupt merchant, who used it as a dowry for his daughters to marry, thus saving them from the fate of being taken by the creditors. The father caught Nicholas, who made him promise not to reveal the source of the gift, thus inspiring the tradition of secret gift-giving on the anniversary of his death. Nicholas entered a monastery and eventually was ordained Bishop of the coastal city of Myra. He was known for miraculous answers to prayer, confronting "Diana" worship and being imprisoned during Roman Emperor Diocletian's persecution of Christians. When Constantine ended the persecution, Nicholas attended the Council of Nicaea and helped write the Nicene Creed. A true Saint, Nicholas died this day, December 6, 343AD. Early American writer Washington Irving, creator of Rip Van Winkle and the Legend of Sleepy Hollow, was instrumental in transforming Saint Nicholas into jolly ol' St. Nick!

American Minute
December 7th

"December 7, 1941 - a date which will live in infamy - the United States of America was suddenly and deliberately attacked by naval and air forces of the Empire of Japan." Thus spoke President Franklin D. Roosevelt, following the surprise attack on Pearl Harbor by over 100 Japanese aircraft. Five American battleships and three destroyers were sunk, 400 planes were destroyed and over 4000 were killed or wounded. President Roosevelt concluded: "No matter how long it may take us to overcome this premeditated invasion, the American people, in their righteous might, will win through to absolute victory...Our people, our territory and our interests are in grave danger. With confidence in our armed forces, with the unbounding determination of our people, we will gain the inevitable triumph. So help us God." (Note: The designers of the new WWII Memorial in Washington, D.C., chose not include the line "So help us God" from FDR's address.)

American Minute
December 8th

On this day, December 8, 1863, President Abraham Lincoln announced his plan to pardon those who had been in the Confederacy. He wrote: "Whereas it is now desired by some persons heretofore engaged in said rebellion to resume their allegiance to the United States...Therefore, I, Abraham Lincoln, President of the United States, do proclaim, declare, and make known to all persons who have, directly or by implication, participated in the existing rebellion...that a full pardon is hereby granted to them and each of them, with restoration of all rights of property...upon the condition that every such person shall take and subscribe an oath...to wit: "I, ____ ____, do solemnly swear, in presence of Almighty God, that I will henceforth faithfully support, protect, and defend the Constitution of the United States and the Union of the States thereunder, and that I will in like manner abide by and faithfully support all acts of Congress passed during the existing rebellion with reference to slaves...and that I will in like manner abide by and faithfully support all proclamations of the President made during the existing rebellion having reference to slaves....So help me God."

American Minute
December 9th

In the year 1891, on this day, December 9th, President Benjamin Harrison wrote: "This Government has found occasion to express...to the Government of the Czar its serious concern because of the harsh measures now being enforced against the Hebrews in Russia. By the revival of antisemitic laws, long in abeyance, great numbers of those unfortunate people have been constrained to abandon their homes and leave the Empire by reason of the impossibility of finding subsistence within the pale to which it is sought to confine them. The immigration of these people to the United States - many others countries being closed to them - is largely increasing....It is estimated that over 1,000,000 will be forced from Russia within a few years. The Hebrew is never a beggar; he has always kept the law - life by toil - often under severe and oppressive civil restrictions. It is also true that no race, sect, or class has more fully cared for its own than the Hebrew race....This consideration, as well as the suggestion of humanity, furnishes ample ground for the remonstrances which we have presented to Russia."

American Minute
December 10th

After slavery ended in the U.S., President Grant spoke to Congress, 1873, regarding "several thousand persons illegally held as slaves in Cuba...by the slaveholders of Havana, who are vainly striving to stay the march of ideas which has terminated slavery in Christendom, Cuba only excepted." In February 1898, the U.S.S. Maine blew up in Havana's Harbor, killing 266 sailors. In April, Congress stated: "The abhorrent conditions which have existed for more than three years in the Island of Cuba, so near our own borders, have shocked the moral sense of the people of the United States, have been a disgrace to Christian civilization...Resolved...the people of the Island of Cuba are, and of right ought to be, free." In May, Commodore Dewey destroyed the Spanish fleet in Manila Bay. In July, Teddy Roosevelt's Rough Riders captured Santiago, Cuba. President William McKinley stated: "With the nation's thanks let there be mingled the nation's prayers that our gallant sons may be shielded from harm alike on the battlefield and in the clash of fleets...while they are striving to uphold their country's honor." The Spanish-American War ended with a Treaty signed this day, December 10, 1898.

American Minute
December 11th

Alexander Solzhenitsyn was born in Russia this day, December 11, 1918. He was arrested for writing a letter criticizing Joseph Stalin and spent eleven years in prisons and labor camps. He began writing and eventually received the Nobel Prize for Literature. Solzhenitsyn wrote: "At the height of Stalin's terror in 1937-38...more than 40,000 persons were shot per month...Over there people are groaning and dying and in psychiatric hospitals. Doctors are making their evening rounds, injecting people with drugs which destroy their brain cells." Solzhenitsyn continued: "You know the words from the Bible: 'Build not on sand, but on rock'.... Lenin's teachings are that anyone is considered to be a fool who doesn't take what's lying in front of him. If you can take it, take it. If you can attack, attack. But if there's a wall, then go back. And the Communist leaders respect only firmness and have contempt and laugh at persons who continually give in to them." Solzhenitsyn concluded: "America...they are trying to weaken you; they are trying to disarm your strong and magnificent country...I call upon you: ordinary working men of America...do not let yourselves become weak."

American Minute
December 12th

*P*ennsylvania - The Continental Congress met there, the Declaration of Independence was signed there, the Liberty Bell was rung there, the Continental Army spent the freezing winter of 1777 at Valley Forge there, and the Constitution was written there. For awhile the United States Capitol was there. While Dr. Benjamin Franklin was the President (Governor) of Pennsylvania, it became the second State to join the Union on this day, December 12, 1787. Pennsylvania's original Constitution read: "Frame of Government, Chapter 2, Section 10. And each member of the legislature, before he takes his seat, shall make and subscribe the following declaration, viz: 'I do believe in one God, the Creator and Governour of the Universe, the Rewarder of the good and Punisher of the wicked, and I do acknowledge the Scriptures of the Old and New Testament to be given by Divine Inspiration.'"

American Minute
December 13th

*P*hillips Brooks was born this day, December 13, 1835. At Harvard, he was taught by Henry Wadsworth Longfellow and Oliver Wendell Holmes. He later became bishop of the Episcopal Church in Massachusetts. But Phillips Brooks is probably best remembered for a song he wrote two years after the Civil War, which goes: "O little town of Bethlehem! How still we see thee lie; Above thy deep and dreamless sleep, The silent stars go by; Yet in thy dark streets shineth, The everlasting Light; The hopes and fears of all the years, Are met in thee tonight."

American Minute
December 14th

*H*e caught a chill riding horseback several hours in the snow while inspecting his Mount Vernon farm. The next morning it developed into acute laryngitis and the doctors were called in. Their response was to bleed him heavily four times, a process of cutting one's arm to let the "bad blood" out. They also had him gargle with a mixture of molasses, vinegar and butter. Despite their best efforts, the doctors could not save former President George Washington and he died this day, December 14, 1799, at the age of sixty-seven. After saying "Doctor, I die hard, but I am not afraid to go" and "I should have been glad, had it pleased God, to die a little easier, but I doubt not it is for my good," George Washington, at about 11pm, uttered his last words: "Father of mercies, take me unto thyself." On Washington's tomb at Mount Vernon is engraved: "I am the Resurrection and the Life; sayeth the Lord. He that believeth in Me, though he were dead yet shall he live. And whosoever liveth and believeth in Me shall never die." The Washington Monument in Washington, D.C., which is 555 feet tall, has engraved on its metal cap the Latin phrase "Laus Deo," which means "Praise be to God."

American Minute
December 15th

Newly independent, the thirteen States were concerned their new government may become too powerful, as King George's was. They insisted handcuffs be place on the power of the Federal Government. We call these the First Ten Amendments or Bill of Rights, ratified this day, December 15, 1791. The First states: "Congress shall make no law respecting an establishment of religion, or prohibiting the free exercise thereof; or abridging the freedom of speech, or of the press; or the right of the people peaceably to assemble, and to petition the Government for a redress of grievances." Regarding this, Thomas Jefferson wrote to Samuel Miller, January 23, 1808: "I consider the government of the U.S. as interdicted by the Constitution from intermeddling with religious institutions, their doctrines, discipline, or exercises. This results not only from the provision that no law shall be made respecting the establishment or free exercise of religion, but from that also which reserves to the states the powers not delegated to the U.S....Every religious society has a right to determine for itself the times for these exercises, and the objects proper for them, according to their own particular tenets."

American Minute
December 16th

The Boston Tea Party took place this day, December 16, 1773, just three years after the Boston Massacre, where the British fired into a crowd, killing five. The British passed unbearable taxes: 1764 Sugar Act -taxing sugar, coffee, wine; 1765 Stamp Act -taxing newspapers, contracts, letters, playing cards and all printed materials; 1767 Townshend Acts -taxing glass, paints, paper; and 1773 Tea Act. While American merchants paid taxes, British allowed the East India Tea Company to sell a half million pounds of tea in the Colonies with no taxes, giving them a monopoly by underselling American merchants. Disguised as Mohawk Indians, a band of patriots called Sons of Liberty, led by Sam Adams, left the South Meeting House toward Griffin's Wharf, boarded the Dartmouth, Eleanor and Beaver, and threw 342 chests of tea into the harbor. The men of Marlborough, Massachusetts, declared: "Death is more eligible than slavery. A free-born people are not required by the religion of Jesus Christ to submit to tyranny, but may make use of such power as God has given them to recover and support their liberties...We implore the Ruler above the skies that He would bare His arm...and let Israel go."

American Minute
December 17th

A contemporary of Mozart and Haydn, he started losing his hearing at age 28, and eventually became totally deaf. Incredibly, though, he continued writing some of the most beautiful symphonies, concertos, sonatas, and quartets of all time. Today, he ranks as one of the greatest composers in history. His name was Ludwig van Beethoven. Presumed to have been born a day earlier, he was baptized this day, December 17, 1770. Beethoven wrote: "No friend have I. I must live by myself alone; but I know well that God is nearer to me than others in my art, so I will walk fearlessly with Him." In the U.S. Supreme Court case of McCollum v. Board of Education (1948), Justice Robert Houghwout Jackson concurred: "It would not seem practical to teach...appreciation of the arts if we are to forbid exposure of youth to any religious influences. Music without sacred music...would be...incomplete, even from a secular point of view."

American Minute
December 18th

The same year twenty-one-year-old George Washington was fighting in the French Indian War, a Christmas carol became popular. It was written by Charles Wesley, born this day, December 18, 1707. He was the brother of John Wesley, the founder of Methodism, and together they served as missionaries among the Indians and settlers in Georgia. Charles Wesley's Christmas carol, written in 1753, begins: "Hark the herald angels sing, Glory to the new-born King; Peace on earth, and mercy mild, God and sinners reconciled. Joyful all ye nations rise, Join the triumph of the skies; With th' angelic host proclaim, Christ is born in Bethlehem."

American Minute
December 19th

Driven into Pennsylvania by the British, it was on this day, December 19, in the freezing winter of 1777, that the Continental Army set up camp at Valley Forge. Lacking supplies, soldiers died at the rate of twelve per day. Quaker Isaac Potts observed General Washington kneeling in prayer in the snow. In a letter written to John Banister, Washington recorded: "To see men without clothes to cover their nakedness, without blankets to lay on, without shoes, by which their marches might be traced by the blood from their feet... and at Christmas taking up their... quarters within a day's march of the enemy... is a mark of patience and obedience which in my opinion can scarce be paralleled."

American Minute
December 20th

The U.S. National Archives in Washington, D.C., houses all the Public Papers of the Presidents. Among them is President Ronald Reagan's nationally broadcast Christmas Address, delivered this day, December 20, 1983. President Reagan stated: "Of all the songs ever sung at Christmastime, the most wonderful of all was the song of exaltation heard by the shepherds while tending their flocks on the night of Christ's birth. An angel of the Lord appeared to them and said: 'Fear not: for behold, I bring you good tidings of great joy, which shall be to all people. For unto you is born this day in the city of David a Savior, which is Christ the Lord.' ...Sometimes, in the hustle and bustle of holiday preparations we forget that the true meaning of Christmas... the birth of the Prince of Peace, Jesus Christ... During this glorious festival let us renew our determination to follow His example. Won't all of you join Nancy and me in a prayer for peace and good will."

American Minute
December 21st

The captain of a slave trading ship, he was so depraved that once in a drunken stupor he fell overboard. His crew, in order to rescue him, threw a harpoon through his leg and reeled him back on board. His constant limp reminded him of God's grace. His name was John Newton, and he died this day, December 21, 1807. Spending the rest of his life working to rid England of slavery, John Newton is best known for writing the song: "Amazing Grace, how sweet the sound, that saved a wretch like me. I once was lost, but now am found, was blind, but now I see."

American Minute
December 22nd

*T*he Battle of the Bulge - The Nazi's amassed three of their armies for an enormous attack against the Allies in the Ardennes Forest. The Germans soon surrounded the 101st Airborne Division in southern Belgium and demanded their surrender. U.S. General Anthony McAuliffe answered in one word: "Nuts." This response confused the Nazi commander, causing him to hesitate. Three days later relief came and the Allies began a counterattack. In his order given this day, December 22, 1944, General Eisenhower stated: "By rushing out from his fixed defenses the enemy may give us the chance to turn his great gamble into his worst defeat. So I call upon every man, of all the Allies, to rise now to new heights of courage... with unshakable faith in the cause for which we fight, we will, with God's help, go forward to our greatest victory." Two days later President Franklin Roosevelt stated: "It is not easy to say 'Merry Christmas' to you, my fellow Americans, in this time of destructive war...We will celebrate this Christmas Day in our traditional American way...because the teachings of Christ are fundamental in our lives...the story of the coming of the immortal Prince of Peace."

American Minute
December 23rd

An essay titled The American Crisis was published this day, December 23, 1776. Signed "Common Sense," it was written by Thomas Paine and it greatly spread the flames of independence. General George Washington ordered it read to his troops. It stated: "These are the times that try men's souls... Tyranny, like hell, is not easily conquered; yet we have this consolation with us, that the harder the conflict, the more glorious the triumph... What we obtain too cheaply, we esteem too lightly... Heaven knows how to put a price upon its goods; and it would be strange indeed if so celestial an article as freedom should not be highly rated... Let it be told to the future world, that in the depth of winter, when nothing but hope and virtue could survive, that the city and the country, alarmed at one common danger, came forth to meet and to repulse it... 'show your faith by your works,' that God may bless you."

American Minute
December 24th

On Christmas eve, December 24, 1492, one of Columbus' ships, the Santa Maria ran aground on the island of Haiti and had to be abandoned. Columbus left 40 men on the Island and named the settlement "La Navidad," meaning "The Nativity," promising to return the following year. On this same day, Columbus wrote in his Journal to the King and Queen of Spain: "In all the world there can be no better or gentler people. Your Highnesses should feel great joy, because presently they will be Christians, and instructed in the good manners of your realms." On December 24, 1946, at the Lighting of the National Christmas Tree on the White House Grounds, President Harry S Truman remarked: "Our...hopes of future years turn to a little town in the hills of Judea where on a winter's night two thousand years ago the prophecy of Isaiah was fulfilled. Shepherds keeping watch by night over their flock heard the glad tidings of great joy from the angels of the Lord singing, 'Glory to God in the Highest and on Earth, peace, good will toward men.'..If we...will accept it, the star of faith will guide us into the place of peace as it did the shepherds on that day of Christ's birth long ago."

American Minute
December 25th

President Eisenhower 1960: "Through the ages men have felt the uplift of the spirit of Christmas. We commemorate the birth of the Christ Child by...giving expression to our gratitude for the great things that His coming has brought about in the world." President Kennedy 1962: "Christmas is the most sacred and hopeful day in our civilization. For nearly 2,000 years the message of Christmas, the message of peace and good will towards all men, has been the guiding star of our endeavors...Pause...on the 25th of December to celebrate the birthday of the Prince of Peace. President Carter 1977: "Christmas has a special meaning for those of us who are Christians, those of us who believe in Christ, those of us who know that almost 2,000 years ago, the Son of Peace was born." President Reagan 1983: "Christmas is a time...to open our hearts to...millions forbidden the freedom to worship a God who so loved the world that He gave us the birth of the Christ Child so that we might learn to love...The message of Jesus is one of hope and joy. I know there are those who recognize Christmas Day as the birthday of a wise teacher...And then there are others of us who believe that he was the Son of God, that he was divine."

American Minute
December 26th

*I*n the first six months of the Revolution, the Continental Army was driven back, out of New York, across New Jersey and into Pennsylvania. The American troops dwindled from a high of nearly 20,000 volunteers down to barely 2000, and half of those were planning on leaving at the end of the year, when their six month enlistment would be over. In a desperate act, Washington crossed the dangerous ice filled Delaware River in the freezing cold on Christmas Day evening, and on this day, December 26, 1776, attacked the Hessian mercenary troops at Trenton, who were not at their highest level of alertness due to the effects of their Christmas celebrations. General Washington captured nearly a thousand of them, and ten days later captured 3,000 British at Princeton. Washington later wrote: "The Hand of Providence has been so conspicuous in all this (the course of the war) that he must be worse than an infidel that lacks faith, and more wicked that has not gratitude to acknowledge his obligations; but it will be time enough for me to turn Preacher when my present appointment ceases."

American Minute
December 27th

*H*e suffered an attack of smallpox when he was four-years-old which left him with crippled hands and poor eyesight. Overcoming those handicaps, he studied Copernicus' works and at age twenty-three became a professor of astronomy. His name was Johannes Kepler, born this day, December 27, 1571. His laws of planetary motion, known as Kepler's Laws, helped Newton formulate the theory of gravity. Regarding his book on astronomy, Kepler stated: "O, Almighty God, I am thinking Thy thoughts after Thee!...The book is written, to be read either now or by posterity, I care not which. It may be well to wait a century for a reader, as God has waited six thousand years for an observer."

American Minute
December 28th

*H*e thought tariffs between countries caused wars, so he worked to repeal them, pushing through the Income Tax to make up for lost Federal revenue. Four years later the United States entered World War I. After the financial Panic of 1907, he promoted the Federal Reserve Act to prevent future national economic disasters. Eight years after he left office the Great Depression began. His name was Woodrow Wilson, born this day, December 28, 1856. While serving as the 28th President, he married Edith Bolling Galt, a direct descendant of Pocahontas. His administration saw the completion of Panama Canal, begun under President Theodore Roosevelt, and the purchase of the Virgin Islands from Denmark. During World War I, in May of 1918, he proclaimed: "I, Woodrow Wilson, President of the United States of America, do hereby proclaim...a day of public humiliation, prayer and fasting, and do exhort my fellow-citizens of all faiths and creeds...to pray Almighty God that He may forgive our sins and...give victory to our armies as they fight for freedom."

American Minute
December 29th

After nearly ten years of being its own nation, the Republic of Texas became the 28th State of the Union this day, December 29, 1845. It later joined the Confederacy, but was readmitted after the Civil War. The Preamble of the Texas Constitution began: "We, the people of the Republic of Texas, acknowledging, with gratitude the grace and beneficence of God, in permitting us to make a choice of our form of government, do... establish this Constitution." It later added: "Nor shall anyone be excluded from holding office on account of his religious sentiments, provided he acknowledge the existence of a Supreme Being."

American Minute
December 30th

The Jungle Book was written by Rudyard Kipling, who was born this day, December 30, 1865, in Bombay, India. Educated in England, he returned to India as a journalist. His notoriety as a writer grew tremendously and in 1907, he received the Nobel Prize for literature. He popular works include: Kim, Wee Willie Winkie, Baa Baa Black Sheep, and Gunga Din. In his Ballad of East and West, Rudyard Kipling wrote: "Oh, East is East, and West is West, And never the twain shall meet, Till earth and sky stand presently, At God's great judgement seat."

American Minute
December 31st

On December 31, 1955, Reverend Martin Luther King, Jr, pastor of the Ebenezer Baptist Church in Atlanta, Georgia, and founder of the Southern Christian Leadership Conference, led a nonviolent protest by boycotting the city buses of Montgomery, AL, Rev. King stated: "If you will protest courageously, and yet with dignity and Christian love, when the history books are written in future generations, the historians will have to pause and say, 'There lived a great people...who injected new meaning and dignity into the veins of civilization.'" At the end of the year, 1962, President John F. Kennedy stated: "We mark the festival of Christmas which is the most sacred and hopeful day in our civilization. For nearly 2,000 years the message of Christmas, the message of peace and good will towards all men, has been the guiding star of our endeavors....the birthday of the Prince of Peace. To the one million men in uniform who will celebrate this Christmas away from their homes...and to all of you I send my very best wishes for a blessed and happy Christmas and a peaceful and prosperous New Year."

ENDNOTES

JANUARY 1. Lincoln, Abraham. Jan. 1, 1863, Emancipation Proclamation. James D. Richardson (U.S. Representative from Tennessee), ed., A Compilation of the Messages & Papers of the Presidents 1789-1897, 10 vols. (Washington, D.C.: U.S. Government Printing Office, published by Authority of Congress, 1897, 1899; Washington, D.C.: Bureau of National Literature & Art, 1789-1902, 11 vols., 1907, 1910), Vol. VI, pp. 157-159. Charles W. Eliot, LL.D., ed., American Historical Documents 1000-1904 (NY: P. F. Collier & Son Co., The Harvard Classics, 1910), Vol. 43, pp. 344-346. Henry Steele Commager, ed., Documents of American History, 2 vols. (NY: F.S. Crofts & Co., 1934; Appleton-Century-Crofts, Inc., 1948, 6th edition, 1958; Englewood Cliffs, NJ: Prentice Hall, Inc., 9th edition, 1973), Vol. I, p, 421. Richard D. Heffner, A Documentary History of the United States (NY: The New American Library of World Literature, Inc., 1952), pp. 150-151. John Bartlett, Bartlett's Familiar Quotations (Boston: Little, Brown & Co., 1855, 1980), p. 522. Vincent J. Wilson, ed., The Book of Great American Documents (Brookfield, MD: American History Research Associates, 1987), p. 69. NOTE: Lincoln issued the Emancipation Proclamation acting in his role as Commander-in-Chief of the military. The Southern States were declared to be in rebellion and therefore war zones. As such the military was in control, and with the President being over the military, his Proclamation had the force of law. Lincoln had no justification for claiming absolute jurisdiction over the Northern States, as they were not considered war zones. The Commander-in-Chief of the military could not arbitrarily make law in the States not 'in rebellion', as the regular legislative process was still in effect. Many thought Lincoln overstepped his Executive power by making "law" through "Proclamation," so after the war was over, Congress passed the 13th Amendment ending slavery throughout the entire country.

JANUARY 2. Ross, Betsy. US: Betsy Ross Day (1776), http://www.scopesys.com/cgi/today2.cgi. http://www.ushistory.org/betsy/flaglife.html.

JANUARY 3. Stiles, Ezra. 1783, in an address before the Assembly of Connecticut. Robert Flood, The Rebirth of America (Philadelphia: Arthur S. DeMoss Foundation, 1986), p. 45.

JANUARY 4. Rush, Benjamin. 1798. 1786, in "Thoughts upon the Mode of Education Proper in a Republic," published in Early American Imprints. Benjamin Rush, Essays, Literary, Moral & Philosophical (Philadelphia: Thomas & Samuel F. Bradford, 1798), p. 8, "Of the Mode of Education Proper in a Republic." The Annals of America, 20 vols. (Chicago, IL: Encyclopedia Britannica, 1968), Vol. 4, pp. 28-29. Stephen McDowell & Mark Beliles, "The Providential Perspective " (Charlottesville, VA: The Providence Foundation, P.O. Box 6759, Charlottesville, Va. 22906, Jan. 1994), Vol. 9, No. 1, p. 3.

JANUARY 5. Carver, George Washington. 1928, Tuskegee Institute. Ethel Edwards, Carver of Tuskegee (Cincinnati, Ohio: Ethel Edwards & James T. Hardwick, a limited edition work compiled in part from over 300 personal letters written by Dr. Carver to James T. Hardwick between 1922-1937, available from the Carver Memorial in Locust Grove, Diamond, Mo., 1971), pp. 157-160.

JANUARY 6. There Really is a Santa Claus! - Origins of the Christmas Holiday by William J. Federer, 1997, p. 10. P.O. Box 4363, St. Louis, MO 63123, fax (314) 487-4395. The Second Council of Tours (can. xi, xvii) proclaims, in 566 or 567, the sanctity of the "twelve days" from Christmas to Epiphany, & the duty of Advent fast; that of Agde (506), in canons 63-64, orders a universal communion, & that of Braga (563) forbids fasting on Christmas Day. Popular merry-making, however, so increased that the "Laws of King Cnut ", fabricated c. 1110, order a fast from Christmas to Epiphany. Cyril Martindale, transcribed by Robert H. Sarkissian & Susanti A. Suastika, The Catholic Encyclopedia, Volume III, V, Copyright 8 1908-9 by Robert Appleton Co., Online Edition Copyright 8 1999 by Kevin Knight.

JANUARY 7. Fillmore, Millard. Benjamin Franklin Morris, The Christian Life & Character of the Civil Institutions of the United States (Philadelphia: George W. Childs, 1864), p. 609.

JANUARY 8. Jackson, Andrew. Jan. 8, 1815, in a letter to his friend Robert Hays at the occasion of the Battle of New Orleans, during the War of 1812. Burke Davis, Old Hickory: A Life of Andrew Jackson (NY: Dial Press, 1977), p. 150. Peter Marshall & David Manuel, From Sea to Shining Sea (Old Tappan, NJ: Fleming H. Revell Co., 1986), p. 169.

JANUARY 9. Nixon, Richard Milhous. Jan. 20, 1969, Inaugural Address. Department of State Bulletin, Feb. 10, 1969. Inaugural Addresses of the Presidents - From George Washington 1789 to Richard Milhous Nixon 1969 (Washington, D.C.: U.S. Government Printing Office, 91st Congress, 1st Session, House Document 91-142, 1969), pp. 275-279. The Annals of America, 20 vols. (Chicago, IL: Encyclopedia Britannica, 1968, 1977), Vol. 19, pp. 8-12. Benjamin Weiss, God in American History: A Documentation of America's Religious Heritage (Grand Rapids, MI: Zondervan, 1966), p. 154. J. Michael Sharman, J.D., Faith of the Fathers (Culpepper, Virginia: Victory Publishing, 1995), pp. 116-117.

JANUARY 10. Beecher, Lyman. In his work titled, Plea for the West (Cincinnati: Truman & Smith, 1835), p. 11. Peter Marshall & David Manuel, From Sea to Shining Sea (Old Tappan, New Jersey: Fleming H. Revell Co., 1985), p. 371.

JANUARY 11. Dwight, Timothy. Timothy Dwight, Travels; in New England & New York (New Haven, 1821-1822), Vol. IV, pp. 403-404. Charles Roy Keller, The Second Great Awakening in Connecticut (New Haven: Yale University Press, 1942), p. 36. Peter Marshall & David Manuel, The Light & the Glory (Old Tappan, New Jersey: Fleming H. Revell Co., 1977), p. 350.

JANUARY 12. Burke, Edmund. Jan. 9, 1795, in a letter to William Smith. John Bartlett, Bartlett's Familiar Quotations (Boston: Little, Brown & Co., 1863, 1980), p. 374. Edward L.R. Elson, D.D., Lit.D., LL.D., America's Spiritual Recovery (Westwood, N.J.: Fleming H. Revell Co., 1954), p. 174. Carroll E. Simcox, comp., 4400 Quotations for Christian Communicators (Grand Rapids, MI: Baker Book House, 1991), p. 124. D.P. Diffine, Ph.D., One Nation Under God - How Close a Separation? (Searcy, AR: Harding University, Belden Center for Private Enterprise Education, 6th edition, 1992), p. 20. Burke, Edmund. 1791, in "A Letter to a Member of the National Assembly." Theodore Roosevelt, "Fifth Annual Message to Congress," Dec. 5, 1905. A Compilation of the Messages & Papers of the Presidents 20 vols. (NY: Bureau of National Literature, Inc., prepared under the direction of the Joint Committee on Printing, of the House & Senate, pursuant to an Act of the 52nd Congress of the United States, 1893, 1923), Vol. XIV, p. 6986. Keith Fournier, In Defense of Liberty (Virginia Beach, VA: Law & Justice, 1993), Vol. 2, No. 2, p. 5. Rush H. Limbaugh III, See, I Told You So (NY: reprinted by permission of Pocket Books, a division of Simon & Schuster Inc., 1993), pp. 73-76.

JANUARY 13. Georgia, Colony of. 1732. Stephen K. McDowell & Mark A. Beliles, America's Providential History (Charlottesville, VA: Providence Press, 1988), p. 55. www.ourgeorgiahistory.com/lists/georgia_settlers.html http://archiver.rootsweb.com/th/read/SOUTHEAST-PIONEERS/2002-04/1020087886 www.allcensus.com/earlygeor/pafg17.htm#707 Henry Herbert died on 15 Jun 1733, Minister at Savannah; embarked Nov. 1732; arrived in the Georgia Colony 1 Feb. 1732-3. This clergyman was bastard son to the Earl of Torrington. He was obliged to leave the Colony on acct. of sickness, and died at sea in his return 15 Jun. 1733. Dead 15 Jun. 1733. The Moravians in Georgia 1735-1740, by Adelaide L. Fries, Winston-Salem, N. C., Hypertext Meanings and Commentaries from the Encyclopedia of the Self by Mark Zimmerman, http://emotional-literacy-education.com/classic-books-online-a/mrvga10.htm Chapter V. The Second Year in Georgia. The English Clergymen. The same day that Bishop Nitschmann left Savannah, John Wesley moved into the parsonage which had just been vacated by his predecessor, Mr. Quincy. A week earlier he had entered upon his ministry at Savannah, being met by so large and attentive an audience that he was much encouraged, and began with zeal to perform his pastoral duties. He was the third Rector of the Savannah Parish, the Rev. Henry Herbert having been the first, and he preached in a rude chapel built on the lot reserved for a house of worship in the original plan of Savannah,-the site of the present Christ Church. Georgia Settlers, Feb. 1733 There are 115 individual names in 40 families on this list. This list is accurate except where question marks appear. Herbert Henry, a minister who appears on some lists did make the trip, offering a prayer when the ship arrived in South Carolina. http://ourgeorgiahistory.com

JANUARY 14. Schweitzer, Albert. Carroll E. Simcox, 3000 Quotations on Christian Themes (Grand Rapids, Michigan: Baker Book House 1989), pp. 204-205.

JANUARY 15. King, Martin Luther, Jr. Apr. 16, 1963, in a message written from his jail cell in Birmingham, AL. Christian Century, Jun. 12, 1963. The Annals of America, 20 vols. (Chicago, IL: Encyclopedia Britannica, 1968), Vol. 18, pp. 143-149.

JANUARY 16. Jefferson, Thomas. Jan. 16, 1786, in a bill written by the Committee on Religion, Virginia Assembly; inscribed on the Jefferson Memorial, Washington D.C. H.A. Washington, ed., The Writings of Thomas Jefferson - Being His Autobiography, Correspondence, Reports, Messages, Addresses, & Other Writings, Official & Private, 9 vols. (Jackson: 1859); (Washington: 1853-54); (Philadelphia: 1871), Vol. 8; (NY: Derby), Vol. VIII, p. 454-56. William Taylor Thom, The Struggle for Religious Freedom in Virginia: The Baptists, Johns Hopkins Studies in Historical & Political Science, Herbert B. Adams, ed., (Baltimore: Johns Hopkins, 1900), p. 79. The Annals of America, 20 vols. (Chicago, IL: Encyclopedia Britannica, 1968), Vol. 3, p. 53. Norman Cousins, In God We Trust - The Religious Beliefs & Ideas of the American Founding Fathers (NY: Harper & Brothers, 1958), p. 124. Tim LaHaye, Faith of Our Founding Fathers (Brentwood, TN: Wolgemuth & Hyatt, Publishers, Inc., 1987), pp. 192-193.

JANUARY 17. Washington, George. Feb. 13, 1781, in a report from British Commander-in-Chief Henry Clinton. William Hosmer, Remember our Bicentennial - 1781 (Foundation for Christian Self-Government Newsletter - Jun. 1981), p. 5. Marshall Foster & Mary-Elaine Swanson, The American Covenant - The Untold Story (Roseburg, OR: Foundation for Christian Self-Government, 1981; Thousand Oaks, CA: The Mayflower Institute, 1983, 1992), p. 166. Washington, George. Aug. 20, 1778, in a letter written from White Plains, New York, to Brigadier-General

Thomas Nelson of Virginia. Jared Sparks, ed., The Writings of George Washington 12 vols. (Boston: American Stationer's Company, 1837; NY: F. Andrew's, 1834-1847), Vol. VI, p. 36. William J. Johnson, George Washington - The Christian (St. Paul, MN: William J. Johnson, Merriam Park, Feb. 23, 1919; Nashville, TN: Abingdon Press, 1919; reprinted Milford, MI: Mott Media, 1976; reprinted Arlington Heights, IL: Christian Liberty Press, 502 West Euclid Avenue, Arlington Heights, Illinois, 60004, 1992), pp. 119-120. John Clement Fitzpatrick, ed., The Writings of George Washington, from the Original Manuscript Sources 1749-1799, 39 vols. (Washington, D.C.: United States Government Printing Office, 1931-1944), Vol. XII, p. 343. Saxe Commins, ed., The Basic Writings of George Washington (NY: Random House, 1948), p. 332. Norman Cousins, In God We Trust - The Religious Beliefs and Ideas of the American Founding Fathers (NY: Harper & Brothers, 1958), p. 54. Paul F. Boller, Jr., George Washington and Religion (Dallas: Southern Methodist University, 1963), p. 106. Edmund Fuller, and David E. Green, God in the White House - The Faiths of American Presidents (NY: Crown Publishers, Inc., 1968), p. 14. John Eidsmoe, Christianity and The Constitution - The Faith of Our Founding Fathers (Baker Book House, 1987), p. 137. "Our Christian Heritage," Letter from Plymouth Rock (Marlborough, NH: The Plymouth Rock Foundation), p. 4. Peter Marshall and David Manuel, The Light and the Glory (Old Tappan, NJ: Fleming H. Revell Company, 1977), p. 332. George Otis, The Solution to the Crisis in America, Revised and Enlarged Edition (Van Nuys, CA.: Fleming H. Revell Company; Bible Voice, Inc., 1970, 1972, foreword by Pat Boone), p. 46. Our home and office are about three blocks from that Yadkin River in NC, which was named for Daniel Boon's indian guide "Yadkin." A little tidbit that we're sure you already know. Blessings and our prayers, Mary Kathryn. TXmedia@aol.com
JANUARY 18. Webster, Daniel. Benjamin Franklin Morris, The Christian Life & Character of the Civil Institutions of the United States of America (Philadelphia: George W. Childs, 1864), p. 270. Henry H. Halley, Halley's Bible Handbook (Grand Rapids, MI: Zondervan Publishing House, 1927, 1965), p. 18. Alfred Armand Montapert, Distilled Wisdom (Englewood Cliffs, NJ: Prentice Hall, Inc., 1965), p. 37. D.P. Diffine, Ph.D., One Nation Under God - How Close a Separation? (Searcy, AR: Harding University, Belden Center for Private Enterprise Education, 6th edition, 1992), p. 13. Stephen McDowell & Mark Beliles, "The Providential Perspective" (Charlottesville, VA: The Providence Foundation, P.O. Box 6759, Charlottesville, Va. 22906, Jan. 1994), Vol. 9, No. 1, p. 7.
JANUARY 19. United States Supreme Court. 1952, Zorach v. Clauson, 343 US 306 307 312-314 (1952), Justice William O. Douglas. Dr. Ed Rowe, The ACLU & America's Freedom (Washington: Church League of America, 1984), pp. 20-21. Tim LaHaye, Faith of Our Founding Fathers (Brentwood, TN: Wolgemuth & Hyatt, Publishers, Inc., 1987), pp. 9-10. Martin Shapiro & Roco Tresolini, eds., American Constitutional Law (NY: Macmillan Publishing, 5th edition, 1979), p. 445. John Whitehead, The Rights of Religious Persons in Public Education (Wheaton IL: Crossway Books, Good News Publishers, 1991), p. 284. Elizabeth Ridenour, Public Schools - Bible Curriculum (Greensboro, N.C.: National Council On Bible Curriculum, 1996), p. 24. The Capitol: A Pictorial History of the Capitol & of the Congress (Washington, D.C.: U.S. Government Printing Office, 1979), p. 24. Gary DeMar, America's Christian History: The Untold Story (Atlanta, GA: American Vision Publishers, Inc., 1993), p. 105. Keith A. Fournier, Religious Cleansing in the American Republic (Washington, D.C.: Liberty, Life, & Family Publications, 1993), p. 33. Gary L. Bauer, Family Research Council Newsletter (Washington, D.C.: Family Research Council, 1996), p. 3.
JANUARY 20. Kennedy, John Fitzgerald. Jan. 20, 1961, Inaugural Address. Inaugural Addresses of the Presidents of the United States - From George Washington 1789 to Richard Milhous Nixon 1969 (Washington, D.C.: U.S. Government Printing Office; 91st Congress, 1st Session, House Document 91-142, 1969), pp. 267-270. Department of State Bulletin (published weekly by the Office of Public Services, Bureau of Public Affairs, Feb. 6, 1961). Davis Newton Lott, The Inaugural Addresses of the American Presidents (NY: Holt, Rinehart & Winston, 1961), p. 269. Charles E. Rice, The Supreme Court & Public Prayer (NY: Fordham University Press, 1964), p. 193. Benjamin Weiss, God in American History: A Documentation of America's Religious Heritage (Grand Rapids, MI: Zondervan, 1966), p. 146. The Annals of America, 20 vols. (Chicago, IL: Encyclopedia Britannica, 1968), Vol. XVIII, pp. 5-7. Lillian W. Kay, ed., The Ground on Which We Stand - Basic Documents of American History (NY: Franklin Watts, Inc, 1969), p. 296. Bob Arnebeck, "FDR Invoked God Too," Washington Post, Sept. 21, 1986. Vincent J. Wilson, ed., The Book of Great American Documents (Brookfield, MD: American History Research Associates, 1987), p. 84. Halford Ross Ryan, American Rhetoric from Roosevelt to Reagan (Prospect Heights, IL: Waveland Press, 1987), p. 156. Jeffrey K. Hadden & Anson Shupe, Televangelism - Power & Politics on God's Frontier (NY: Henry Holt & Co., 1988), p. 272. Ronald Reid, ed., Three Centuries of American Rhetorical Discourse: An Anthology & a Review (Prospect Heights, Il: Waveland Press, Inc., 1988), p. 711. William Safire, ed., Lend Me Your Ears - Great Speeches in History (NY: W.W. Norton & Co. 1992), p. 812.
JANUARY 21. DeMille, Cecil Blount. 1956, at the New York opening of the film The Ten Commandments.
JANUARY 22. USA Today, Friday, Aug. 11, 1995, p. 3A. "Roe's litigant's about face: 'I'm Prolife'" Jeannine Lee

& Masud Khan. ABC's World News Tonight, Aug. 10, 1995.
JANUARY 23. John Carroll University, 20700 North Park Blvd, University Heights, Ohio 44118, (216) 397-1886.
http://www1.jcu.edu/library/johncarr/jced.htm
JANUARY 24. Madison, James. Jan. 24, 1774, in a letter to William Bradford. James Madison, The Papers of
James Madison, William T. Hutchinson & William M. Rachal, eds., (Chicago: University of Chicago Press), I:104-
6. John Eidsmoe, Christianity & the Constitution - The Faith of Our Founding Fathers (Grand Rapids, MI: Baker
Book House, A Mott Media Book, 1987, 6th printing 1993), p. 105. Jun. 12, 1776, Virginia Bill of Rights, Article
XVI. Frances Newton Thorpe, ed., Federal & State Constitutions, Colonial Charters, & Other Organic Laws of the
States, Territories, & Colonies now or heretofore forming the United States, 7 vols. (Washington: Government
Printing Office, 1905-9; St. Clair Shores, MI: Scholarly Press, 1968), Vol. VII, p. 3814. Henry Steele Commager,
ed., Documents of American History, 2 vols. (NY: F.S. Crofts & Co., 1934; Appleton Century Crofts, Inc., 1948,
6th edition, 1958; Englewood Cliffs, NJ: Prentice Hall, Inc., 9th edition, 1973), pp. 103104. Anson Phelps Stokes
& Leo Pfeffer, Church & State in United States (NY: Harper & Row, Pub., 1950, revised one vol ed, 1964), p. 42.
Annals of America, 20 vols. (Chicago, IL: Encyclopedia Britannica, 1968), Vol. 2, p. 433. Charles Fadiman, ed.,
The American Treasury (NY: Harper & Brothers, Pub., 1955), p. 121.
JANUARY 25. Reagan, Ronald. Jan. 25, 1985, State of the Union Address. David R. Shepherd, ed., Ronald Reagan:
In God I Trust (Wheaton, IL: Tyndale House Publishers, Inc., 1984), pp. 72, 137.
JANUARY 26. MacArthur, Douglas. May 12, 1962, in a speech delivered at the U.S. Military Academy at West
Point. William Safire, ed., Lend Me Your Ears - Great Speeches in History (NY: W.W. Norton & Co., 1992), p. 76.
JANUARY 27. Wilson, Woodrow. Jan.. 11, 1916, in a Proclamation of a Contribution Day for the aid of stricken
Jewish people. A Compilation of the Messages & Papers of the Presidents 20 vols. (NY: Bureau of National
Literature, Inc., prepared under the direction of the Joint Committee on Printing, of the House & Senate, pursuant
to an Act of the Fifty-Second Congress of the United States, 1893, 1923), Vol. XVII, p. 8174-8175.
JANUARY 28. Reagan, Ronald. Jan. 28, 1986, Address to the Nation after the Challenger Space Shuttle disaster.
Frederick J. Ryan, Jr., ed., Ronald Reagan - The Wisdom & Humor of The Great Communicator (San Francisco:
Collins Publishers, A Division of Harper Collins Publishers, 1995), p. 27.
JANUARY 29. Frost, Robert. In an interview on radio station WQED, Pittsburgh, quoted in Collier's, Apr. 27,
1956.
JANUARY 30. Roosevelt, Franklin Delano. 1935, Radio broadcast. Gabriel Sivan, The Bible & Civilization (NY:
Quadrangle/The New York Times Book Co., 1973), p. 178. Gary DeMar, America's Christian History: The Untold
Story (Atlanta, GA: American Vision Publishers, Inc., 1993), p. 60.
JANUARY 31. Duche', Jacob. Sept. 7, 1774, Rev. Mr. Duche' reading Psalm 35. "Our Christian Heritage," Letter
from Plymouth Rock (Marlborough, NH: The Plymouth Rock Foundation), pp. 2-3. Adams, John. Sept. 7, 1774,
in a letter to his wife Abigail relating the events of the First Continental Congress. John & Abigail Adams, Vol. I,
pp. 23-24. Charles Francis Adams (son of John Quincy Adams & grandson of John Adams), ed., Letters of John
Adams - Addressed To His Wife (Boston: Charles C. Little & James Brown, 1841), Vol. I, pp. 23-24. Edmund
Fuller & David E. Green, God in the White House - The Faiths of American Presidents (NY: Crown Publishers, Inc.,
1968), pp. 21-22. L.H. Butterfield, Marc Frielander, & Mary-Jo King, eds., The Book of Abigail & John - Selected
Letters of The Adams Family 1762-1784 (Cambridge, Massachusetts & London, England: Harvard University
Press, 1975), p. 76. Phyllis Lee Levin, Abigail Adams (NY: St. Martin's Press, 1987), p. 55.
FEBRUARY 1. Howe, Julia Ward. Feb., 1862, The Battle Hymn of the Republic (Massachusetts: The Atlantic
Monthly, Feb. 1862), Vol. IX, No. LII, p. 10, Entered according to Act of Congress by Ticknor & Fields, in the
Clerk's Office of the District Court of the District of Massachusetts. Mark Galli, Christian History (Carol Stream, IL:
Christian History, 1992, Issue 33), Vol. XI, No. 1, p. 19. D.P. Diffine, Ph.D., One Nation Under God - How Close
a Separation? (Searcy, AR: Harding University, Belden Center for Private Enterprise Education, 6th edition, 1992),
p. 14.
FEBRUARY 2. United States Congress. 1848, Peace Treaty with Mexico which ended the Mexican War; concluded
at Guadalupe Hidalgo, Feb. 2, 1848; ratified with amendments by U.S. Senate, Mar. 10, 1848; ratified by President,
Mar. 16, 1848; ratifications exchanged at Queretaro, May 30, 1848; proclaimed Jul. 4, 1848. Charles W. Eliot,
LL.D., ed., American Historical Documents 1000-1904 (NY: P. F. Collier & Son Co., The Harvard Classics, 1910),
Vol. 43, pp. 309-326.
FEBRUARY 3. Four Chaplains Day. http://www.fourchaplains.org. On the evening of Feb. 2, 1943, the U.S.A.T.
Dorchester, overcrowded with 902 servicemen, merchant seamen & civilian workers, was torpedoed by a German
submarine off the coast of Newfoundland. The transport sank in fire & smoke in 27 minutes. The ship's crew launched
lifeboats & rafts. Many servicemen jumped into the water. Two of the three escort ships, the Coast Guard cutters

Comanche & Escanaba, circled the Dorchester rescuing 231 survivors. The third cutter, CGC Tampa, continued on, escorting the remaining two ships in the convoy. According to those present, four Army chaplains aboard the Dorchester brought hope in despair & light in darkness. Those chaplains were Lt. George L. Fox, Methodist; Lt. Alexander D. Goode, Jewish; Lt. John P. Washington, Roman Catholic; & Lt. Clark V. Poling, Dutch Reformed. Quickly & quietly the four chaplains spread out among the soldiers. There they tried to calm the frightened, tend the wounded & guide the disoriented toward safety. When most of the men were topside, the chaplains opened a storage locker & began distributing life jackets. When there were no more lifejackets in the locker, the chaplains removed theirs & gave them to four frightened young men. As the ship went down, survivors in nearby rafts could see the four chaplains-arms linked & braced against the slanting deck. Their voices could also be heard offering prayers. The Distinguished Service Cross & Purple Heart were awarded posthumously on Dec. 19, 1944, to the next of kin by Lt. Gen. Brehon B. Somervell, Commanding General of the Army Service Forces, in a ceremony at the post chapel at Fort Myer, VA. http://www.goags.com/~c-r-ffl/archives/199805/msg01618.html. .Dwight David Eisenhower, Feb. 7, 1954, Remarks from the White House at 2:30 P.M., as part of the American Legion "BACK-TO-GOD" Program. Public Papers of the Presidents (Washington, D.C., U.S. Government Printing Office).

FEBRUARY 4. Lindbergh, Charles Augustus. Feb. 1, 1954, in an address at the Institute of Aeronautical Sciences dinner, news summaries. James Beasely Simpson, Best Quotes of '54 '55 '56 (NY: Thomas Y. Crowell Co., 1957), p. 84.

FEBRUARY 5. Williams, Roger. The World Book Encyclopedia, 18 vols. (Chicago, IL: Field Enterprises, Inc., 1957; W.F. Quarrie & Co., 8 vols., 1917; World Book, Inc., 22 vols., 1989), Vol. 14, p. 6931; Vol. 18, pp. 8780-8781. Lynn R. Buzzard & Samuel Ericsson, The Battle for Religious Liberty (Elgin, IL: David C. Cook, 1982), p. 51. John Eidsmoe, Christianity & the Constitution - The Faith of Our Founding Fathers (Grand Rapids, MI: Baker Book House, A Mott Media Book, 1987, 6th printing 1993), pp. 215, 243. Senator Henry Bowen Anthony delivers the Eulogy of Roger Williams in Congress. Stephen Abbott Northrop, D.D., A Cloud of Witnesses (Portland, OR: American Heritage Ministries, 1987; Mantle Ministries, 228 Still Ridge, Bulverde, TX), p. 16.

FEBRUARY 6. Reagan, Ronald Wilson. Aug. 23, 1984 at an ecumenical prayer breakfast at the Reunion Arena in Dallas, on the occasion of the enactment of the Equal Access Bill of 1984. Jeremiah O'Leary, "Reagan Declares that Faith Has Key Role in Political Life," The Washington Times (Aug. 24, 1984). Walter Shapiro, "Politics & the Pulpit," Newsweek (Sept. 17, 1984), p. 24. The Speech That Shook The Nation (Forerunner, Dec. 1984), p. 12. Nadine Strossen, "A Constitutional Analysis of the Equal Access Act's Standards Governing School Student's Religious Meetings," Harvard Journal on Legislation, Winter, 1987. p. 118. David R. Shepherd, Ronald Reagan: In God We Trust (Wheaton, IL: Tyndale House Publishers, Inc., 1984), p. 146.

FEBRUARY 7. Douglass, Frederick. Page Smith, The Nation Comes of Age (NY: McGraw-Hill Book Co., 1981), Vol. 4, p. 584. Peter Marshall & David Manuel, The Glory of America (Bloomington, MN: Garborg's Heart'N Home, Inc., 1991), 2.20.

FEBRUARY 8. Boy Scouts of America. Feb. 8, 1910, the Boy Scout Oath. "Boy Scouts of America," The World Book Encyclopedia, 18 vols. (Chicago, IL: Field Enterprises, Inc., 1957; W.F. Quarrie & Co., 8 vols., 1917; World Book, Inc., 22 vols., 1989), Vol. 2, pp. 948-951. John Wilson Taylor, M.A., Ph.D, editor, Lincoln Library of Essential Information (Buffalo, NY: The Frontier Press Co., 1935), pp. 1717, 2048. Harvey L. Price, Chief Scout Executive, The Official Boy Scout Handbook (Irving, TX: The Boy Scouts of America), pp. 26-41. D.P. Diffine, Ph.D., One Nation Under God - How Close a Separation? (Searcy, AR: Harding University, Belden Center for Private Enterprise Education, 6th edition, 1992), p. 16.

FEBRUARY 9. Harrison, William H. Mar. 4, 1841, Inaugural Address. James D. Richardson (U.S. Representative from Tennessee), ed., A Compilation of the Messages & Papers of the Presidents 1789-1897, 10 vols. (Washington, D.C.: U.S. Government Printing Office, published by Authority of Congress, 1897, 1899; Washington, D.C.: Bureau of National Literature & Art, 1789-1902, 11 vols., 1907, 1910), Vol. 4, pp. 6-20. Benjamin Franklin Morris, The Christian Life & Character of the Civil Institutions of the United States (Philadelphia: George W. Childs, 1864), p. 605. Inaugural Addresses of the Presidents of the United States - From George Washington 1789 to Richard Milhous Nixon 1969 (Washington, D.C.: U.S. Government Printing Office; 91st Congress, 1st Session, House Document 91-142, 1969), pp. 71-87. Davis Newton Lott, The Inaugural Addresses of the American Presidents (NY: Holt, Rinehart & Winston, 1961), p. 86. Charles E. Rice, The Supreme Court & Public Prayer (NY: Fordham University Press, 1964), p. 182. Arthur Schlesinger Jr., ed., The Chief Executive (NY: Chelsea House Publishers, 1965), pp. 93-94. Stephen Abbott Northrop, D.D., A Cloud of Witnesses (Portland, OR: American Heritage Ministries, 1987; Mantle Ministries, 228 Still Ridge, Bulverde, TX), p. 215. Peter Marshall & David Manuel, The Glory of America (Bloomington, MN: Garborg's Heart 'N Home, Inc., 1991), 4.4. J. Michael Sharman, J.D., Faith of the Fathers (Culpepper, Virginia: Victory Publishing, 1995), pp. 43-44.

FEBRUARY 10. Cortez, Hernando. Feb. 10, 1519, in an address to his men as they embark for Mexico. Henry Morton Robinson, Stout Cortez: A Biography of the Spanish Conquest (NY: Century Co., 1931), pp. 47-48. John Eidsmoe, Columbus & Cortez, Conquerors for Christ (Green Forest, AR: New Leaf Press, 1992), p. 165-166.

FEBRUARY 11. Lincoln, Abraham. Feb. 11, 1861, Springfield, IL., in a Farewell Address to his home as he left for Washington, D.C. Weekly Illinois State Journal, Springfield, IL., Feb. 13, 1861. William J. Johnson, How Lincoln Prayed (NY: Abingdon Press, 1931), p. 27. John Bartlett, Bartlett's Familiar Quotations (Boston: Little, Brown & Co., 1855, 1980), p. 521. Roy P. Basler, ed., The Collected Works of Abraham Lincoln (New Brunswick, N.J.: Rutgers University Press, 1953), Vol. IV, p. 191. Christine F. Hart, One Nation Under God (NJ: American Tract Society, reprinted by Gospel Tract Society, Inc., Independence, Mo.), p. 3. Carroll E. Simcox, 3000 Quotations on Christian Themes (Grand Rapids, MI: Baker Book House, 1989), p. 12, No. 115.

FEBRUARY 12. Lincoln, Abraham. Apr. 24, 1865, a Memorial Address delivered by Schuyler Colfax, Speaker of the House of Representatives. Colfax, Lincoln, p. 180. Peter Marshall & David Manuel, The Glory of America (Bloomington, MN: Garborg's Heart 'N Home, Inc., 1991), 4.24. D.P. Diffine, Ph.D., One Nation Under God - How Close a Separation? (Searcy, AR: Harding University, Belden Center for Private Enterprise Education, 6th edition, 1992), p. 15. In 1955, the Congress of the United States passed a bill, signed by President Eisenhower, providing that all United States currency should bear the words "In God We Trust." The World Book Encyclopedia, 18 vols. (Chicago, IL: Field Enterprises, Inc., 1957; W.F. Quarrie & Co., 8 vols., 1917; World Book, Inc., 22 vols., 1989), Vol. 11, p. 5182.

FEBRUARY 13. Solzhenitsyn, Alexander. Jun. 30, 1975, while speaking in Washington, D.C. Society, Nov.-Dec. 1975. The Annals of America, 20 vols. (Chicago, IL: Encyclopedia Britannica, 1968), Vol. 20, pp. 174-182.

FEBRUARY 14. Valentine, Saint. American Holidays & Special Days, George & Virginia Schaun, 1986. The Book of Festivals & Holidays the World Over, Marguerite Ickis, 1970. Stories of the World's Holidays, Grace Humphrey, 1924, reprinted 1990. Hearts, Cupids & Red Roses-The Story of the Valentines Symbols, Edna Barth, 1974. The Valentine & Its Origins, Frank Staff, 1969. "Saints for Young People for Every Day of the Year - Vol. 1 (St. Paul Editions, Daughters of St. Paul, 1984).

FEBRUARY 15. McKinley, William. Apr. 20, 1898, approved a Joint Resolution of Congress. James D. Richardson (U.S. Representative from Tennessee), ed., A Compilation of the Messages & Papers of the Presidents 1789-1897, 10 vols. (Washington, D.C.: U.S. Government Printing Office, published by Authority of Congress, 1897, 1899; Washington, D.C.: Bureau of National Literature & Art, 1789-1902, 11 vols., 1907, 1910), Vol. X, p. 155.

FEBRUARY 16. United States Congress. Jun. 7, 1797, Treaty with Tripoli. Dr. C. Snouck Hurgronje of Leyden, Netherlands in his 1930 retranslation of the original treaty from Arabic into English. Gary DeMar, "The Treaty of Tripoli " (Atlanta, GA: The Biblical Worldview, An American Vision Publication - American Vision, Inc., Dec. 1992), Vol. 8, No. 12, pp. 7-12. Gary DeMar, America's Christian History: The Untold Story (Atlanta, GA: American Vision Publishers, Inc., 1993), p. 80. John W. Whitehead, "The Treaty of Tripoli " (The Rutherford Institute (Jan/Feb 1985), pp. 10-11.

FEBRUARY 17. Sunday, William Ashley "Billy ". Tryon Edwards, D.D., The New Dictionary of Thoughts - A Cyclopedia of Quotations (Garden City, NY: Hanover House, 1852; revised & enlarged by C.H. Catrevas, Ralph Emerson Browns & Jonathan Edwards descendent, along with Tryon, of Jonathan Edwards (1703-1758), president of Princeton, 1891; The Standard Book Co., 1955, 1963), p. 93.

FEBRUARY 18. Bunyan, John. Charles W. Eliot, LLD, editor, The Harvard Classics (NY: P. F. Collier & Son Co., 1909) Vol. 15, pp. 3-4.

FEBRUARY 19. Judson, Adoniram. Heros of Faith-Adoniram Judson (Oak Brook, IL: Institute of Basic Life Principles, 1990), pp. 1-14.

FEBRUARY 20. Prescott, William. 1774, in writing to the citizens of Boston on the occasion of the British blockade. George Bancroft, History of the United States of America, 6 vols. (Boston: Charles C. Little & James Brown, Third Edition, 1838), Vol. VII, p. 99. Lucille Johnston, Celebrations of a Nation (Arlington, VA: The Year of Thanksgiving Foundation, 1987), p. 76. Peter Marshall & David Manuel, The Glory of America (Bloomington, MN: Garborg's Heart 'N Home, 1991), 7.27.

FEBRUARY 21. Washington, George. Apr. 30, 1789. In the President's Oath of Office given at his inauguration. John Eidsmoe, Christianity & The Constitution - The Faith of Our Founding Fathers (Baker Book House, 1987), p. 117. The World Book Encyclopedia 22 vols. (Chicago, IL: Field Enterprises Educational Corporation, 1976; Field Enterprises, Inc., 1957; W.F. Quarrie & Co., 8 vols., 1917), Vol. 21, p. 79. Edmund Fuller & David E. Green, God in the White House - The Faiths of American Presidents (NY: Crown Publishers, Inc., 1968), p. 15. Lucille Johnston, Celebrations of a Nation (Arlington, VA: The Year of Thanksgiving Foundation, 1987), p. 142. Pat Robertson, America's Dates with Destiny (Nashville: Thomas Nelson Publishers, 1986), p. 102.

FEBRUARY 22. Washington, George. First Inaugural Address, Apr. 30, 1789, Federal Hall, New York City.

FEBRUARY 23. Taft, William H.. Dec. 6, 1912, Annual Message to Congress, part II. A Compilation of the Messages & Papers of the Presidents 20 vols. (NY: Bureau of National Literature, Inc., prepared under the direction of the Joint Committee on Printing, of the House & Senate, pursuant to an Act of the 52nd Congress of the United States, 1893, 1923), Vol. XVI, p. 7808.

FEBRUARY 24. Texas, Declaration of Independence of. Mar. 2, 1836, in General Convention at the Town of Washington. Printed by Baker & Bordens, San Felipe de Austin. Historical Documents Co., (8 North Preston Street, Philadelphia, Pa. 19104), 1977.

FEBRUARY 25. Dulles, John Foster. Statement. Charles Wallis, ed., Our American Heritage (NY: Harper & Row, Publishers, Inc., 1970), p. 23. Dulles, John Foster. Apr. 11, 1955, in a speech delivered to the Fifth Annual All-Jesuit Alumni Dinner, during his tenure as Secretary of State. Charles Hurd, ed., A Treasury of Great American Speeches (NY: Hawthorne Books, 1959), pp. 325-330.

FEBRUARY 26. Hugo, Victor Marie. William Neil, Ph.D., D.D., Concise Dictionary of Religious Quotations (Grand Rapids, MI: William B. Eerdmans Publishing Co., 1974), p. 9.

FEBRUARY 27. Longfellow, Henry Wadsworth. Bless Your Heart (series II) (Eden Prairie, MN: Heartland Sampler, Inc., 1990), 6.12

FEBRUARY 28. Stockton, Richard. Last Will & Testament. Edward J. Giddings, American Christian Rulers, p. 463. Stephen Abbott Northrop, D.D., A Cloud of Witnesses (Portland, OR: American Heritage Ministries, 1987; Mantle Ministries, 228 Still Ridge, Bulverde, TX), pp. 431-432. D.P. Diffine, Ph.D., One Nation Under God - How Close a Separation? (Searcy, AR: Harding University, Belden Center for Private Enterprise Education, 6th edition, 1992), p. 7.

FEBRUARY 29. Columbus, Christopher. Columbus, Libro de las profecias (Book of Prophecies). Kay Brigham, Christopher Columbus - His life & discovery in the light of his prophecies (Terrassa, Barcelona: CLIE Publishers, 1990), p. 97. Peter Marshall & David Manuel, The Glory of America (Bloomington, MN: Garborg's Heart'N Home, Inc., 1991), 10.13.

MARCH 1. Articles of Confederation. Nov. 15, 1777, proposed by the Continental Congress; signed Jul. 9, 1778; ratified Mar. 1, 1781. Charles W. Eliot, LL.D., ed., American Historical Documents 1000-1904 (NY: P. F. Collier & Son Co., The Harvard Classics, 1910), Vol. 43, pp. 168-179. John Wilson Taylor, M.A., Ph.D., et al., The Lincoln Library of Essential Information (Buffalo, NY: The Frontier Press Co., 1935), pp. 1392-1394. "Our Christian Heritage," Letter from Plymouth Rock (Marlborough, NH: The Plymouth Rock Foundation), p. 3. Michael R. Farris, Esq., Constitutional Law (Paeonian Springs, VA: Home School Legal Defense Association, 1991), pp. 20-29.

MARCH 2. Texas, Declaration of Independence of. Mar. 2, 1836, in General Convention at the Town of Washington. Printed by Baker & Bordens, San Felipe de Austin. Historical Documents Co., (8 North Preston Street, Philadelphia, Pa. 19104), 1977.

MARCH 3. Colfax, Schuyler. Apr. 24, 1865, a Memorial Address for President Lincoln delivered by Schuyler Colfax, Speaker of the House of Representatives. Colfax, Lincoln, p. 180. Peter Marshall & David Manuel, The Glory of America (Bloomington, MN: Garborg's Heart 'N Home, Inc., 1991), 4.24. D.P. Diffine, Ph.D., One Nation Under God - How Close a Separation? (Searcy, AR: Harding University, Belden Center for Private Enterprise Education, 6th edition, 1992), p. 15. In 1955, the Congress of the United States passed a bill, signed by President Eisenhower, providing that all United States currency should bear the words "In God We Trust." The World Book Encyclopedia, 18 vols. (Chicago, IL: Field Enterprises, Inc., 1957; W.F. Quarrie & Co., 8 vols., 1917; World Book, Inc., 22 vols., 1989), Vol. 11, p. 5182.

MARCH 4. Jefferson, Thomas. Mar. 4, 1801, First Inaugural Address. James D. Richardson (U.S. Representative from Tennessee), ed., A Compilation of the Messages & Papers of the Presidents 1789-1897, 10 vols. (Washington, D.C.: U.S. Government Printing Office, published by Authority of Congress, 1897, 1899; Washington, D.C.: Bureau of National Literature & Art, 1789-1902, 11 vols., 1907, 1910), Vol. I, p. 322-324. Jackson, Andrew. Mar. 4, 1833, Inaugural Address. James D. Richardson (U.S. Representative from Tennessee), ed., A Compilation of the Messages & Papers of the Presidents 1789-1897, 10 vols. (Washington, D.C.: U.S. Government Printing Office, published by Authority of Congress, 1897, 1899; Washington, D.C.: Bureau of National Literature & Art, 1789-1902, 11 vols., 1907, 1910), Vol. III, p. 5. Lincoln, Abraham. Mar. 4, 1865, Second Inaugural Address. James D. Richardson (U.S. Representative from Tennessee), ed., A Compilation of the Messages & Papers of the Presidents 1789-1897, 10 vols. (Washington, D.C.: U.S. Government Printing Office, published by Authority of Congress, 1897, 1899; Washington, D.C.: Bureau of National Literature & Art, 1789-1902, 11 vols., 1907, 1910), Vol. VI, pp. 276-277. Roosevelt, Franklin Delano. Mar. 4, 1933, First Inaugural Address. Inaugural Addresses of the Presidents of the United States - From George Washington 1789 to Richard Milhous Nixon 1969 (Washington, D.C.: U.S. Government Printing Office; 91st Congress, 1st Session, House Document 91-142, 1969), pp. 235-239. Coolidge, (John) Calvin. Mar. 4, 1925, Inaugural Address. Inaugural Addresses of the Presidents of the United States - From George Washington 1789 to Richard Milhous Nixon 1969 (Washington, D.C.: U.S. Government Printing Office; 91st Congress, 1st Session, House Document 91-142, 1969), pp. 215-223. Kennedy, John Fitzgerald. Jan. 20, 1961, Inaugural Address. Inaugural Addresses of the Presidents of the United States - From George Washington 1789 to Richard Milhous Nixon 1969 (Washington, D.C.: U.S. Government Printing Office; 91st Congress, 1st Session, House Document 91-142, 1969), pp. 267-270.

MARCH 5. Hancock, John. Mar. 5, 1774, in an oration on the Boston Massacre. The Magazine of History, with Notes & Queries, Vol. 24, No. 95 (1923), pp 125, 136. Ronald Reid, ed., Three Centuries of American Rhetorical Discourse: An Anthology & a Review (Prospect Heights, Ill: Waveland Press, Inc., 1988), pp. 101, 107-8.

MARCH 6. Washington, George. Mar. 6, 1776, from the headquarters at Cambridge, in his command for a Day of Prayer, Fasting, & Humiliation. Dorothy Dudley, The Cambridge of 1776, with the diary of Dorothy Dudley, (1876), p. 59. William J. Johnson, George Washington - The Christian (St. Paul, MN: William J. Johnson, Merriam Park, Feb. 23, 1919; Nashville, TN: Abingdon Press, 1919; reprinted Milford, MI: Mott Media, 1976; reprinted Arlington Heights, IL: Christian Liberty Press, 502 West Euclid Ave., Arlington Heights, IL., 60004, 1992), p. 77. John Eidsmoe, Christianity & The Constitution - The Faith of Our Founding Fathers (Baker Book House, 1987), p. 139.

MARCH 7. Prescott, William. 1774, in writing to the citizens on the occasion of the British blockade. George Bancroft, History of the United States of America, 6 vols. (Boston: Charles C. Little & James Brown, Third Edition, 1838), Vol. VII, p. 99. Lucille Johnston, Celebrations of a Nation (Arlington, VA: The Year of Thanksgiving Foundation, 1987), p. 76. Peter Marshall & David Manuel, The Glory of America (Bloomington, MN: Garborg's Heart 'N Home, 1991), 7.27.

MARCH 8. Holmes, Oliver Wendell, Jr. Mar. 8, 1931, in reply to a reporter's question on his ninetieth birthday. John Bartlett, Bartlett's Familiar Quotations (Boston: Little, Brown & Co., 1855, 1980), p. 645. The Annals of America 20 Vols. (Chicago, IL: Encyclopedia Britannica, Inc., 1976), Vol. 14, p. 166, Oliver Wendell Holmes, Jr. stated: "My boy, about seventy-five years ago I learned I was not God."

MARCH 9. Coolidge, (John) Calvin. May 29, 1926, at the dedication of the statue of John Ericsson, Washington, D.C. Calvin Coolidge, Foundations of the Republic - Speeches & Addresses (NY: Charles Scribner's Sons, 1926), pp. 415-425.

MARCH 10. Penn, William. Aug. 18, 1681, Letter to the Indians before his arrival. Pennsylvania Historical Society Collection, Philadelphia.

MARCH 11. Sumner, Charles. E.C. Lester, Life & Public Services of Charles Sumner, pp. 321, 171. Stephen Abbott Northrop, D.D., A Cloud of Witnesses (Portland, OR: American Heritage Ministries, 1987; Mantle Ministries, 228 Still Ridge, Bulverde, TX), p. 436.

MARCH 12. Girl Scouts. The World Book Encyclopedia-Vol 7 (Chicago: Field Enterprises, 1957), pp. 2999-3003.

MARCH 13. Anthony, Susan B. The World Book Encyclopedia-Vol 1 (Chicago: Field Enterprises, 1957), p. 327. Jun. Sochen, "Anthony, Susan Brownell," World Book Online Americas Edition, http://www.aolsvc.worldbook.aol.com/wbol/wbPage/na/ar/co/023980, Oct. 8, 2001. http://www.compleatheretic.com/pubs/letters/020624.html http://www.family.org/fofmag/sl/a0024084.cfm http://www.crosswalk.com/news/1185972.html?view=print

MARCH 14. Einstein, Albert. Engraved over the fireplace in Fine Hall, Princeton, N.J. Burton Stevenson, The Home Book of Quotations - Classical & Modern (NY: Dodd, Mead & Co., 1967). ("Raffiniert ist der Herr Gott, aber Boshaft ist er nicht,"- "The Lord God is subtle, but malicious he is not.") John Bartlett, Bartlett's Familiar Quotations (Boston: Little, Brown & Co., 1855, 1980), p. 764.

MARCH 15. Reagan, Ronald Wilson. May 20, 1984, on a School Prayer amendment to the Constitution. David R. Shepherd, ed., Ronald Reagan: In God I Trust (Wheaton, IL: Tyndale House Publishers, Inc., 1984), pp. 79-80. Reagan, Ronald Wilson. Aug. 23, 1984 at an ecumenical prayer breakfast at the Reunion Arena in Dallas, on the occasion of the enactment of the Equal Access Bill of 1984. Jeremiah O'Leary, "Reagan Declares that Faith Has Key Role in Political Life," The Washington Times (Aug. 24, 1984). Walter Shapiro, "Politics & the Pulpit," Newsweek (Sept. 17, 1984), p. 24. The Speech That Shook The Nation (Forerunner, Dec. 1984), p. 12. Nadine Strossen, "Constitutional Analysis of the Equal Access Act's Standards Governing School Student's Religious Meetings," Harvard Journal on Legislation, Winter, 1987. p. 118. David R. Shepherd, Ronald Reagan: In God We Trust (Wheaton, IL: Tyndale House Publishers, Inc., 1984), p. 146.

MARCH 16. Madison, James. Jun. 20, 1785. James Madison, A Memorial & Remonstrance (Washington, D.C.: Library of Congress, Rare Book Collection, delivered to the General Assembly of the State of Virginia, 1785; Massachusetts: Isaiah Thomas, 1786). Robert Rutland, ed., The Papers of James Madison (Chicago: University of Chicago Press, 1973), Vol. VIII, pp. 299, 304. Stephen McDowell & Mark Beliles, "The Providential Perspective " (Charlottesville, VA: The Providence Foundation, P.O. Box 6759, Charlottesville, Va. 22906, Jan. 1994), Vol. 9, No. 1, p. 5.

MARCH 17. Patrick, Confessions, Letter to Coroticus, The Writings of Patrick; Book of Armagh. Robert G. Clouse, Patrick (Grand Rapids, MI: Eerdman's Handbook to the History of Christianity. W.H. Eerdman's Publishing Co., 1988), pp. 211-212.

MARCH 18. Venable, William Henry. In Johnny Appleseed, st. 25. John Bartlett, Bartlett's Familiar Quotations (Boston: Little, Brown & Co., 1855, 1980), p. 765.

MARCH 19. Bradford, William. Nov. 11, 1620, in his record of the Pilgrims' landing at Cape Cod, Massachusetts. William Bradford (Governor of Plymouth Colony), The History of Plymouth Plantation 1608-1650 (Boston, Massachusetts: Massachusetts Historical Society, 1856; Boston, Massachusetts: Wright & Potter Printing Co., 1898, 1901, from the Original Manuscript, Library of Congress Rare Book Collection, Washington, D.C.; rendered in Modern English, Harold Paget, 1909; NY: Russell & Russell, 1968; NY: Random House, Inc., Modern Library College edition, 1981; San Antonio, TX: American Heritage Classics, Mantle Ministries, 228 Still Ridge, Bulverde, TX, 1988), p. 66. Sacvan Bercovitch, ed., Typology & Early American Literature (Cambridge: University of Massachusetts Press, 1972), p. 104. Peter Marshall & David Manuel, The Glory of America (Bloomington, MN: Garborg's Heart'N Home, Inc., 1991), 11.28. (note: reference to these first settlers as "pilgrims" is owed to this passage.)

MARCH 20. Newton, Sir Isaac. 1704, in Optics. John Bartlett, Bartlett's Familiar Quotations (Boston: Little, Brown and Company, 1855, 1980), p. 313. T.H.L. Leary, Short Biographies of the People - Life of Sir Isaac Newton, Vol. VI. Stephen Abbott Northrop, D.D., A Cloud of Witnesses (Portland, OR: American Heritage Ministries, 1987; Mantle Ministries, 228 Still Ridge, Bulverde, TX), p. 338.

MARCH 21. Bach, Johann Sebastian. Statement regarding music. G. Schirmer Music Publishing Catalogue. Bush, George H. W.., Feb. 22, 1990, Presidential Proclamation of 1990 the International Year of Bible Reading, at the request of Congress, Senate Joint Resolution 164. Courtesy of Bruce Barilla, Christian Heritage Week Ministry (P.O. Box 58, Athens, W.V. 24712; 304-384-7707, 304-384-9044 fax). U.S. Supreme Court. 1948, McCollum v. Board of Education of School District Number 71, 333 U.S. 203, 236 (1948). Elizabeth Ridenour, Public Schools - Bible Curriculum (Greensboro, N.C.: National Council On Bible Curriculum, 1996), p. 13, 14-15, 28, 42. Robert K. Skolrood, The National Legal Foundation, letter to National Council on the Bible Curriculum in Public Schools, Sept. 13, 1994, p. 2.

MARCH 22. Franklin, Benjamin. 1739. Benjamin Franklin, The Autobiography of Benjamin Franklin (NY: Books, Inc., 1791), p. 146. Benjamin Franklin, Autobiography, 1771-75 (Reprinted Garden City, NY: Garden City Publishing Co., Inc., 1916), Vol. 1, pp. 191-192. John Pollack, George Whitefield & the Great Awakening (Garden City NJ: Doubleday & Co., 1972), p. 117. John Eidsmoe, Christianity & The Constitution - The Faith of Our Founding Fathers (Grand Rapids, MI: Baker Book House, 1987), p. 204. Tim LaHaye, Faith of Our Founding Fathers (Brentwood, TN: Wolgemuth & Hyatt, Publishers, Inc., 1987), p. 116. Peter Marshall & David Manuel, The Glory of America (Bloomington, MN: Garborg's Heart 'N Home, 1991), 12.18.

MARCH 23. Henry, Patrick. Mar. 23, 1775, in The Second Virginia Convention given at St. John's Church in Richmond Virginia. The Annals of America, 20 vols. (Chicago, IL: Encyclopedia Britannica, 1968), Vol. 2, pp. 322-333. William Wirt Henry (grandson of Patrick Henry), editor, Sketches of the Life & Character of Patrick Henry (Philadelphia: Claxton, 1818; Revised edition, NY: M'Elrath & Sons, 1835), pp. 137-142. George Bancroft, History of the United States of America, 6 vols. (Boston: Charles C. Little & James Brown, 3rd Ed., 1838), p. 29. Frederick C. Packard, Jr., ed., Are You an American? - Great Americans Speak (NY: Charles Scribner's Sons, 1951), pp. 1-4. A. Craig Baird, American Public Addresses (NY: McGraw Hill, 1956), complete speech, pp. 29-36. Ronald Reid, ed., Three Centuries of American Rhetorical Discourse - An Anthology & a Review (Prospect Heights, Ill: Waveland Press, Inc., 1988), pp. 115-116. Peter Marshall & David Manual, The Light & the Glory (Old Tappan, NJ: Fleming Revell Co., 1977), p. 269. William Safire, ed., Lend Me Your Ears - Great Speeches in History (NY: W.W. Norton & Co. 1992), pp. 86-89.

MARCH 24. King, Rufus. M.E. Bradford, A Worthy Company (Marlborough, NH: Plymouth Rock Foundation, 1982), p. 15. Tim LaHaye, Faith of Our Founding Fathers (Brentwood, TN: Wolgemuth & Hyatt, Publishers, Inc., 1987), p. 161.

MARCH 25. Jackson, Andrew. Mar. 25, 1835, in a letter. Robert V. Remini, Andrew Jackson & the Course of American Freedom, 1822-1832 (NY: Harper & Row, 1981), Vol. 2, p. 251. Peter Marshall & David Manuel, The Glory of America (Bloomington, MN: Garborg's Heart 'N Home, Inc., 1991), 3.25.

MARCH 26. Allen, Richard. Edgar Allan Toppin, "Allen, Richard," World Book Online Americas Edition, http://www.aolsvc.worldbook.aol.com/wbol/wbPage/na/ar/co/013810, Oct. 8, 2001.

MARCH 27. Adams, Henry. 1889-1891. Henry Adams, History of the United States, 9 vols. (Ithaca, NY: Cornell University Press, Great Seal Books, 1889-1891; 1960), p. 127. Peter Marshall & David Manuel, From Sea to Shining Sea (Old Tappan, New Jersey: Fleming H. Revell Co., 1985), p. 48.

MARCH 28. Booth, William. Peter W. Williams, "Booth, William," World Book Online Americas Edition, http://www.aolsvc.worldbook.aol.com/wbol/wbPage/na/ar/co/070150, Oct. 8, 2001 President Lyndon B. Johnson, 1 p.m. Dec. 9, 1965, from the LBJ Ranch, Johnson City, TX, gave Telephone Remarks Upon Accepting an Award From the Salvation Army Association of New York, which was meeting in the New York Hilton Hotel. In his opening words he referred to Walker G. Buckner, Chairman of the Salvation Army Advisory Board, & Frederick R. Kappel, Chairman of the Board, American Telephone & Telegraph Co., & member of the Salvation Army Advisory Board: "Mr. Buckner and my good friend, Fred Kappel, ladies & gentlemen: I feel a very special gratitude in receiving this honor today-because I think I know something of the men and women who extend it. Your standard of service is high, your record of accomplishment proud and long. For a century now, the Salvation Army has offered food to the hungry and shelter to the homeless-in clinics and children's homes, through disaster relief, in prison and welfare work, and a thousand other endeavors. In that century you have proved time and again the power of a handshake, a meal, and a song. But you have not stopped there. You have demonstrated also the power of a great idea. The voice of the Salvation Army has reminded men that physical well-being is just not enough; that spiritual rebirth is the most pressing need of our time and of every time; that the world cannot be changed unless men change. That voice has been clear and courageous-and it has been heard. Even when other armies have disbanded, I hope that this one will still be on the firing line: an army whose foes are hunger and hopelessness; an army whose happy battle cry is a call to 'brighten the corner where you are.' With a pledge to heed that good advice, and with genuinely warm appreciation, I proudly accept your award."

MARCH 29. Tyler, John. Apr. 13, 1841, in a Proclamation recommending a National Day of Fasting & Prayer in respect of the death of President William Henry Harrison, issued from Washington, D.C. James D. Richardson (U.S. Representative from Tennessee), ed., A Compilation of the Messages & Papers of the Presidents 1789-1897, 10 vols. (Washington, D.C.: U.S. Government Printing Office, pub. by Authority of Congress, 1897, 1899; Washington, D.C.: Bureau of National Literature & Art, 1789-1902, 11 vols., 1907, 1910), Vol. IV, p. 32. Benjamin Franklin Morris, The Christian Life & Character of the Civil Institutions of the United States (Philadelphia: George W. Childs, 1864), pp. 550-551.

MARCH 30. Lincoln, Abraham. Mar. 30, 1863, in a Proclamation of a National Day of Humiliation, Fasting & Prayer. James D. Richardson (U.S. Representative from Tennessee), ed., A Compilation of the Messages & Papers of the Presidents 1789-1897, 10 vols. (Washington, D.C.: U.S. Government Printing Office, published by Authority of Congress, 1897, 1899; Washington, D.C.: Bureau of National Literature & Art, 1789-1902, 11 vols., 1907, 1910), Vol. VI, pp. 164-165. Benjamin Franklin Morris, The Christian Life & Character of the Civil Institutions of the United States (Philadelphia: George W. Childs, 1864), pp. 558-559. Anson Phelps Stokes, Church & State in the United States (NY: Harper & Brothers, 1950), Vol. III, p. 186. Roy P. Basler, ed., The Collected Works of Abraham Lincoln, 9 vols. (New Brunswick, NJ: Rutgers University Press, 1953), Vol. 6, p. 179. Benjamin Weiss, God in American History: A Documentation of America's Religious Heritage (Grand Rapids, MI: Zondervan, 1966), p. 92. Willard Cantelon, Money Master of the World (Plainfield, NJ: Logos International, 1976), p. 120. Gary DeMar, God & Government, A Biblical & Historical Study (Atlanta, GA: American Vision Press, 1984), p. 128-29. "Our Christian Heritage," Letter from Plymouth Rock (Marlborough, NH: The Plymouth Rock Foundation), p. 6. D.P. Diffine, Ph.D., One Nation Under God - How Close a Separation? (Searcy, AR: Harding University, Belden Center for Private Enterprise Education, 6th edition, 1992), pp. 14-15. Gary DeMar, America's Christian History: The Untold Story (Atlanta, GA: American Vision Publishers, Inc., 1993), pp. 53, 99. George Otis, The Solution to the Crisis in America, Revised & Enlarged Edition (Van Nuys, CA.: Fleming H. Revell Co.; Bible Voice, Inc., 1970, 1972, foreword by Pat Boone), pp. 47-48.

MARCH 31. Ka'ahumanu, Queen Regent-Prime Minister of Hawaii. 1832, in her last words to Rev. Hiram Bingham. "Hawaii's heroes of the faith," (Hawaii: University of the Nations Newsletter, Youth With a Mission, 1993), p. 8.

APRIL 1. MacArthur, Douglas. Sept. 2, 1945, in a prayer given aboard the battleship USS Missouri in Tokyo Bay, at a meeting with leaders of Allied forces to sign the treaty of surrender of Japan. Charles Colson, Kingdoms in

Conflict (Grand Rapids, MI: Zondervan Publishing House, 1987), p. 178.
APRIL 2. Morse, Samuel Finley Breese. 1844. Webster's Family Encyclopedia, 13 vols. (NY: Ottenheimer Publishers, Inc., 1988), Vol. 8, p. 1763. Sarah K. Bolton, Famous Men of Science. Stephen Abbott Northrop, D.D., A Cloud of Witnesses (Portland, OR: American Heritage Ministries, 1987; Mantle Ministries, 228 Still Ridge, Bulverde, TX), p. 327-328.
APRIL 3. Hale, Everett. Robert Flood, The Rebirth of America (Philadelphia: Arthur S. DeMoss Foundation, 1986), p. 223.
APRIL 4. King, Martin Luther, Jr. Aug. 28, 1963, on the occasion of the Civil Rights Mar. on Washington. The SCLC Story in Words & Pictures, 1964, pp. 50-51. The Annals of America, 20 vols. (Chicago, IL: Encyclopedia Britannica, Inc., 1976), Vol. 18, pp. 156-159. John Bartlett, Bartlett's Familiar Quotations (Boston: Little, Brown & Co., 1855, 1980), p. 909.
APRIL 5. Washington, Booker Taliaferro. Kevin A. Miller, "Fashionable or Forceful," (Carol Streams, IL: Christian History, 465 Gunderson Dr., Carol Streams, IL, 60188, 1990), Issue 26. Vol. IX, No. 2,p. 2.
APRIL 6. Wilson, Woodrow. Oct. 19, 1917, Proclamation of a National Day of Supplication & Prayer. A Compilation of the Messages & Papers of the Presidents 20 vols. (NY: Bureau of National Literature, Inc., prepared under the direction of the Joint Committee on Printing, of the House & Senate, pursuant to an Act of the 52nd Congress of the United States, 1893, 1923), Vol. XVII, pp. 8377-8378.
APRIL 7. Barnum, Phineas Taylor. Statement. Perry Tanksley, To Love is to Give (Jackson, Mississippi: Allgood Books, Box 1329; Parthenon Press, 201 8th Ave., South, Nashville, Tennessee, 1972), p. 25.
APRIL 8. Bradley, Omar. Nov. 11, 1948, in an address he delivered on Armistice Day, or Veteran's Day. John Bartlett, Bartlett's Familiar Quotations (Boston: Little, Brown & Co., 1855, 1980), p. 825.
APRIL 9. Lee, Robert Edward. Apr. 10, 1865, Final Order to the Army of Northern Virginia. Charles W. Eliot, LL.D., ed., American Historical Documents 1000-1904 (NY: P.F. Collier & Son Co., The Harvard Classics, 1910), Vol. 43, p. 449. Raymond A. St. John, American Literature for Christian Schools (Greenville, SC: Bob Jones University Press, Inc., 1979), p. 388. Lillian W. Kay, ed., The Ground on Which We Stand - Basic Documents of American History (NY: Franklin Watts., Inc, 1969), p. 207.
APRIL 10. Booth, William. Norman H. Murdoch, "Sayings of William Booth," (Carol Streams, IL: Christian History, 465 Gunderson Drive, Carol Streams, IL, 60188, 1990), Issue 26, Vol. IX, No. 2, p. 7.
APRIL 11. Apollo 13. Author/Curator: Dr. David R. Williams, dwilliam"nssdc.gsfc.nasa.gov, NSSDC, Mail Code 633, NASA Goddard Space Flight Center, Greenbelt, MD 20771, 1-301-286-1258. Jim Bickford, American Dreams, 3950 Koval Lane, #3029, Las Vegas, NV 89109, Phone: 702-732-1971, Fax: 702-732-2815, Email: jimb@usdreams.com, Web: http://www.usdreams.com, http://www.ozcraft.com/scifidu/apollo13.html, http://www.ksc.nasa.gov/history/apollo/apollo-13/apollo-13.html.
APRIL 12. Lincoln, Abraham. In statement to Noah Brooks, as related by Judge Henry C. Whitney. Tryon Edwards, D.D., The New Dictionary of Thoughts - A Cyclopedia of Quotations (Garden City, NY: Hanover House, 1852; revised & enlarged by C.H. Catrevas, Ralph Emerson Browns & Jonathan Edwards descendent, along with Tryon, of Jonathan Edwards (1703-1758), president of Princeton, 1891; The Standard Book Co., 1955, 1963), p. 486. John G. Holland, Life of Abraham Lincoln (1866), p 435. Trueblood, Abraham Lincoln: Theologian of American Anguish, p. 76. William J. Johnson, How Lincoln Prayed (NY: Abingdon, Press, 1931), p. 63. Robert Flood, The Rebirth of America (Philadelphia: Arthur S. DeMoss Foundation, 1986), p. 182. Bless Your Heart (series II) (Eden Prairie, MN: Heartland Sampler, Inc., 1990), 12.18. Christianity Today, Feb. 11, 1991. Peter Marshall & David Manuel, The Glory of America (Bloomington, MN: Garborg's Heart'N Home, Inc., 1991), 5.24.
APRIL 13. Jefferson, Thomas. A Summary View of the Rights of British America: "God...liberty." Notes on the State of Virginia: "Can...God?" Notes on the State of Virginia: "commerce...despotism." The Autobiography: "Nothing...free." Letter to George Wythe, Aug. 13, 1780 (?): "Establish...people." Letter to George Washington, Jan. 4, 1786: "This...plan." http://www.geocities.com/Athens/7842/archives/memorial.htm 1781, Notes on the State of Virginia, Query XVIII, 1781, 1782, p. 237. Paul Leicester Ford, The Writings of Thomas Jefferson (NY: G.P. Putnam's Sons, the Knickerbocker Press, 1894), 3:267. A.A. Lipscomb & Albert Bergh, eds., The Writings of Thomas Jefferson 20 vols. (Washington, D.C.: The Thomas Jefferson Memorial Association, 1903-1904). Vol. IX, Vol. II, p. 227. Saul K. Padover, ed., The Complete Jefferson (NY: Tudor Publishing, 1943), p. 677. Robert Byrd, U.S. Senator from West Virginia, Jul. 27, 1962, in a message delivered in Congress two days after the Supreme Court declared prayer in schools unconstitutional. Merrill D. Peterson, ed., Jefferson Writings (NY: Literary Classics of the United States, Inc., 1984) p. 289. Robert Flood, The Rebirth of America (Philadelphia: Arthur S. DeMoss Foundation, 1986), pp. 66-69. Tim LaHaye, Faith of Our Founding Fathers (Brentwood, TN: Wolgemuth & Hyatt,

Publishers, Inc., 1987), pp. 192-193. George Grant, Third Time Around (Brentwood, TN: Wolgemuth & Hyatt, Inc., 1991), p. 103. D.P. Diffine, Ph.D., One Nation Under God - How Close a Separation? (Searcy, AR: Harding University, Belden Center for Private Enterprise Education, 6th edition, 1992), p. 10. Gary DeMar, America's Christian History: The Untold Story (Atlanta, GA: American Vision Publishers, Inc., 1993), p. 56. Stephen McDowell & Mark Beliles, "The Providential Perspective " (Charlottesville, VA: The Providence Foundation, P.O. Box 6759, Charlottesville, Va. 22906, Jan. 1994), Vol. 9, No. 1, p. 5.

APRIL 14. Webster, Noah. An American Dictionary of the English Language - with pronouncing vocabularies of Scripture, classical & geographical names (New Haven), preface. Noah Webster's First Edition of an American Dictionary of the English Language (San Francisco, CA: Foundation for American Christian Education, 1980), p. 12. Peter Marshall & David Manuel, From Sea to Shining Sea (Old Tappan, N.J.: Fleming H. Revell Co., 1986), p. 412.

APRIL 15. Lincoln, Abraham. Feb. 22, 1861, in a speech at Independence Hall, Philadelphia. John Bartlett, Bartlett's Familiar Quotations (Boston: Little, Brown & Co., 1863, 1980), pp. 520-524. Pat Robertson, America's Dates With Destiny (Nashville, TN: Thomas Nelson Publishers, 1986), p. 156. Lincoln, Abraham. Sept. 22, 1862, in commenting to his Cabinet after the massive Confederate Army lost to the Union troops at the Battle at Antietam, just prior to the issuance of the Emancipation Proclamation, as reported by Secretary of the Treasury, Salmon Portland Chase. Frank B. Carpenter, Six Months at the White House (1866), p. 89. William J. Johnson, How Lincoln Prayed (NY: Abingdon Press, 1931), p. 48. Peter Marshall & David Manuel, The Glory of America (Bloomington, MN: Garborg's Heart'N Home, Inc., 1991), 9.22.

APRIL 16. Tocqueville, Alexis de. Statement. Alexis de Tocqueville, The Republic of the United States of America & Its Political Institutions, Reviewed & Examined, Henry Reeves, trans., (Garden City, NY: A.S. Barnes & Co., 1851), Vol. I, p. 337. Alexis de Tocqueville, Democracy in America (NY: Vintage Books, 1945), Vol. I, p. 319. Tim LaHaye, Faith of Our Founding Fathers (Brentwood, TN: Wolgemuth & Hyatt, Publishers, Inc., 1987), p. 97. Francis J. Grund, a publicist, wrote his work The Americans in Their Moral, Social & Political Relations in 1837, in which he observed the trends of religious influence in America: "The religious habits of the Americans form not only the basis of their private & public morals, but have become so thoroughly interwoven with their whole course of legislation, that it would be impossible to change them, without affecting the very essence of their government." Francis J. Grund, The Americans in Their Moral, Social & Political Relations, (1837), Vol. I, pp. 281, 292, 294. Anson Phelps Stokes & Leo Pfeffer, Church & State in the United States (NY: Harper & Row, Publishers, 1950, revised one-volume edition, 1964), p. 210.

APRIL 17. Franklin, Benjamin. James H. Hutson, Ph.D., Chief, Manuscript Division, Library of Congress, "Franklin, Benjamin," World Book Online Americas Edition, http://www.aolsvc.worldbook.aol.com/wbol/wbPage/na/ar/co/209260, Oct. 9, 2001.

APRIL 18. Bradford, William. 1643, in recounting the death of Mr. William Brewster. William Bradford (Governor of Plymouth Colony), The History of Plymouth Plantation 1608-1650 (Boston, Massachusetts: Massachusetts Historical Society, 1856; Boston, Massachusetts: Wright & Potter Printing Co., 1898, from the original manuscript; rendered in Modern English, Harold Paget, 1909; NY: Russell & Russell, 1968; San Antonio, TX: American Heritage Classics, Mantle Ministries, 228 Still Ridge, Bulverde, TX, 1988), p. 314.

APRIL 19. MacArthur, Douglas. Apr. 19, 1951, in a speech to a Joint Session of Congress in which he announced his retirement. Frederick C. Packard, Jr., ed., Are You an American? - Great Americans Speak (NY: Charles Scribner's Sons, 1951), p. 105. Charles Hurd, ed., A Treasury of Great American Speeches (NY: Hawthorne Books, 1959), p. 296. William Safire, ed., Lend Me Your Ears - Great Speeches in History (NY: W.W. Norton & Co. 1992), p. 379.

APRIL 20. Brainerd, David. "Brainerd, David," World Book Online Americas Edition, http://www.aolsvc.worldbook.aol.com/wbol/wbPage/na/ar/co/723264, Oct. 9, 2001. Mark A. Knoll, A History of Christianity in the United States & Canada (Grand Rapids, MI: William B. Eerdmans Publishing Co., 1992), pp. 105-106. Christian Classics Ethereal Library, Calvin College, Grand Rapids, Michigan. http://www.ccel.org/e/edwards/works/vol2/david_brainerd/brainerd.htm

APRIL 21. Twain, Mark. Henry & Dana Thomas, 1942. Charles E. Jones, The Books You Read (Harrisburg, PA: Executive Books, 1985), p. 133.

APRIL 22. Oklahoma, State of. 1907, Constitution, Preamble. Charles E. Rice, The Supreme Court & Public Prayer (NY: Fordham University Press, 1964), p. 174; "Hearings, Prayers in Public Schools & Other Matters," Committee on the Judiciary, U.S. Senate (87th Cong., 2nd Sess.), 1962, pp. 268 et seq.

APRIL 23. Shakespeare, William. 1616, first clause in his last will. Stephen Abbott Northrop, D.D., A Cloud of Witnesses (Portland, OR: American Heritage Ministries, 1987; Mantle Ministries, 228 Still Ridge, Bulverde, TX), p. 405. See also: inscription on his tombstone, 1616, Holy Trinity Church, Stratford-on-Avon, England. The World

Book Encyclopedia, 18 vols. (Chicago, IL: Field Enterprises, Inc., 1957; W.F. Quarrie & Co., 8 vols., 1917; World Book, Inc., 22 vols., 1989), Vol. 15, p. 7372.

APRIL 24. Library of Congress. Jul. 27, 1962, Senator Robert Byrd of West Virginia, in a message delivered in Congress two days after the Supreme Court declared prayer in schools unconstitutional. Robert Flood, The Rebirth of America (Philadelphia: Arthur S. DeMoss Foundation, 1986), pp. 66-69. Gary DeMar, America's Christian History: The Untold Story (Atlanta, GA: American Vision Publishers, Inc., 1993), p. 55.

APRIL 25. Marshall, Peter. Jul. 3, 1947, in a prayer before the 80th Congress. Catherine Marshall, ed., The Prayers of Peter Marshall (NY: McGraw Hill Book Co., Inc., 1949), p. 186. Robert Flood, The Rebirth of America (The Arthur S. DeMoss Foundation, 1986), back cover.

APRIL 26. Virginia, First Charter of. 1606, granted by King James I. Ebenezer Hazard, editor, Historical Collections: Consisting of State Papers & other Authentic Documents; Intended as Materials for an History of the United States of America (Philadelphia: T. Dobson, 1792), Vol. I, pp. 50-51. Church of the Holy Trinity v. United States, 143 US 457, 458, 465-471, 36 L ed 226, (1892), Justice David Josiah Brewer. Henry Steele Commager, ed., Documents of American History, 2 vols. (NY: F.S. Crofts & Co., 1934; Appleton-Century-Crofts, Inc., 1948, 6th edition, 1958; Englewood Cliffs, NJ: Prentice Hall, Inc., 9th edition, 1973), p. 8. Gary DeMar, God & Government - A Biblical & Historical Study (Atlanta, GA: American Vision Press, 1984), p. 127. "Our Christian Heritage," Letter from Plymouth (Marlborough, NH: The Plymouth Rock Foundation), pp. 1, 6. Robert Flood, The Rebirth of America (Philadelphia: Arthur S. DeMoss Foundation, 1986), p. 46. Gary DeMar, America's Christian History: The Untold Story (Atlanta, GA: American Vision Publishers, Inc., 1993), p. 37.

APRIL 27. Grant, Ulysses Simpson. Jun. 26, 1876, in a Proclamation of a National Day of Public Thanksgiving. James D. Richardson (U.S. Representative from Tennessee), ed., A Compilation of the Messages & Papers of the Presidents 1789-1897, 10 vols. (Washington, D.C.: U.S. Government Printing Office, published by Authority of Congress, 1897, 1899; Washington, D.C.: Bureau of National Literature & Art, 1789-1902, 11 vols., 1907, 1910), Vol. 7, p. 392.

APRIL 28. Monroe, James. Dec. 2, 1817, First Annual Message. James D. Richardson (U.S. Representative from Tennessee), ed., A Compilation of the Messages & Papers of the Presidents 1789-1897, 10 vols. (Washington, D.C.: U.S. Government Printing Office, published by Authority of Congress, 1897, 1899; Washington, D.C.: Bureau of National Literature & Art, 1789-1902, 11 vols., 1907, 1910), Vol. II, p. 12.

APRIL 29. Farragut, David Glasgow. Loyall Farragut, the son of Admiral D.G. Farragut, Life & Letters of Admiral D.C. Farragut, p. 548. Stephen Abbott Northrop, D.D., A Cloud of Witnesses (Portland, OR: American Heritage Ministries, 1987; Mantle Ministries, 228 Still Ridge, Bulverde, TX), p. 148. Per Rolf Briegel, LT, USNR, inactive, Mt. Lebanon High School, Pittsburgh, PA RBriegel@mtlsd.net "The actual quote was 'Damn the torpedoes, ring four bells!', four bells being the signal to the engine room to crank the engine up as much as possible."

APRIL 30. Bonaparte, Napoleon. At St. Helena, to Count de Motholon. Major General Alfred Pleasonton. Stephen Abbott Northrop, D.D., A Cloud of Witnesses (Portland, OR: American Heritage Ministries, 1987; Mantle Ministries, 228 Still Ridge, Bulverde, TX), pp. 361-362. Vernon C. Grounds, The Reason for Our Hope (Chicago: Moody Press), p. 37. Willard Cantelon, New Money or None? (Plainfield, NJ: Logos International, 1979), p. 246.

MAY 1. Diocletion. EUSEBIUS, Hist. Eccl. in P.G., XX; De Mart. Palæstinæ, P.G., XX, 1457-1520; LACTANTIUS, Divinæ Institutiones, V, in P.L., VI; De Mortibus Persecutorum, P.L., VII; GIBBON, Decline & Fall of the Roman Empire, xiii, xvi; ALLARD, Le persécution de Dioclétien et le triomphe de l'eglise (Paris, 1890); IDEM, Le christianisme et l'empire romain (Paris, 1898); IDEM, Ten Lectures on the Martyrs, tr. (London, 1907); DUCHESNE, Histoire ancienne de l'eglise (Paris, 1907), II. T.B. SCANNELL, Transcribed by WGKofron, With thanks to St. Mary's Church, Akron, Ohio. The Catholic Encyclopedia, Volume V. Copyright 8 1909 by Robert Appleton Co.. Online Edition Copyright 8 1999 by Kevin Knight, Nihil Obstat, May 1, 1909. Remy Lafort, Censor, Imprimatur. +John M. Farley, Archbishop of New York. Eusebius, The History of the Church from Christ to Constantine, translated by G.A. Williamson (NY: Dorset Press, a division of Marboro Books Corporation, 1965), pp. 346, 355. Ronald Reagan, Feb. 2, 1984, National Prayer Breakfast. David R. Shepherd, ed., Ronald Reagan: In God I Trust (Wheaton, Illinois: Tyndale House Publishers, Inc., 1984), pp. 73-75. The writings of Theodoret, Bishop of Cyrus (393-457 A.D.). Theodoret's Ecclesiastical History covers the period of time up until 429 A.D. (the early fifth century). Theodoret of Cyrus, The Ecclesiastical History Book V, Chapter XXVI: Of Honorius the Emperor and Telemachus the monk. "Honorius, who inherited the empire of Europe, put a stop to the gladiatorial combats which had long been held at Rome. The occasion of his doing so arose from the following circumstance. A certain man of the name of Telemachus had embraced the ascetic life. He had set out from the East and for this reason had repaired to Rome. There, when the abominable spectacle was being exhibited, he went himself into the stadium, and stepping down into the arena, endeavored to stop the men who were wielding their weapons against one another. The spectators of the slaughter were indignant, and inspired by the triad fury of the demon who delights in those bloody deeds, stoned the peacemaker to death. When the admirable emperor was informed of this he numbered Telemachus in the number of victories martyrs, and put an end to that impious spectacle."

MAY 2. Hoover, J. (John) Edgar. Herbert V. Prochnow, 5100 Quotations for Speakers & Writers (Grand Rapids, MI: Baker Book House, 1992), p. 489.

MAY 3. McHenry, James. Bernard Steiner, One Hundred & Ten Years of Bible Society in Maryland (Maryland: Maryland Bible Society, 1921), p. 14. Tim LaHaye, Faith of Our Founding Fathers (Brentwood, TN: Wolgemuth & Hyatt, Publishers, Inc., 1987), pp. 171-172. Peter Marshall & David Manuel, The Glory of America (Bloomington, MN: Garborg's Heart 'N Home, 1991), 8.17.

MAY 4. McGuffey, William. Holmes. William Ellery Channing, "Religion The Only Basis of Society" William Holmes McGuffey, McGuffey's Fifth Eclectic Reader (Cincinnati & New York: Van Antwerp, Bragg & Co., revised edition, 1879), lesson XCIII, pp. 284-286.

MAY 5. Truman, Harry S. Jun. 17, 1952, issued Proclamation 2978, declaring an annual National Day of Prayer, in concurrence with the Congressional Resolution, Public Law 82-324; 66 Stat. 64). Edmund Fuller & David E. Green, God in the White House - The Faiths of American Presidents (NY: Crown Publishers, Inc., 1968), p. 210. Reagan, Ronald Wilson. Feb. 3, 1988, in a Proclamation of a National Day of Prayer. Filed with the Office of the Federal Register, 11:21 a.m., Feb. 4, 1988. Frederick J. Ryan, Jr., ed., Ronald Reagan - The Wisdom and Humor of the Great Communicator (San Francisco: Collins Publishers, A Division of Harper Collins Publishers, 1995), p. 115.

MAY 6. Patroons, Charter Of Freedoms & Exemptions To. Jun. 7, 1629, Article XXVII. E.B. O'Callagnhan, ed., Documents Relative to the Colonial History of the State of New York (Boston: Old South Leaflets, published by the Directors of the Old South Work, Old South meeting House, n.d.), II:553 ff. Henry Steele Commager, ed., Documents of American History, 2 vols. (NY: F.S. Crofts & Co., 1934; Appleton-Century-Crofts, Inc., 1948, 6th edition, 1958; Englewood Cliffs, NJ: Prentice Hall, Inc., 9th edition, 1973), Vol. I, pp. 20, 26-27. The Annals of America 20 vols. (Chicago, IL: Encyclopedia Britannica, 1968), Vol. 1, p. 106.

MAY 7. Eisenhower, Dwight David. May 7th. Eisenhower, Dwight David. Feb. 20, 1955, Remarks recorded & broadcast over radio & television 8:00pm-8:30pm for the "Back to God" Programs of the American Legion. Quoted by President Gerald Rudolph Ford, Thursday, Dec. 5, 1974, in a National Day of Prayer, 1974, Proclamation 4338. Mrs. James Dobson (Shirley), chairman, The National Day of Prayer Information Packet (Colorado Springs, CO: National Day of Prayer Tack Force, May 6, 1993).

MAY 8. Truman, Harry S. Feb. 15, 1950, at 10:05 a.m., in an address given to the Attorney General's Conference on Law Enforcement Problems in the Department of Justice Auditorium, Washington. DC.; organizations present included the Department of Justice, the National Association of Attorneys, the U.S. Conference of Lawyers, & the National Institute of Municipal Law Officers. Public Papers of the Presidents: Harry S. Truman, 1950 - Containing Public Messages, Speeches, & Statements of the President, Jan. 1 to Dec. 31, 1950 (Washington, DC: U.S. Government Printing Office, 1965), Item 37, p. 157. Steve C. Dawson, God's Providence in America's History (Rancho Cordova, CA: Steve Dawson, 1988), p. 13:1. Gary DeMar, America's Christian History: The Untold Story (Atlanta, GA: American Vision Publishers, Inc., 1993), p. 60.

MAY 9. Wilson, Woodrow. May 9, 1914, in a Proclamation of Mother's Day. A Compilation of the Messages & Papers of the Presidents 20 vols. (NY: Bureau of National Literature, Inc., prepared under the direction of the Joint Committee on Printing, of the House & Senate, pursuant to an Act of the 52nd Congress of the United States, 1893, 1923), Vol. XVI, p. 7941.

MAY 10. Allen, Ethan. May 10, 1775, statement made in demanding that Captain de la Place surrender Fort Ticonderoga on Lake Champlain to the Green Mountain Boys of the Continental Army. Ethan Allen, A Narrative of Colonel Ethan Allen's Captivity (Burlington: 1779, 4th ed., 1846). Washington Irving, Life of Washington (1855-1859), Vol. 1, ch. 38. John Bartlett, Bartlett's Familiar Quotations (Boston: Little, Brown & Co., 1855, 1980), p. 385. Charles Fadiman, ed., The American Treasury (NY: Harper & Brothers, Publishers, 1955), p. 371. Henry Steele Commager & Richard B. Morris, eds., The Spirit of 'Seventy-Six (NY: Bobbs-Merrill Co., Inc., 1958; reprinted, NY: Harper & Row, Publishers, 1967), p. 103. Burton Stevenson, The Home Book of Quotations - Classical & Modern (NY: Dodd, Mead & Co., 1967), p. 61. Peter Beilenson, ed., Spirit of '76 (NY: Peter Pauper Press, 1974), p. 35. Boston Globe, Jun. 8, 1975, p. 15. Peter Marshall & David Manuel, The Light & the Glory (Old Tappan, New Jersey: Fleming H. Revell Co., 1977), p. 276. Peter Marshall & David Manuel, The Glory of America (Bloomington, MN: Garborg's Heart'N Home, Inc., 1991), 2.11.

MAY 11. Berlin, Irving. 1938, in the patriotic hymn he composed titled, God Bless America. John Bartlett,

Bartlett's Familiar Quotations (Boston: Little, Brown & Co., 1855, 1980), p. 802. Tim LaHaye, Faith of Our Founding Fathers (Brentwood, TN: Wolgemuth & Hyatt, Inc., 1987), p. 96. (ed. note: The song may actually have been written about 20 years earlier, but Berlin felt it was not the right time for its release. - from Larry King Live, taped 12-27-94).

MAY 12. Howe, Julia Ward. Feb., 1862, The Battle Hymn of the Republic (Massachusetts: The Atlantic Monthly, Feb. 1862), Vol. IX, No. LII, p. 10, Entered according to Act of Congress by Ticknor & Fields, in the Clerk's Office of the District Court of the District of Massachusetts. Mark Galli, Christian History (Carol Stream, IL: Christian History, 1992, Issue 33), Vol. XI, No. 1, p. 19. D.P. Diffine, Ph.D., One Nation Under God - How Close a Separation? (Searcy, AR: Harding University, Belden Center for Private Enterprise Education, 6th edition, 1992), p. 14.

MAY 13. Virginia, Colony of. 1607. Inscription of original 1607 Settler's testimony engraved upon the bronze Robert Hunt Memorial, Jamestown Island, Virginia.

MAY 14. Truman, Harry S. Nov. 29, 1948, in a personal letter to Dr. Chaim Weizmann, President of the State of Israel. Harry S. Truman, Memoirs by Harry S. Truman - Volume Two: Years of Trial & Hope (Garden City, NY: Doubleday & Co., Inc., 1956), pp. 168-169. President Harry S. Truman wrote: "I remember well our conversations about the Negeb, to which you referred in your letter. I agree fully with your estimate of the importance of the area to Israel, and I deplore any attempt to take it away from Israel. I had thought that my position would have been clear to all the world, particularly in the light of the specific wording of the Democratic Party Platform.... I have interpreted my re-election as a mandate from the American people to carry out the Democratic platform - including, of course, the plank on Israel. I intend to do so.... Thank you so much for your warm congratulations and good wishes on my re-election....In closing, I want to tell you how happy and impressed I have been at the remarkable progress made by the new State of Israel." Public Papers of the Presidents, President Lyndon B. Johnson Remarked at the 125th Anniversary Meeting of B'nai B'rith, Sept. 10, 1968: "Our society is illuminated by the spiritual insights of the Hebrew prophets. America and Israel have a common love of human freedom, and they have a common faith in a democratic way of life....That small land in the eastern Mediterranean saw the birth of your faith and your people thousands and thousands of years ago. Down through the centuries, through dispersion and through very grievous trials, your forefathers clung to their Jewish identity and clung to their ties with the land of Israel. As the prophet Isaiah foretold-'And He shall set up an ensign for the nations, and He shall assemble the outcasts of Israel and gather together the dispersed of Judah from all the four corners of the earth.' History knows no more moving example of persistence against the cruelest odds. But conflict has surrounded the modern state of Israel since its very beginning. It is now more than a year that has passed since the 6-day war between Israel and its neighbors-a tragic and an unnecessary war which we tried in every way we could to prevent. That war was the third round of major hostilities in the Middle East since the United Nations established Israel just 21 years ago-the third round-and it just must be the last round."

MAY 15. http://www.af.mil/news/May1995/n19950517_498.html, William J. Perry, Secretary of Defense, SECDEF Armed Forces Day message, May 17, 1995, Air Force News (http://www.af.mil/news/May1995/): "Fifty years ago, in World War II, the United States Armed Forces helped defeat the forces of aggression and oppression on two sides of the globe. For the next 45 years, in the Cold War, we faced down the global Soviet threat. Today, our forces stand guard, at home and abroad, against a range of potential threats to American interests. And on Armed Forces Day, the nation says thank you to our men and women in uniform, their families, and the communities that support them. The dedication, spirit, courage, and patriotism of our forces make them a beacon of freedom in a turbulent world. Around the world, there is a growing sense of peace and cooperation among nations that once struggled against oppression. From Eastern Europe to Southwest Asia to nations in our own hemisphere, this growing sense of peace and cooperation is a testament to the service of American forces. You have helped to share the blessings of liberty we enjoy with more people around the world. Daniel Webster said, "God grants liberty only to those who love it and are always ready to guard and defend it.' America loves liberty. And we are proud of our forces, who are always ready to guard and defend our liberty. We sleep better each night knowing our nation's security is in sure and strong hands." Webster, Daniel. Apr. 6, 1830, in presenting argument on the murder of Captain White. John Bartlett, Bartlett's Familiar Quotations (Boston: Little, Brown and Company, 1855, 1980), p. 451.

MAY 16. Seward, William Henry. 1836, address as Vice-President of the American Bible Society. George E. Baker, Life of William Henry Seward. Stephen Abbott Northrop, D.D., A Cloud of Witnesses (Portland, OR: American Heritage Ministries, 1987; Mantle Ministries, 228 Still Ridge, Bulverde, TX), p. 404. D.P. Diffine, Ph.D., One Nation Under God - How Close a Separation? (Searcy, AR: Harding University, Belden Center for Private Enterprise Education, 6th edition, 1992), p. 11.

MAY 17. Jay, John. Dec. 23, 1776, in an address before the New York Convention. William Jay, Life of John Jay, with Selections from His Correspondence, 2 vols. (NY: Harper, 1833), Vol. I, pp. 55-56. John Eidsmoe, Christianity & The Constitution - The Faith of Our Founding Fathers (Grand Rapids, MI: Baker Book House, 1987), pp. 166-167.

MAY 18. Pope John Paul II. Aug. 12, 1993, in an address at Regis University, Denver, Colorado. John Wheeler, "Pope Defends Unborn Life " (Chesapeake, VA: Christian American, Sept. 1993), p. 10. Pope John Paul II met in Rome with Haggai Institute alumnus Hrayr Jebehjian in Sept. of 2002 and stated: "Whatever differences remain between us, the promotion of the Bible is one point where Christians can work closely together for the glory of God and the good of the human family." The website carried this article in Sept. 2002, a few days before the 9/11 tragedy http://www.haggai-institute.com/News/NewsItem.asp?ItemID=727

MAY 19. Spanish Armada. Carla Rahn Phillips, Ph.D., Professor of History, University of Minnesota, Twin Cities Campus. William D. Phillips, Jr., Ph.D., Professor of History, University of Minnesota, Twin Cities Campus. Carla Rahn Phillips & William D. Phillips, Jr., "Spanish Armada," World Book Online Americas Edition, http://www.aolsvc.worldbook.aol.com/wbol/wbPage/na/ar/co/522940, Oct. 9, 2001. Mark A. Beliles & Stephen K. McDowell, America's Providential History (Providence Foundation, P.O. Box 6759, Charlottesville, Virginia 22906, 1989), pp. 57-58.

MAY 20. Lindbergh, Charles Aug.us. Feb. 1, 1954, in an address at the Institute of Aeronautical Sciences dinner, news summaries. James Beasely Simpson, Best Quotes of '54 '55 '56 (NY: Thomas Y. Crowell Co., 1957), p. 84.

MAY 21. Wilson, Woodrow. May 18, 1918, at the opening of the Second Red Cross Drive in New York City. A Compilation of the Messages & Papers of the Presidents 20 vols. (NY: Bureau of National Literature, Inc., prepared under the direction of the Joint Committee on Printing, of the House & Senate, pursuant to an Act of 52nd Congress of the United States, 1893, 1923), Vol. XVII, pp. 8503-8504.

MAY 22. Williamson, Hugh. Joan R. Gundersen, Ph.D., Professor of History, California State University, San Marcos. Joan R. Gundersen, "Williamson, Hugh," World Book Online Americas Edition, http://www.aolsvc.worldbook.aol.com/wbol/wbPage/na/ar/co/604940, Oct. 9, 2001. John Neal, Trinity College Historical Society Papers, Series 13 (NY: AMS Press, 1915), pp. 62-63. Tim LaHaye, Faith of Our Founding Fathers (Brentwood, TN: Wolgemuth & Hyatt, Publishers, Inc., 1987), p. 182. William J. Federer, American Quotations (St. Louis, MO: www.amerisearch.net, 1-888-USA-WORD, 2001). Report of the committee including Hugh Williamson, Apr. 14, 1785-An Ordinance for ascertaining the mode of disposing of lands in the Western territory. There shall be reserved the Central section of every township for the maintenance of public schools and the Section immediately to the Northward for the support of religion, the profits arising therefrom in both instances to be applied for ever according to the will of the majority of male residents of full age within the same." Journals of the Continental Congress, Vol. 28, pp 291-296.

MAY 23. Carson, Christopher "Kit". Statement made during his last illness. Jessie Benton Fremont, The Will & the Way Stories (Boston: D. Lathrop Co., 1891), pp. 44-48. Thelma S. Guild & Henry L. Carter, Kit Carson - A Pattern for Heros (Lincoln, NE: University of Nebraska Press, 1984), p. 280.

MAY 24. Garrison, William Lloyd. Jan. 1, 1831, The Liberator. Richard D. Heffner, A Documentary History of the United States (NY: New American Library of World Literature, Inc., 1961), pp. 110-111.

MAY 25. Emerson, Ralph Waldo. Charles Wallis, ed., Our American Heritage (NY: Harper & Row, Publishers, Inc., 1970), p. 57.

MAY 26. Wayne, John. Rachel Gallagher, B.A., Author, Games in the Street. Rachel Gallagher, "Wayne, John," World Book Online Americas Edition, http://www.aolsvc.worldbook.aol.com/wbol/wbPage/na/ar/co/595925, Oct. 9, 2001. "Face the Flag," narrated by John Wayne, Copyright 81973, Devere Music Corporation (ASCAP), Batjac Music Co. (ASCAP), Music: Billy Liebert Words: Bill Ezellpeace, http://www.fromtheheartpostcards.com/ICQ/FacetheFlag.html, http://www.dukelestweforget.com/john_wayne_face%20the%20flag.htm

MAY 27. Marshall, Peter. Jul. 3, 1947, in a prayer before the 80th Congress. Catherine Marshall, ed., The Prayers of Peter Marshall (NY: McGraw Hill Book Co., Inc., 1949), p. 186. Robert Flood, The Rebirth of America (The Arthur S. DeMoss Foundation, 1986), back cover.

MAY 28. Webster, Noah. 1832. The History of the United States (New Haven: Durrie & Peck, 1832), p. 309, paragraph 53. Gary DeMar, God & Government, A Biblical & Historical Study (Atlanta, GA: American Vision Press, 1984), p. 4. "Our Christian Heritage," Letter from Plymouth Rock (Marlborough, NH: The Plymouth Rock Foundation), p. 5. Noah Webster, The American Dictionary of the English Language (NY: S. Converse, 1828; reprinted, San Francisco: Foundation for American Christian Education, facsimile edition, 1967), preface, p. 22. Gary DeMar, God & Government - A Biblical & Historical Study (Atlanta: American Vision Press, 1982), p. 4. Robert Flood, The Rebirth of America (The Arthur S. DeMoss Foundation, 1986), p. 33.

MAY 29. Kennedy, John Fitzgerald. Jan. 20, 1961, Inaugural Address. Inaugural Addresses of the Presidents of the

United States - From George Washington 1789 to Richard Milhous Nixon 1969 (Washington, D.C.: U.S. Government Printing Office; 91st Congress, 1st Session, House Document 91-142, 1969), pp. 267-270. Department of State Bulletin (published weekly by the Office of Public Services, Bureau of Public Affairs, Feb. 6, 1961). Davis Newton Lott, The Inaugural Addresses of the American Presidents (NY: Holt, Rinehart & Winston, 1961), p. 269. Charles E. Rice, The Supreme Court & Public Prayer (NY: Fordham University Press, 1964), p. 193. Benjamin Weiss, God in American History: A Documentation of America's Religious Heritage (Grand Rapids, MI: Zondervan, 1966), p. 146. The Annals of America, 20 vols. (Chicago, IL: Encyclopedia Britannica, 1968), Vol. XVIII, pp. 5-7. Lillian W. Kay, ed., The Ground on Which We Stand - Basic Documents of American History (NY: Franklin Watts., Inc, 1969), p. 296. Willard Cantelon, Money Master of the World (Plainfield, NJ: Logos International, 1976), p. 121-122. Bob Arnebeck, "FDR Invoked God Too," Washington Post, Sept. 21, 1986. Vincent J. Wilson, ed., The Book of Great American Documents (Brookfield, MD: American History Research Associates, 1987), p. 84. Halford Ross Ryan, American Rhetoric from Roosevelt to Reagan (Prospect Heights, IL: Waveland Press, 1987), p. 156. Jeffrey K. Hadden & Anson Shupe, Televangelism - Power & Politics on God's Frontier (NY: Henry Holt & Co., 1988), p. 272. Ronald Reid, ed., Three Centuries of American Rhetorical Discourse: An Anthology & a Review (Prospect Heights, Il: Waveland Press, Inc., 1988), p. 711. William Safire, ed., Lend Me Your Ears - Great Speeches in History (NY: W.W. Norton & Co. 1992), p. 812. Peter Marshall & David Manuel, The Glory of America (Bloomington, MN: Garborg's Heart 'N Home, Inc., 1991), 1.20. J. Michael Sharman, J.D., Faith of the Fathers (Culpepper, Virginia: Victory Publishing, 1995), pp. 111-112.

MAY 30. Tomb of the Unknown Soldier. Nov. 11, 1932, inscription on back panel. Thomas Vorwerk, The Unknown Soldier (Springfield, MO: Pentecostal Evangel, Jun. 28, 1992), p. 12. Vice-President Calvin Coolidge, May 31, 1923, Memorial Day Address, "The Destiny of America," The Price of Freedom - Speeches and Addresses (NY: Charles Scribner's Sons, 1924), pp. 331-353.

MAY 31. Coolidge, (John) Calvin. May 31, 1923, Memorial Day, as Vice-President under President Harding, speaking on the motives of the Puritan forefathers in his message titled "The Destiny of America." Calvin Coolidge, The Price of Freedom - Speeches & Addresses (NY: Charles Scribner's Sons, 1924), pp. 331-353. The Annals of America, 20 vols. (Chicago, IL: Encyclopedia Britannica, 1968, 1977), Vol. XIV, pp. 410-414. Peter Marshall & David Manuel, From Sea to Shining Sea (Old Tappan, NJ: Fleming H. Revell Co., 1986) and The Glory of America (Bloomington, MN: Garborg's Heart'N Home, Inc., 1991), 1.5, 5.30. D.P. Diffine, Ph.D., One Nation Under God - How Close a Separation? (Searcy, AR: Harding Univ., Belden Center for Private Enterprise Education, 6th ed., 1992), p. 17.

JUNE 1. Perry, Oliver Hazard. Tucker, Poltroons, pp. 331-332. Peter Marshall & David Manuel, The Glory of America (Bloomington, MN: Garborg's Heart'N Home, Inc., 1991), 9.10.

JUNE 2. Cleveland, Grover. Mar. 4, 1893, Second Inaugural Address. James D. Richardson (U.S. Representative from Tennessee), ed., A Compilation of the Messages & Papers of the Presidents 1789-1897, 10 vols. (Washington, D.C.: U.S. Government Printing Office, published by Authority of Congress, 1897, 1899; Washington, D.C.: Bureau of National Literature & Art, 1789-1902, 11 vols., 1907, 1910), Vol. IX, pp. 389, 393. Inaugural Addresses of the Presidents of the United States - From George Washington 1789 to Richard Milhous Nixon 1969 (Washington, D.C.: U.S. Government Printing Office; 91st Congress, 1st Session, House Document 91-142, 1969), pp. 163-167. Charles E. Rice, The Supreme Court & Public Prayer (NY: Fordham University Press, 1964), p. 187. Benjamin Weiss, God in American History - A Documentation of America's Religious Heritage (Grand Rapids, MI: Zondervan, 1966), p. 109. Willard Cantelon, Money Master of the World (Plainfield, NJ: Logos International, 1976), p. 120. J. Michael Sharman, J.D., Faith of the Fathers (Culpepper, Virginia: Victory Publishing, 1995), p. 77.

JUNE 3. "Staten Island," Microsoft7 Encarta7 Online Encyclopedia 2000, http://encarta.msn.com 8 1997-2000 Microsoft Corporation. All rights reserved. http://odur.let.rug.nl/usanew/E/newnetherlands/nl5.htm, The United States of America & the Netherlands, 6/14 The towns of New Netherland, By George M. Welling: In the early sixties of the seventeenth century, Pieter Plockhoy of Zeeland province, The Netherlands, started the first of the many Utopias which shine in the pages of American history. In 1662 he sailed from Holland with twenty-four families, to establish his colony of 'universal Christian brotherhood,' ... to raise up an universal magistrate in Christendom, that can suffer all sorts of people (of what religion soever they are) in any one country, as God suffers the same in all the countries of the world.' The city of Amsterdam met the expenses of the expedition. The place chosen was on the Delaware River, & the following year forty more immigrants joined those already there. Plockhoy's Utopia was soon to come to a terrible end. It resisted the British troops of Sir Robert Carr which landed in New Netherland in 1664, & was destroyed 'to a very naile.'

JUNE 4. Battle of Midway. Jun. 4-6, 1942. Robert C. Kiste, Ph.D., Director & Professor, University of Hawaii Center for Pacific Islands Studies, "Midway Island," World Book Online Americas Edition, ttp://

www.aolsvc.worldbook.aol.com/wbol/wbPage/na/ar/co/360580, Oct. 20, 2001. James L. Stokesbury, Ph.D., Former Professor of History, Acadia University; author, Navy & Empire & A Short History of Air Power, "World War II," World Book Online Americas Edition, http://www.aolsvc.worldbook.aol.com/wbol/wbPage/na/ar/co/610460, Oct. 20, 2001.

JUNE 5. Ben-Gurion, David. Oct. 5, 1956, comment in an interview with Edward R. Murrow, "Person to Person," CBS-TV. James Beasely Simpson, Best Quotes of '54, '55, '56 (NY: Thomas Y. Crowell Co., 1957), p. 302. Public Papers of the Presidents: Toasts of the President & Prime Minister Eshkol at a Dinner at the LBJ Ranch. Jan. 7, 1968, "Mr. Prime Minister, Mrs. Eshkol: Welcome to our family table. We are honored and happy to have you here in our home. Here, we ask only that you enjoy the warm ties of friendship and partnership that mean so much to each of us, and both our peoples. Our peoples, Mr. Prime Minister, share many qualities of mind and heart. We both rise to challenge. We both admire the courage and the resourcefulness of the citizen-soldier. We each draw strength and purpose for today from our heroes of yesterday. We both know the thrill of bringing life from a hard but a rewarding land. But all Americans-and all Israelis-also know that prosperity is not enough-that none of our restless generation can ever live by bread alone. For we are equally nations in search of a dream. We share a vision and purpose far brighter than our abilities to make deserts bloom. We have been born and raised to seek and find peace. In that common spirit of our hopes, I respect our hope that a just and lasting peace will prevail between Israel and her neighbors. This past year has been a busy one for America's peacemakers-in the Middle East, in Cyprus, in Vietnam. Wherever conscience and faith have carried them, they have found a stubborn truth confirmed. Making peace is punishing work. It demands enormous courage, flexibility, and imagination. It is ill served by hasty slogans or half-solutions. I know you understand this, sir, better than most men. One of your ancestors said it for all men almost 2,000 years ago: 'Other precepts are performed when the occasion arises . . . but for peace it is written, '"pursue it."' That is our intention in the Middle East and throughout our world. To pursue peace. To find peace. To keep peace forever among men. If we are wise, if we are fortunate, if we work together-perhaps our Nation and all nations may know the joys of that promise God once made about the children of Israel: 'I will make a covenant of peace with them . . . it shall be an everlasting covenant.' Let that be our toast to each other-our Governments and our peoples-as this new year begins. Its days are brighter, Mr. Prime Minister, because you lighten them with your presence here and the spirit you will leave behind."

JUNE 6. Eisenhower, Dwight David. Jun. 6, 1944, in his "D-day Orders of the Day." Dwight D. Eisenhower, Crusade in Europe (Garden City, NY: Doubleday & Co., Inc., 1948), back cover.

JUNE 7. Boone, Daniel. Oct. 1816, to Sarah Boone. Rolla P. Andrae, A True, Brief History of Daniel Boone (Defiance, MO: Daniel Boone Home, 1985), p. 59.

JUNE 8. Jackson, Andrew. Jun. 8, 1845. Henry Halley, Halley's Bible Handbook (Grand Rapids, MI: Zondervan, 1927, 1965), p. 18. Alfred Armand Montapert, Distilled Wisdom (Englewood Cliffs, NJ: Prentice Hall, Inc., 1965), p. 36. George Sivan, The Bible & Civilization (NY: Quadrangle/The New York Times Book Co., 1973), p. 178. George Herbert Walker Bush, Feb. 22, 1990, at the request of Congress, Senate Joint Resolution 164, in a Presidential Proclamation declaring 1990 the International Year of Bible Reading. Courtesy of Bruce Barilla, Christian Heritage Week Ministry (P.O. Box 58, Athens, W.V. 24712; 304-384-7707, 304-384-9044 fax). "Our Christian Heritage," Letter from Plymouth Rock (Marlborough, NH: The Plymouth Rock Foundation), p. 5. Gary DeMar, America's Christian History: The Untold Story (Atlanta, GA: American Vision Publishers, Inc., 1993), p. 59. Stephen McDowell & Mark Beliles, "The Providential Perspective" (Charlottesville, VA: The Providence Foundation, P.O. Box 6759, Charlottesville, Va. 22906, Jan.1994), Vol. 9, No. 1, p. 6.

JUNE 9. Kennedy, John Fitzgerald, Apr. 20, 1961, Special Message on Taxation, Apr. 20, 1961. Public Papers of the Presidents-Containing Public Messages, Speeches & Statements of the President, (Wash., DC: U.S. Gov. Printing Office.) Jackson, Andrew. May 27, 1830, Veto Message to Congress. James D. Richardson (U.S. Representative from Tennessee), ed., A Compilation of the Messages & Papers of the Presidents 1789-1897, 10 vols. (Washington, D.C.: U.S. Government Printing Office, published by Authority of Congress, 1897, 1899; Washington, D.C.: Bureau of National Literature & Art, 1789-1902, 11 vols., 1907, 1910), Vol. II, p. 489.

JUNE 10. Bancroft, George. Address titled, "The Progress of Mankind." George Bancroft, Literary & Historical Miscellanies, pp. 502, 504. Stephen Abbot Northrop, D.D., A Cloud of Witnesses (Portland, OR: American Heritage Ministries, 1987; Mantle Ministries, 228 Still Ridge, Bulverde, TX), pp. 24-25.

JUNE 11. Warren, Joseph. Mar. 5, 1772, Principles & Acts of the Revolution in America. Oration Delivered at Boston, on the second anniversary of the Boston Massacre. The Annals of America, 20 vols. (Chicago, IL: Encyclopedia Britannica, 1968), Vol. 2, p. 216. Hezekiah Niles, ed., Principles & Acts of the Revolution in America (Baltimore: William Ogden Niles, 1822; reprinted, NY: S.A. Barnes & Co., Centennial Edition, 1876).

JUNE 12. Bush, George Herbert Walker. Jan. 20, 1989, Inaugural Address. J. Michael Sharman, J.D., Faith of the

Fathers (Culpepper, Virginia: Victory Publishing, 1995), p. 127.

JUNE 13. Washington, George. Jul. 28, 1791, in a letter written from Philadelphia to Marquis de Lafayette. Jared Sparks, ed., The Writings of George Washington 12 vols. (Boston: American Stationer's Co., 1837; NY: F. Andrew's, 1834-1847), Vol. X, p. 179. William J. Johnson, George Washington - The Christian (St. Paul, MN: William J. Johnson, Meriam Park, Feb. 23, 1919; Nashville, TN: Abingdon Press, 1919; reprinted Milford, MI: Mott Media, 1976; reprinted Arlington Heights, IL: Christian Liberty Press, 502 West Euclid Ave., Arlington Heights, IL., 60004, 1992), p. 201. William Barclay Allen, ed., George Washington - A Collection (Indianapolis: Liberty Classics, Liberty Fund, Inc., 7440 N. Shadeland, Indianapolis, IN 46250, 1988; based on materials reproduced from The Writings of George Washington from original manuscript sources, 1745-1799/John Clement Fitzpatrick, editor), pp. 553-555. John Clement Fitzpatrick, ed., The Writings of George Washington, from the Original Manuscript Sources 1749-1799, 39 vols. (Washington, D.C.: U.S. Government Printing Office, 1931-1944).

JUNE 14. Eisenhower, Dwight David. Jun. 14, 1954, on signing the Act of Congress, (bill introduced by Representative Louis Rabout of Michigan - May 6, 1954) which added the phrase "under God" to the Pledge of Allegiance. James Beasley Simpson, Best Quotes of '54, '55, '56 (NY: Thomas Y. Crowell Co., 1957), p. 73. Supreme Court Dismisses Pledge Case on Technicality, Mon. Jun 14, 2004, WASHINGTON (Reuters) - The U.S. Supreme Court dismissed on Monday a constitutional challenge to the words "under God" in the Pledge of Allegiance recited by schoolchildren, without deciding the key church-state issue. The justices ruled that California atheist Michael Newdow lacked the legal right to bring the challenge in the first place. "We conclude that Newdow lacks standing," Justice John Paul Stevens declared in the opinion. The ruling came down on the 50th anniversary of the addition of the words "under God" to the pledge. Congress adopted the Jun. 14, 1954, law in an effort to distinguish America's religious values and heritage from those of communism, which is atheistic. Jun. 14, 2004 A Unanimous Supreme Court Vacates Ninth Circuit Court Of Appeals Decision Striking Down "Under God" In The Pledge Of Allegiance WASHINGTON, D.C. - Today, the United States Supreme Court held, in a unanimous decision, that Michael Newdow, an atheist from California who had challenged the constitutionality of the words "Under God" in the pledge of allegiance, did not have standing to bring his case. The legal effect of the Supreme Court's ruling is to vacate the Ninth Circuit Court of Appeals decision that struck the words "Under God" from the pledge. Liberty Counsel, a nationwide civil liberties legal defense and education organization headquartered in Orlando, Florida, filed an Amicus Brief at the United States Supreme Court in the case. The Supreme Court decision held that Michael Newdow lacked standing to bring his case because he did not have the legal authority to speak on behalf of his daughter. Mr. Newdow is currently involved in a custody battle with his ex-wife. Justices Rehnquist, Thomas and O'Connor issued a concurring opinion agreeing that Mr. Newdow lacked standing, but also arguing that the phrase "Under God" in the pledge is constitutional. The legal effect of the Supreme Court's ruling is to vacate the Ninth Circuit's earlier decision holding the pledge to be unconstitutional. After today's ruling, it is as if Mr. Newdow had never brought his case in the courts. Prior to today's ruling by the Supreme Court, schoolchildren in states covered by the Ninth Circuit (Alaska, Arizona, California, Hawaii, Idaho, Montana, Nevada, Oregon and Washington) were barred from saying the pledge of allegiance with the inclusion of the phrase "Under God." Now, there is no prohibition against saying the entire pledge in those states. Mathew Staver, President and General Counsel of Liberty Counsel, stated, "We are pleased that the effect of the Supreme Court's decision is to uphold the constitutionality of the pledge of allegiance. Schoolchildren in states covered by the Ninth Circuit can now say the entire pledge of allegiance without fear of censorship." Staver continued, "Justices Rehnquist, Thomas and O'Connor are correct that the pledge of allegiance is constitutional. Our history is not complete without God. If "under God" were removed, many history books and founding documents will be in jeopardy, not the least of which is the Declaration of Independence." ### The United States Supreme Court's Opinion will be posted on its web site later today. Read the brief filed by Liberty Counsel before the Supreme Court. Liberty Counsel, headquartered in Orlando, Florida, is a national public interest law firm dedicated to advancing religious freedom, the sanctity of human life and the traditional family. On the campus of Liberty University School of Law in Lynchburg, Virginia, Liberty Counsel's Center for Constitutional Litigation and Policy trains attorneys, law students, policymakers, legislators, clergy and world leaders in constitutional principles and government policies. Mathew D. Staver, Esq., Liberty Counsel, PO Box 540774, Orlando, FL 32854, 800-671-1776

http://www.lc.org/donations.html

JUNE 15. Magna Carta. 1215. Benjamin Hart, Faith & Freedom - The Christian Roots of American Liberty (Dallas, TX: Lewis & Stanley, 1988), p. 17.

JUNE 16. Braun, Wernher Magnus Maximillan von. Statement. Charles E. Jones, The Books You Read (Harrisburg, PA: Executive Books, 1985), p. 120.

JUNE 17. Prescott, William. 1774, in writing to the citizens on the occasion of the British blockade. George Bancroft, History of the United States of America, 6 vols. (Boston: Charles C. Little & James Brown, Third Edition, 1838), Vol. VII, p. 99. Lucille Johnston, Celebrations of a Nation (Arlington, VA: The Year of Thanksgiving Foundation, 1987), p. 76. Peter Marshall & David Manuel, The Glory of America (Bloomington, MN: Garborg's Heart 'N Home, 1991), 7.27.

JUNE 18. Madison, James. Jun. 19, 1812, in a Proclamation of War between Great Britain & the United States. James D. Richardson (U.S. Representative from Tennessee), ed., A Compilation of the Messages & Papers of the Presidents 1789-1897, 10 vols. (Washington, D.C.: U.S. Government Printing Office, published by Authority of Congress, 1897, 1899; Washington, D.C.: Bureau of National Literature & Art, 1789-1902, 11 vols., 1907, 1910), Vol. I, p. 512.

JUNE 19. Fathers Day. Jun. 19, 1910. The first formal "Father's Day" celebrated in Spokane, Washington, by Sonora Louise Smart Dodd. In 1972, President Richard M. Nixon established Father's Day as a permanent national observance of on the third Sunday of Jun.. Sharron G. Uhler, B.Phil., Archivist, Colorado Springs Pioneers Museum; former Curator, Hallmark Historical Collection, "Father's Day," World Book Online Americas Edition, http://www.aolsvc.worldbook.aol.com/wbol/wbPage/na/ar/co/192440, Oct. 20, 2001. http://www.geocities.com/Heartland/2328/father1.htm, http://www.arose4ever.com/roses/fathersday.htm, http://morning-glow.com/holidays/father/father.html

JUNE 20. Maryland, Charter of. Jun. 20, 1632, issued by King Charles I to Cecilius Calvert, Second Lord Baltimore. Ebenezer Hazard, Historical Collection: Consisting of State Papers & other Authentic Documents: Intended as Materials for an History of the United States of America (Philadelphia: T. Dobson, 1792), Vol. I, pp. 327-328. William McDonald, editor, Select Charters & Other Documents (NY: The Macmillan Co., 1899), pp. 53-54. Frances Newton Thorpe, ed., Federal & State Constitutions, Colonial Charters, & Other Organic Laws of the States, Territories, & Colonies now or heretofore forming the United States, 7 vols. (Washington: Government Printing Office, 1905; 1909; St. Clair Shores, MI: Scholarly Press, 1968), Vol. III, pp. 1677 ff. Henry Steele Commager, ed., Documents of American History, 2 vols. (NY: F.S. Crofts & Co., 1934; Appleton-Century-Crofts, Inc., 1948, 6th ed, 1958; Englewood Cliffs, NJ: Prentice Hall, Inc., 9th edition, 1973), Vol. I, p. 21. William McDonald, ed., Documentary Source Book of American History, 1606-1889 (NY: Macmillan Co., 1909), p. 32. Charles E. Rice, The Supreme Court & Public Prayer (NY: Fordham University Press, 1964), pp. 160-161. Richard L. Perry, ed., Sources of Our Liberties: Documentary Origins of Individual Liberties in the United States Constitution & Bill of Rights (Chicago: American Bar Foundation, 1978; NY: 1952), p. 105. Pat Robertson, America's Dates With Destiny (Nashville, TN: Thomas Nelson Publishers, 1986), pp. 31-32.

JUNE 21. Franklin, Benjamin. Jun. 28, 1787. James Madison, Notes of Debates in the Federal Convention of 1787 (NY: W.W. Morton & Co., Original 1787 reprinted 1987), Vol. I, p. 504, 451-21. James Madison, Notes of Debates in the Federal Convention of 1787 (Athens, Ohio: Ohio University Press, 1966, 1985), pp. 209-10. Henry D. Gilpin, editor, The Papers of James Madison (Washington: Langtree & O' Sullivan, 1840), Vol. II, p. 985. George Bancroft, Bancroft's History of the Constitution of the United States vols. I-X (Boston: Charles C. Little & James Brown, 1838), Vol. II. Albert Henry Smyth, ed., The Writings of Benjamin Franklin (NY: The Macmillan Co., 1905-7), Vol. IX, pp. 600-601. Gaillard Hunt & James B. Scott, ed., The Debates in the Federal Convention of 1787 Which Framed the Constitution of the United States of America, reported by James Madison (NY: Oxford University Press, 1920), pp. 181-182. Andrew M. Allison, W. Cleon Skousen, & M. Richard Maxfield, The Real Benjamin Franklin (Salt Lake City, Utah: The Freeman Institute, 1982, pp. 258-259. John Eidsmoe, Christianity & the Constitution - The Faith of Our Founding Fathers (Grand Rapids, MI: Baker Book House, A Mott Media Book, 1987, 6th printing 1993), pp. 12-13, 208. Tim LaHaye, Faith of Our Founding Fathers (Brentwood, TN: Wolgemuth & Hyatt, Publishers, Inc., 1987), pp. 122-124. Stephen Abbott Northrop, D.D., A Cloud of Witnesses (Portland, OR: American Heritage Ministries, 1987; Mantle Ministries, 228 Still Ridge, Bulverde, TX), p. 159-160. D.P. Diffine, Ph.D., One Nation Under God - How Close a Separation? (Searcy, AR: Harding University, Belden Center for Private Enterprise Education, 6th edition, 1992), p. 8. Stephen McDowell & Mark Beliles, "The Providential Perspective" (Charlottesville, VA: The Providence Foundation, P.O. Box 6759, Charlottesville, Va. 22906, Jan. 1994), Vol. 9, No. 1, pp. 5-6.

JUNE 22. Nixon, Richard Milhous. Jan. 20, 1969, Inaugural Address. Department of State Bulletin, Feb. 10, 1969. Inaugural Addresses of the Presidents - From George Washington 1789 to Richard Milhous Nixon 1969 (Washington, D.C.: U.S. Government Printing Office, 91st Congress, 1st Session, House Document 91-142, 1969), pp. 275-279. The Annals of America, 20 vols. (Chicago, IL: Encyclopedia Britannica, 1968, 1977), Vol. 19, pp. 8-12. Benjamin Weiss, God in American History: A Documentation of America's Religious Heritage (Grand Rapids, MI: Zondervan,

1966), p. 154. Willard Cantelon, Money Master of the World (Plainfield, NJ: Logos International, 1976), p. 122. J. Michael Sharman, J.D., Faith of the Fathers (Culpepper, Virginia: Victory Publishing, 1995), pp. 116-117.

JUNE 23. Penn, William. Aug. 18, 1681, Letter to the Indians before his arrival. Pennsylvania Historical Society Collection, Philadelphia.

JUNE 24. Smith, Jedediah Strong. Dec. 24, 1829, in writing to his brother, Ralph Smith in Richland County. Dale L. Morgan, Jedediah Smith - & the Opening of the West (Lincoln, Nebraska: University of Nebraska Press, Bobbs - Merrill Co., 1953; Bison Books, 1964), pp. 352-353.

JUNE 25. MacArthur, Douglas. John Stormer, The Death of a Nation (Florissant, MO: Liberty Bell Press, 1968), p. 128. John Eidsmoe, God & Caesar-Christian Faith & Political Action (Westchester, IL: Crossway Books, a Division of Good News Publishers, 1984), p. 68. George Otis, The Solution to the Crisis in America, Revised & Enlarged Edition (Van Nuys, CA.: Fleming H. Revell Co.; Bible Voice, Inc., 1970, 1972, foreword by Pat Boone), pp. 41-42.

JUNE 26. Harry S Truman, Address to the United Nations Conference in San Francisco, Apr. 25, 1945, 7:35 p.m., Delivered from the White House by direct wire and broadcast over the major networks. Dwight Eisenhower's Dwight Eisenhower's "Atoms for Peace" Address to the UN General Assembly Dec. 8 1953, Congressional Record, vol. 100, Jan. 7, 1954, pp. 61-63. Hoover, Herbert Clark. Apr. 27, 1950, speech to American Newspaper Publishers Association. Charles Hurd, ed., A Treasury of Great American Speeches (NY: Hawthorne Books, 1959), pp. 289-291.

JUNE 27. Keller, Helen Adams. Bless Your Heart (series II) (Eden Prairie, MN: Heartland Samplers, Inc., 1990), 3.2.

JUNE 28. Franklin, Benjamin. Jun. 28, 1787. James Madison, Notes of Debates in the Federal Convention of 1787 (NY: W.W. Morton & Co., Original 1787 reprinted 1987), Vol. I, p. 504, 451-21. James Madison, Notes of Debates in the Federal Convention of 1787 (Athens, Ohio: Ohio University Press, 1966, 1985), pp. 209-10. Henry D. Gilpin, editor, The Papers of James Madison (Washington: Langtree & O' Sullivan, 1840), Vol. II, p. 985. George Bancroft, Bancroft's History of the Constitution of the United States vols. I-X (Boston: Charles C. Little & James Brown, 1838), Vol. II. Albert Henry Smyth, ed., The Writings of Benjamin Franklin (NY: The Macmillan Co., 1905-7), Vol. IX, pp. 600-601. Gaillard Hunt & James B. Scott, ed., The Debates in the Federal Convention of 1787 Which Framed the Constitution of the United States of America, reported by James Madison (NY: Oxford University Press, 1920), pp. 181-182. Andrew M. Allison, W. Cleon Skousen, & M. Richard Maxfield, The Real Benjamin Franklin (Salt Lake City, Utah: The Freeman Institute, 1982, pp. 258-259. John Eidsmoe, Christianity & the Constitution - The Faith of Our Founding Fathers (Grand Rapids, MI: Baker Book House, A Mott Media Book, 1987, 6th printing 1993), pp. 12-13, 208. Tim LaHaye, Faith of Our Founding Fathers (Brentwood, TN: Wolgemuth & Hyatt, Publishers, Inc., 1987), pp. 122-124. Stephen Abbott Northrop, D.D., A Cloud of Witnesses (Portland, OR: American Heritage Ministries, 1987; Mantle Ministries, 228 Still Ridge, Bulverde, TX), p. 159-160. D.P. Diffine, Ph.D., One Nation Under God - How Close a Separation? (Searcy, AR: Harding University, Belden Center for Private Enterprise Education, 6th edition, 1992), p. 8. Stephen McDowell & Mark Beliles, "The Providential Perspective" (Charlottesville, VA: The Providence Foundation, P.O. Box 6759, Charlottesville, Va. 22906, Jan. 1994), Vol. 9, No. 1, pp. 5-6.

JUNE 29. Clay, Henry. The World Book Encyclopedia, 18 vols. (Chicago, IL: Field Enterprises, Inc., 1957; W.F. Quarrie & Co., 8 vols., 1917; World Book, Inc., 22 vols., 1989), Vol. 3, p. 1472. Clay, Henry. 1829, in a speech at Frankfort to the Kentucky Colonization Society. Stephen Abbott Northrop, D.D., A Cloud of Witnesses (Portland, OR: American Heritage Ministries, 1987; Mantle Ministries, 228 Still Ridge, Bulverde, TX), p. 87.

JUNE 30. Florida, St. Johns River Settlement. Jun. 30, 1564, as recorded by French Huguenot leader, Rene de Laudonniere. Diana Karter Appelbaum, Thanksgiving: An American Holiday, An American History (NY: Facts on File Publications, 1984), pp. 14-15. Gary DeMar, America's Christian History: The Untold Story (Atlanta, GA: American Vision Publishers, Inc., 1993), p. 22.

JULY 1. McKinley, William. Jul. 6, 1898, in a Proclamation of a National Day of Thanksgiving. James D. Richardson (U.S. Representative from Tennessee), ed., A Compilation of the Messages & Papers of the Presidents 1789-1897, 10 vols. (Washington, D.C.: U.S. Government Printing Office, published by Authority of Congress, 1897, 1899; Washington, D.C.: Bureau of National Literature & Art, 1789-1902, 11 vols., 1907, 1910), Vol. X, pp. 213-214. A Compilation of the Messages & Papers of the Presidents 20 vols. (NY: Bureau of National Literature, Inc., prepared under the direction of the Joint Committee on Printing, of the House & Senate, pursuant to an Act of the 52nd Congress of the United States, 1893, 1923), Vol. XIII, pp. 6573-6574.

JULY 2. Garfield, James Abram. 1876, in a speech commemorating the centennial of the Declaration of Independence. "A Century of Congress," by James A. Garfield, published in Atlantic, Jul. 1877. John M. Taylor, Garfield of Ohio - The Available Man (NY: W.W. Norton & Co., Inc.), p. 180.

JULY 3. Lincoln, Abraham. 1863, in conversation with a General who was wounded at the Battle of Gettysburg, Jul. 1-3, 1863, relating the panic in Washington, D.C., as General Robert E. Lee was leading his army of 76,000 men into Pennsylvania. Thomas Fleming, Lincoln's Journey in Faith" (Carmel, NY: Guideposts, Feb. 1994), p. 36.

JULY 4. Adams, Samuel. 1776, statement made while the Declaration of Independence was being signed. Charles E. Kistler, This Nation Under God (Boston: Richard G. Badger, The Gorham Press, 1924), p. 71. Peter Marshall & David Manuel, The Light & the Glory (NJ: Fleming H. Revell Co., 1977), p. 309. "Our Christian Heritage," Letter from Plymouth Rock (Marlborough, NH: The Plymouth Rock Foundation), p. 8. D.P. Diffine, Ph.D., One Nation Under God - How Close a Separation? (Searcy, AR: Harding University, Belden Center for Private Enterprise Education, 6th edition, 1992), p. 6.

JULY 5. Adams, John Quincy. Jul. 11, 1826, in an Executive Order. James D. Richardson (U.S. Representative from Tennessee), ed., A Compilation of the Messages & Papers of the Presidents 1789-1897, 10 vols. (Washington, D.C.: U.S. Government Printing Office, published by Authority of Congress, 1897, 1899; Washington, D.C.: Bureau of National Literature & Art, 1789-1902, 11 vols., 1907, 1910), Vol. II, pp. 347-348.

JULY 6. Republican Party. Jul. 6, 1854, first state convention, Jackson, Michigan. First local meeting in Ripon, Wisconsin, Feb. 28, 1854; first national convention in Philadelphia, Jun. 1856. World Book Encyclopedia 18 volumes (Chicago: Field Enterprises, Inc., 1957) Vol. 14, pp. 6882-6883.

JULY 7. Ka'ahumanu, Queen Regent-Prime Minister of Hawaii. The State Motto of Hawaii, first uttered by Queen Ke'opuolani, wife of King Kamehameha II, as she was baptized into the Christian faith before her death in 1825, & reiterated by King Kamehameha III at Kawaiaha'o Church for the return of his kingdom in 1843. The State of Hawaii, Dec. 30, 1993, issued an Executive Proclamation declaring Feb. 12 - 22, 1994, as "Christian Heritage Week," signed by Governor John Waihee, in the Capitol City of Honolulu. Courtesy of Bruce Barilla, Christian Heritage Week Ministry (P.O. Box 58, Athens, W.V. 24712; 304-384-7707, 304-384-9044 fax).

JULY 8. Liberty Bell. Committee on the Restoration of Independence Hall, Mayor's Office. Report. Philadelphia, Jun. 12, 1873. Library of Congress Rare Book Collection, Washington, D.C., pp. 2-3. Liberty Bell. "Our Christian Heritage," Letter from Plymouth Rock (Marlborough, NH: The Plymouth Rock Foundation), p. 2. D.P. Diffine, Ph.D., One Nation Under God - How Close a Separation? (Searcy, AR: Harding University, Belden Center for Private Enterprise Education, 6th edition, 1992), p. 5.

JULY 9. Taylor, Zachary. Jul. 4, 1849, at a Sabbath-school celebration in the city of Washington. Benjamin Franklin Morris, The Christian Life & Character of the Civil Institutions of the United States (Philadelphia: George W. Childs, 1864), p. 608.

JULY 10. Fillmore, Millard. Jul. 10, 1850, in an address to Congress after assuming the Presidency the day after President Zachary Taylor died. James D. Richardson (U.S. Representative from Tennessee), ed., A Compilation of the Messages & Papers of the Presidents 1789-1897, 10 vols. (Washington, D.C.: U.S. Government Printing Office, published by Authority of Congress, 1897, 1899; Washington, D.C.: Bureau of National Literature & Art, 1789-1902, 11 vols., 1907, 1910), Vol. 5, p. 64.

JULY 11. Hamilton, Alexander. Apr. 16-21, 1802, writing to James Bayard. Claude G. Bowers, Jefferson & Hamilton: The Struggle for Democracy in America (Boston: Houghton Mifflin Co., 1925, 1937), p. 40. Broadus Mitchell, Alexander Hamilton: The National Adventure 1788-1804 (NY: MacMillan, 1962), pp. 513-514. Allan M. Hamilton, The Intimate Life of Alexander Hamilton (Philadelphia: Richard West, 1979), p. 335. Morton J. Frisch, ed., Selected Writings & Speeches of Alexander Hamilton, (Washington, D.C.: American Enterprise Institute for Public Policy Research, 1985), p. 511, Apr. 16-21, 1802. Henry Cabot Lodge, American Statesmen Series. Stephen Abbott Northrop, D.D., A Cloud of Witnesses (Portland, OR: American Heritage Ministries, 1987; Mantle Ministries, 228 Still Ridge, Bulverde, TX), p. 208. Tim LaHaye, Faith of Our Founding Fathers (Brentwood, TN: Wolgemuth & Hyatt, Publishers, Inc., 1987), p. 140. John Eidsmoe, Christianity & the Constitution - The Faith of Our Founding Fathers (Grand Rapids, MI: Baker Book House, Mott Media Book, 1987; 6th printing, 1993), p. 146.

JULY 12. Carver, George Washington. 1921, in an address before the Senate Ways & Means Committee.. Charles E. Jones, The Books You Read (Harrisburg, PA: Executive Books, 1985), p. 132.

JULY 13. Washington, George. Jul. 13, 1798, from Mount Vernon, in a letter to President John Adams, accepting the commission of Commander in Chief of the Armies of the United States. James D. Richardson (U.S. Representative from Tennessee), ed., A Compilation of the Messages & Papers of the Presidents 1789-1897, 10 vols. (Washington, D.C.: U.S. Government Printing Office, published by Authority of Congress, 1897, 1899; Washington, D.C.: Bureau of National Literature & Art, 1789-1902, 11 vols., 1907, 1910), Vol. I, pp. 267-268. Eulogies & Orations on the Life & Death of General George Washington (1800), p. 258. William J. Johnson, George Washington - The Christian (St. Paul, MN: William J. Johnson, Merriam Park, Feb. 23, 1919; Nashville, TN: Abingdon Press, 1919; reprinted Milford, MI: Mott Media, 1976; reprinted Arlington Heights, IL: Christian Liberty Press, 502 West Euclid

Ave., Arlington Heights, IL., 60004, 1992), p. 226.

JULY 14. Ford, Gerald Rudolph. Aug. 9, 1974, after swearing in as the 38th President of the United States, in an address to Chief Justice Warren E. Burger, members of Congress & the citizens of America. Weekly Compilation of Presidential Documents, Aug. 12, 1974. The Annals of America, 20 vols. (Chicago, IL: Encyclopedia Britannica, 1968, 1977), Vol. 20, pp. 30-32. Benjamin Weiss, God in American History: A Documentation of America's Religious Heritage (Grand Rapids, MI: Zondervan, 1966), p. 158. Willard Cantelon, Money Master of the World (Plainfield, NJ: Logos International, 1976), p. 122.

JULY 15. Aitken, Robert. Jan. 21, 1781, statement presented in Congress. Memorial of Robert Aitken to Congress (Washington, D.C.: National Archives, Jan. 21, 1781). "Our Christian Heritage," Letter from Plymouth Rock (Marlborough, NH: The Plymouth Rock Foundation), p. 4. Robert Flood, The Rebirth of America (Philadelphia: Arthur S. DeMoss Foundation, 1986), p. 39. Aitken, Robert. Sept. 10, 1782, the Continental Congress granted approval to print an edition of the Bible. Bible for the Revolution (NY: Arno Press, 1782, reprinted 1968), cover page. Journals of Continental Congress 1774-1789 (Washington, D.C.: Government Printing Office, 1905), Vol. XXIII, 1782, p. 574. Robert Flood, The Rebirth of America (Philadelphia: Arthur S. DeMoss Foundation, 1986), p. 39. "Our Christian Heritage," Letter from Plymouth Rock (Marlborough, NH: The Plymouth Rock Foundation), p. 4.

JULY 16. Nixon, Richard Milhous. Jan. 20, 1969, Inaugural Address. Department of State Bulletin, Feb. 10, 1969. Inaugural Addresses of the Presidents - From George Washington 1789 to Richard Milhous Nixon 1969 (Washington, D.C.: U.S. Government Printing Office, 91st Congress, 1st Session, House Document 91-142, 1969), pp. 275-279. The Annals of America, 20 vols. (Chicago, IL: Encyclopedia Britannica, 1968, 1977), Vol. 19, pp. 8-12. Benjamin Weiss, God in American History: A Documentation of America's Religious Heritage (Grand Rapids, MI: Zondervan, 1966), p. 154. Willard Cantelon, Money Master of the World (Plainfield, NJ: Logos International, 1976), p. 122. J. Michael Sharman, J.D., Faith of the Fathers (Culpepper, Virginia: Victory Publishing, 1995), pp. 116-117.

JULY 17. de Las Casas, Bartolome'. 1550-1563, in the prologue of his book, Historia de las Indias, translated by Rachel Phillips. John Bartlett, Bartlett's Familiar Quotations (Boston: Little, Brown & Co., 1855, 1980), p. 154.

JULY 18. Washington, George. Jul. 18, 1755. George Washington, in a letter to his brother. Jared Sparks, ed., The Writings of George Washington 12 vols. (Boston: American Stationer's Co., 1837, NY: F. Andrew's, 1834-1847), Vol. II, p. 89. Joseph Banvard, Tragic Scenes in the History of Maryland & the Old French War (Boston: Gould & Lincoln, 1856), p. 153. George Washington, Programs & Papers (Washington: U.S. George Washington Bicentennial Commission, 1932), p. 33. William J. Johnson, George Washington - The Christian (St. Paul, MN: William J. Johnson, Merriam Park, Feb. 23, 1919; Nashville, TN: Abingdon Press, 1919; reprinted Milford, MI: Mott Media, 1976; reprinted Arlington Heights, IL: Christian Liberty Press, 502 West Euclid Ave., Arlington Heights, IL., 60004, 1992), p. 40. John F. Schroeder, ed., Maxims of Washington (Mt. Vernon: Mt. Vernon Ladies' Association, 1942), p. 275. Tim LaHaye, Faith of Our Founding Fathers (Brentwood, TN: Wolgemuth & Hyatt, Publishers, Inc., 1987), pp. 102-104.

JULY 19. Churchill, Winston, British Prime Minister, Jul. 19, 1941, in a speech before the House of Commons launching his campaign against Hitler on this day, Jul. 19, 1941.

JULY 20. Armstrong, Neil Alden. Sept. 16, 1969, in an address before a joint session of Congress. Congressional Record, 91st Congress, 1st Session, Sept. 16, 1969. The Annals of America, 20 vols. (Chicago, IL: Encyclopedia Britannica, 1968, 1977), Vol. 19, p. 46.

JULY 21. Bryan, Williams Jennings. William Jennings Bryan, "The Prince of Peace." Charles Fadiman, ed., The American Treasury (NY: Harper & Brothers, Publishers, 1955), p. 124.

JULY 22. Sandburg, Carl. Carroll E. Simcox, comp., 4400 Quotations for Christian Communicators (Grand Rapids, MI: Baker Book House, 1991), p. 23. Sandburg, Carl, quoted by President Ronald Reagan, Jan. 25, 1985, State of the Union Address. David R. Shepherd, ed., Ronald Reagan: In God I Trust (Wheaton, IL: Tyndale House Publishers, Inc., 1984), pp. 72, 137.

JULY 23. Sherman, Roger. M.E. Bradford, A Worthy Company - Brief Lives of the Framers of the United States Constitution (Marlborough, NH: Plymouth Rock Foundation, 1982), p. 25.

JULY 24. Johnson, Andrew. Sept. 7, 1867; May 29, 1865, in Proclamations of Amnesty & Pardon to the participants of the Confederate insurrection; also Dec. 8, 1863, Mar. 26, 1864 in Proclamations of Amnesty & Pardon issued by President Abraham Lincoln. James D. Richardson (U.S. Representative from Tennessee), ed., A Compilation of the Messages & Papers of the Presidents 1789-1897, 10 vols. (Washington, D.C.: U.S. Government Printing Office, published by Authority of Congress, 1897, 1899; Washington, D.C.: Bureau of National Literature & Art, 1789-1902, 11 vols., 1907, 1910), Vol. VI, pp. 213-215, 310-311, 548-549. Charles W. Eliot, LL.D., ed., American

Historical Documents 1000-1904 (NY: P.F. Collier & Son Co., The Harvard Classics, 1910), Vol. 43, p. 443.
JULY 25. Grant, Ulysses Simpson. Jun. 6, 1876, in a letter from Washington during his term as President, to the Editor of the Sunday School Times in Philadelphia. Stephen Abbott Northrop, D.D., A Cloud of Witnesses (Portland, OR: American Heritage Ministries, 1987; Mantle Ministries, 228 Still Ridge, Bulverde, TX), p. 195. Peter Marshall & David Manuel, The Glory of America (Bloomington, MN: Garborg's Heart 'N Home, Inc., 1991), 4.27. Tryon Edwards, D.D., The New Dictionary of Thoughts - A Cyclopedia of Quotations (Garden City, NY: Hanover House, 1852; revised & enlarged by C.H. Catrevas, Ralph Emerson Browns & Jonathan Edwards descendent, along with Tryon, of Jonathan Edwards (1703-1758), president of Princeton, 1891; The Standard Book Co., 1955, 1963), p. 48. Henry Halley, Halley's Bible Handbook (Grand Rapids, MI: Zondervan, 1927, 1965), p. 18. W. David Stedman & LaVaughn G. Lewis, Our Ageless Constitution (Asheboro, NC: W. Stedman Associates, 1987), p. 162. Gary DeMar, America's Christian History: The Untold Story (Atlanta, GA: American Vision Publishers, Inc., 1993), pp. 59-60. Edmund Fuller & David E. Green, God in the White House - The Faiths of American Presidents (NY: Crown Publishers, Inc., 1968), p. 130. D.P. Diffine, Ph.D., One Nation Under God - How Close a Separation? (Searcy, AR: Harding University, Belden Center for Private Enterprise Education, 6th edition, 1992), p. 16.
JULY 26. Franklin, Benjamin. May 1757, in Poor Richard's Almanac. Carroll E. Simcox, comp., 4400 Quotations for Christian Communicators (Grand Rapids, MI: Baker Book House, 1991), p. 297. John Bartlett, Bartlett's Familiar Quotations (Boston: Little, Brown & Co., 1855, 1980), p. 347.
JULY 27. Eisenhower, Dwight David. Mrs. Mamie Geneva Doud Eisenhower, in a conversation at the Doud home, 750 La Fayette St., Denver, Colorado. Jessie Clayton Adams, More Than Money (San Antonio, TX: The Naylor Co., 1953), p. 9. Courtesy of the personal library Michael Gross.
JULY 28. Bach, Johann Sebastian. Statement regarding music. G. Schirmer Music Publishing Catalogue. Footnote: U.S. Supreme Court. 1948, Justice Frankfurter, McCollum v. Board of Education of School District Number 71, 333 U.S. 203, 236 (1948). Elizabeth Ridenour, Public Schools - Bible Curriculum (Greensboro, N.C.: National Council On Bible Curriculum, 1996), p. 13, 14-15, 28, 42. Robert K. Skolrood, The National Legal Foundation, letter to National Council on the Bible Curriculum in Public Schools, Sept. 13, 1994, p. 2.
JULY 29. Tocqueville, Alexis de. 1835, 1840. Alexis de Tocqueville, The Republic of the United States & Its Political Institutions, Reviewed & Examined, Henry Reeves, translator (Garden City, NY: A.S. Barnes & Co., 1851), Vol. I, p. 331-332. Alexis de Tocqueville, Democracy in America, 2 vols. (NY: Alfred A. Knopf, 1945), Vol. I, p. 303. Alexis de Tocqueville, Democracy in America (NY: Vintage Books, 1945), Vol. I, pp. 314-315. Gary DeMar, "The Christian America Debate " (Atlanta, GA: The Biblical Worldview, An American Vision Publication - American Vision, Inc., Feb. 1993), Vol. 9, No. 2, p. 14. Tim LaHaye, Faith of Our Founding Fathers (Brentwood, TN: Wolgemuth & Hyatt, Pub., Inc., 1987), p. 97.
JULY 30. Penn, William. World Book Encyclopedia, 18 vols. (Chicago, IL: Field Enterprises, Inc., 1957; W.F. Quarrie & Co., 8 vols., 1917; World Book, Inc., 22 vols., 1989), Vol. 13, pp. 6181-6183, 6192-6195.
JULY 31. Christopher Columbus. Jul. 31, 1498, on his third voyage, naming the Island of Trinidad off the coast of Venezuela. World Book Encyclopedia - 18 Volumes (Chicago: Field Enterprises, Inc., 1957), Vol. 16, p. 8170, Vol. 3, pp. 1615-1616.
AUGUST 1. Melville, Herman. 1851. Herman Melville, Moby Dick, p. XXVI. Charles Fadiman, ed., The American Treasury (NY: Harper & Brothers, Publishers, 1955).
AUGUST 2. Kennedy, John Fitzgerald. Jan. 20, 1961, Inaugural Address. Inaugural Addresses of the Presidents of the United States - From George Washington 1789 to Richard Milhous Nixon 1969 (Washington, D.C.: U.S. Government Printing Office; 91st Congress, 1st Session, House Document 91-142, 1969), pp. 267-270. Department of State Bulletin (published weekly by the Office of Public Services, Bureau of Public Affairs, Feb. 6, 1961). Davis Newton Lott, The Inaugural Addresses of the American Presidents (NY: Holt, Rinehart & Winston, 1961), p. 269. Charles E. Rice, The Supreme Court & Public Prayer (NY: Fordham University Press, 1964), p. 193. Benjamin Weiss, God in American History: A Documentation of America's Religious Heritage (Grand Rapids, MI: Zondervan, 1966), p. 146. The Annals of America, 20 vols. (Chicago, IL: Encyclopedia Britannica, 1968), Vol. XVIII, pp. 5-7. Lillian W. Kay, ed., The Ground on Which We Stand - Basic Documents of American History (NY: Franklin Watts., Inc, 1969), p. 296. Willard Cantelon, Money Master of the World (Plainfield, NJ: Logos International, 1976), p. 121-122. Bob Arnebeck, "FDR Invoked God Too," Washington Post, Sept. 21, 1986. Vincent J. Wilson, ed., The Book of Great American Documents (Brookfield, MD: American History Research Associates, 1987), p. 84. Halford Ross Ryan, American Rhetoric from Roosevelt to Reagan (Prospect Heights, IL: Waveland Press, 1987), p. 156. Jeffrey K. Hadden & Anson Shupe, Televangelism - Power & Politics on God's Frontier (NY: Henry Holt and Co.,

1988), p. 272. Ronald Reid, ed., Three Centuries of American Rhetorical Discourse: An Anthology & a Review (Prospect Heights, Il: Waveland Press, Inc., 1988), p. 711. William Safire, ed., Lend Me Your Ears - Great Speeches in History (NY: W.W. Norton & Co., 1992), p. 812.

AUGUST 3. Columbus, Christopher. 1492, in the opening of the journal of his first voyage. Samuel Eliot Morison, Journals & Other Documents on the Life & Voyage of Christopher Columbus (NY: Heritage Press, 1963), pp. 47-48. John Eidsmoe, Columbus & Cortez, Conquerors for Christ (Green Forest, AR: New Leaf Press, 1992), p. 84.

AUGUST 4. The original words & music were written by Captain Francis S. Van Boskerck, USCG in 1927. The first line of each chorus was changed in 1969. www.uscg.mil/sounds/sempara.html. Semper Paratus (Always Ready) Words & Music by Captain Francis Saltus Van Boskerck, USCG Words & Music Copyright by Sam Fox Publishing Co, Inc. Current Version. Verse. Reagan, Ronald Wilson. May 18, 1988, at the U.S. Coast Guard Academy Commencement Ceremony, New London, Connecticut. Frederick J. Ryan, Jr., ed., Ronald Reagan - The Wisdom & Humor of the Great Communicator (San Francisco: Collins Publishers, A Division of Harper Collins Publishers, 1995), p. 43.

AUGUST 5. Eliot, John. 1659 John Eliot, The Christian Commonwealth: or, The Civil Policy of the Rising Kingdom of Jesus Christ, 1659. John Eliot, Massachusetts Historical Collections, 3rd ser,. Vol. 9, pp. 133-134, 163. Benjamin Fletcher Wright, Jr., American Interpretations of Natural Law (NY: Russell & Russell, 1962), pp. 19-21. John Eidsmoe, Christianity & the Constitution - The Faith of Our Founding Fathers (Grand Rapids, MI: Baker Book House, A Mott Media Book, 1987; 6th printing, 1993), pp. 33-34. Gary DeMar, America's Christian History: The Untold Story (Atlanta, GA: American Vision Publishers, Inc., 1993), pp. 125-126.

AUGUST 6. Tennyson, Alfred, Lord. 1864, in Enoch Arden, line 222. John Bartlett, Bartlett's Familiar Quotations (Boston: Little, Brown & Co., 1855, 1980), p. 535.

AUGUST 7. McGready, James. Jun. 1800, as accounted by Rev. Moses Hodge. "The Return of the Spirit" (Carol Stream, IL: Christian History), Vol. VIII, No. 3, Issue 23, p. 25-26.

AUGUST 8. Nixon, Richard Milhous. Aug. 8, 1974, Thursday, in a private farewell to the members of his Cabinet, members of the White House Staff & friends. Weekly Compilation of Presidential Documents, Aug. 12, 1974. The Annals of America, 20 vols. (Chicago, IL: Encyclopedia Britannica, 1968, 1977), Vol. 20, pp. 25-27.

AUGUST 9. Judson, Adoniram. Heros of Faith-Adoniram Judson (Oak Brook, IL: Institute of Basic Life Principles, 1990), pp. 1-14.

AUGUST 10. Hoover, Herbert Clark. Oct. 18, 1931, in an address beginning a nation-wide drive to aid the private relief agencies during the Great Depression. Herbert Hoover, The Memoirs of Herbert Hoover - The Great Depression 1929-1941 (NY: The MacMillan Co., 1952), p. 151. "My own suggestion is that Iraq might be financed to complete this great land development on the consideration that it be made the scene of resettlement of the Arabs from Palestine. This would clear Palestine completely for Jewish immigration and colonization." Herbert Hoover, New York World-Telegram, Nov. 19, 1945. Solomon Goldman, president of the Zionist Organization of America, wrote to David Ben-Gurion on Apr. 6, 1939, quoting a letter from President Roosevelt to Justice Louis Brandeis: "He wrote about the transfer of several hundred thousand Arabs from Palestine to Iraq. In order to finance this transfer, he suggested the establishment of a fund of three hundred million dollars. He thought that it was possible to collect one hundred million from the Jews, the British Government would loan one hundred and the American Government would loan a third of the required sum." Henry Morgenthau, Roosevelt's Secretary of the Treasury, wrote in his diary in 1942 of a conversation with FDR in which the president said: "I actually would put a barbed wire around Palestine, and I would begin to move the Arabs out of Palestine....I would provide land for the Arabs in some other part of the Middle East....Each time we move out an Arab we would bring in another Jewish family....There are lots of places to which you could move the Arabs. All you have to do is drill a well because there is a large underground water supply, and we can move the Arabs to places where they can really live." (John Morton Blum, Roosevelt and Morgenthau: From the Morgenthau Diaries [Boston, 1970], 519-520.)

AUGUST 11. Reagan, Ronald Wilson. Aug. 23, 1984 at an ecumenical prayer breakfast at the Reunion Arena in Dallas, on the occasion of the enactment of the Equal Access Bill of 1984. Jeremiah O'Leary, A Reagan Declares that Faith Has Key Role in Political Life," The Washington Times (Aug. 24, 1984). Walter Shapiro, "Politics & the Pulpit," Newsweek (Sept. 17, 1984), p. 24. The Speech That Shook The Nation (Forerunner, Dec. 1984), p. 12. Nadine Strossen, "A Constitutional Analysis of the Equal Access Act's Standards Governing School Student's Religious Meetings," Harvard Journal on Legislation, Winter, 1987. p. 118. David R. Shepherd, Ronald Reagan: In God We Trust (Wheaton, IL: Tyndale House Publishers, Inc., 1984), p. 146.

AUGUST 12. Bates, Katherine Lee. 1892, verses in the song she composed titled, America the Beautiful. Michael Drury, Why She Wrote America's Favorite Song (NY: Woman's Day, Jan. 1978, reprinted: Pleasantville, NY:

Reader's Digest, The Reader's Digest Association, Inc., Jul. 1993). Robert Flood, The Rebirth of America (Philadelphia: Arthur S. DeMoss Foundation, 1986), p. 13. Tim LaHaye, Faith of Our Founding Fathers (Brentwood, TN: Wolgemuth & Hyatt, Publishers, Inc., 1987), p. 96.

AUGUST 13. Wells, Herbert George "H.G.". 1920. H.G. Wells, The Outline of History, 2 Vol. (H.G. Wells: 1920, reprinted, Garden City, NJ: Garden City Books, 1956), p. 840. D. James Kennedy, "The Bible & the Constitution" (Fort Lauderdale, FL: Coral Ridge Ministries), p. 6.

AUGUST 14. Cummings, William Thomas. 1942, in a field sermon at Bataan. Carlos P. Romulo, I Saw the Fall of the Philippines (1942). John Bartlett, Bartlett's Familiar Quotations (Boston: Little, Brown & Co., 1855, 1980), p. 857.

AUGUST 15. Bonaparte, Napoleon. At St. Helena, to Count de Motholon. Major General Alfred Pleasonton. Stephen Abbott Northrop, D.D., A Cloud of Witnesses (Portland, OR: American Heritage Ministries, 1987; Mantle Ministries, 228 Still Ridge, Bulverde, TX), pp. 361-362. Vernon C. Grounds, The Reason for Our Hope (Chicago: Moody Press), p. 37. Willard Cantelon, New Money or None? (Plainfield, NJ: Logos International, 1979), p. 246.

AUGUST 16. Finney, Charles Grandison. "In the Wake of the Second Great Awakening" (Carol Stream, IL: Christian History), Vol. VIII, No. 3, Issue 23, p. 31.

AUGUST 17. Eisenhower, Dwight David. Aug. 17, 1955, the text of the code of conduct for war prisoners to be put into effect in the armed services by Presidential order. James Beasley Simpson, Best Quotes of '54 '55 '56 (NY: Thomas Y. Crowell Co., 1957), p. 224.

AUGUST 18. Hand, (Billings) Learned. 1944, in an address titled, "The Spirit of Liberty," delivered at an "I Am an American Day" program in New York's Central Park. Charles Fadiman, ed., The American Treasury (NY: Harper & Brothers, Publishers, 1955), p. 149-150. William Safire, ed., Lend Me Your Ears - Great Speeches in History (NY: W.W. Norton & Co., 1992), p. 63.

AUGUST 19. Jefferson, Thomas. Aug. 19, 1785, in a letter to Peter Carr. John Bartlett, Bartlett's Familiar Quotations (Boston: Little, Brown & Co., 1855, 1980), p. 388.

AUGUST 20. Bassett, Richard. M.E. Bradford, A Worthy Company (Marlborough, NH: Plymouth Rock Foundation, 1982), p. 110-111. Tim LaHaye, Faith of Our Founding Fathers (Brentwood, TN: Wolgemuth & Hyatt, Publishers, Inc., 1987), p. 148. M.E. Bradford, Religion & The Framers: The Biographical Evidence (Marlborough, NH: The Plymouth Rock Foundation, 1991), p. 6.

AUGUST 21. Wilson, James. 1789-1791, in his Lectures on Law, delivered at the College of Philadelphia. James DeWitt Andres, Works of Wilson (Chicago,1896), 1:91-93. Charles Page Smith, James Wilson: Founding Father (Chapel Hill: University of North Carolina Press, 1956), p. 329. John Eidsmoe, Christianity & the Constitution - The Faith of Our Founding Fathers (Grand Rapids, MI: Baker Book House, A Mott Media Book, 1987, 6th printing 1993), pp. 44-45.

AUGUST 22. Schwarzkopf, H. Norman. 1991, in an interview with David Frost. Peter Marshall & David Manuel, The Glory of America (Bloomington, MN: Garborg's Heart'N Home, Inc., 1991), 5.29.

AUGUST 23. Perry, Oliver Hazard. Tucker, Poltroons, pp. 331-332. Peter Marshall & David Manuel, The Glory of America (Bloomington, MN: Garborg's Heart'N Home, Inc., 1991), 9.10.

AUGUST 24. Gutenberg, Johannes. Alphonse De Lamartine, Memories of Celebrated Characters, p. 277. Stephen Abbott Northrop, D.D., A Cloud of Witnesses (Portland, OR: American Heritage Ministries, 1987; Mantle Ministries, 228 Still Ridge, Bulverde, TX), p. 202. Gary DeMar, God & Government (Atlanta, GA: American Vision Press, 1984), Vol. 2, p. vi. Also rendered from the German tongue as, "Religious truth is captive in a small number of little manuscripts, which guard the common treasures instead of expanding them. Let us break the seal which binds these holy things; let us give wings to truth that it may fly with the Word, no longer prepared at vast expense, but multiplied everlasting by a machine which never wearies - to every soul which enters life." Gary DeMar, America's Christian History: The Untold Story (Atlanta, GA: American Vision Publishers, Inc., 1993), p. 44.

AUGUST 25. Herschel, Sir William. Henry M. Morris, Men of Science-Men of God (El Cajon, CA: Masters Books, A Division of Creation Life Publishers, Inc., 1990), pp. 29-30.

AUGUST 26. Howe, Julia Ward. Feb., 1862, The Battle Hymn of the Republic (Massachusetts: The Atlantic Monthly, Feb. 1862), Vol. IX, No. LII, p. 10, Entered according to Act of Congress by Ticknor & Fields, in the Clerk's Office of the District Court of the District of Massachusetts. Mark Galli, Christian History (Carol Stream, IL: Christian History, 1992, Issue 33), Vol. XI, No. 1, p. 19. D.P. Diffine, Ph.D., One Nation Under God - How Close a Separation? (Searcy, AR: Harding University, Belden Center for Private Enterprise Education, 6th edition, 1992), p. 14.

AUGUST 27. Washington, George. Aug. 27, 1776. John Fiske, The American Revolution, 2 vols. (Boston & New York: Houghton, Mifflin & Co., 1898), Vol. I, p. 212. Marshall Foster & Mary-Elaine Swanson, The American

Covenant - The Untold Story (Roseburg, OR: Foundation for Christian Self-Government, 1981; Thousand Oaks, CA: The Mayflower Institute, 1983, 1992), p. 41. George F. Scheer & Hugh F. Rankin, Rebels & Redcoats (NY: The World Publishing Co., 1957), p. 171. Peter Marshall & David Manuel, The Light & the Glory (Old Tappan, NJ: Fleming H. Revell Co., 1977), p. 315.

AUGUST 28. King, Martin Luther, Jr. Aug. 28, 1963, on the occasion of the Civil Rights Mar. on Washington. The SCLC Story in Words & Pictures, 1964, pp. 50-51. The Annals of America, 20 vols. (Chicago, IL: Encyclopedia Britannica, Inc., 1976), Vol. 18, pp. 156-159. John Bartlett, Bartlett's Familiar Quotations (Boston: Little, Brown & Co., 1855, 1980), p. 909.

AUGUST 29. Washington, George. Aug. 29, 1796, from the city of Philadelphia in a "Talk" to the Cherokee Nation. William Barclay Allen, ed., George Washington - A Collection (Indianapolis: Liberty Classics, Liberty Fund, Inc., 7440 N. Shadeland, Indianapolis, IN 46250, 1988; based almost entirely on materials reproduced from The Writings of George Washington from the original manuscript sources, 1745-1799/John Clement Fitzpatrick, editor), pp. 647-648. John Clement Fitzpatrick, ed., The Writings of George Washington, from the Original Manuscript Sources 1749-1799, 39 vols. (Washington, D.C.: U.S. Government Printing Office, 1931-1944). In a lecture by Theodore Parker, 1858, the tradition of the New York Indians concerning George Washington is related: "Alone, of all white men, he has been admitted to the Indian Heaven, because of his justice to the Red Man. He lives in a great palace, built like a fort. All the Indians, as they go to Heaven, pass by, & he himself is in his uniform, a sword at his side, walking to and fro. They bow reverently with great humility. He returns the salute, but says nothing." William S. Baker, Character Portraits of Washington, 1887, p. 284. William J. Johnson, George Washington - The Christian (St. Paul, MN: William J. Johnson, Merriam Park, Feb. 23, 1919; Nashville, TN: Abingdon Press, 1919; reprinted Milford, MI: Mott Media, 1976; reprinted Arlington Heights, IL: Christian Liberty Press, 502 West Euclid Ave., Arlington Heights, IL., 60004, 1992), p. 258.

AUGUST 30. Washington, George. Sept. 26, 1780, General Orders from his headquarters in Orangetown. John Clement Fitzpatrick, ed., The Writings of George Washington, from the Original Manuscript Sources 1749-1799, 39 vols. (Washington, D.C.: U.S. Government Printing Office, 1931-1944), Vol. XX, pp. 94-95. Saxe Commins, ed., The Basic Writings of George Washington (NY: Random House, 1948), p. 410. Richard Wheeler, Voices of 1776 (Greenwich: Fawcett Premier Book, 1972), p. 382. Peter Marshall & David Manuel, The Light & the Glory (Old Tappan, NJ: Fleming H. Revell Co., 1977), pp. 328-329.

AUGUST 31. Bunyan, John (Nov. 1628-Aug. 31, 1688), was an English author who wrote the classic work, The Pilgrim's Progress, 1678. Born in Bedford, England, he was a poor, unskilled tinker by trade. In 1657, he became a Baptist minister and was imprisoned over 12 years, 1660-72, 1675, for preaching without a license. It was during this time that he did much of his writing, while supporting his family by making shoelaces. The Pilgrim's Progress, 1678, which is an allegory of a Christian's journey to the Celestial City, has been translated into over 100 languages and, after the Bible, has held the position as the world's best-seller for hundreds of years, It, along with the Bible and Fox's Book of Martyrs, was found in nearly every home in colonial New England.

SEPTEMBER 1. Madison, James. Sept. 1, 1814, in a National Proclamation after the British had invaded the Capitol. Nile's Weekly Register, Vol. 7, p. 2. James D. Richardson, ed., A Compilation of the Messages & Papers of the Presidents 1789-1897, 10 vols. (Washington, D.C.: U.S. Government Printing Office, published by Authority of Congress, 1897, 1899; Washington, D.C.: Bureau of National Literature & Art, 1789-1902, 11 vols., 1907, 1910), Vol. I, pp. 545-546.

SEPTEMBER 2. Bush, George Herbert Walker. Jan. 20, 1989, Inaugural Address. J. Michael Sharman, J.D., Faith of the Fathers (Culpepper, Virginia: Victory Publishing, 1995), p. 127.

SEPTEMBER 3. Confederation, Congress of the. Jan. 14, 1784, under the Articles of Confederation, ratified the peace treaty with Great Britain, which had been signed in Paris on Sept. 3, 1783, by D. Hartley, John Adams, B. Franklin, & John Jay, thereby officially ending the Revolutionary War. William M. Malloy, compiler, Treaties, Conventions, International Acts, Protocols & Agreements between the United States of America & Other Powers, 1776-1909, 4 vols. (NY: Greenwood Press, 1910, 1968), 2:1786. Charles W. Eliot, LL.D., ed., American Historical Documents 1000-1904 (NY: P.F. Collier & Son Co., The Harvard Classics, 1910), Vol. 43, pp. 185-191. Gary DeMar, America's Christian History: The Untold Story (Atlanta, GA: American Vision Publishers, Inc., 1993), p. 84.

SEPTEMBER 4. Harding, Warren Gamaliel. Jul. 3, 1923, in a speech about the Oregon Trail given at Meacham, Oregon. "Harding, Warren Gamaliel; A Government Document," Washington, D.C.: Government Printing Office, 1923. A Compilation of the Messages & Papers of the Presidents 20 vols. (NY: Bureau of National Literature, Inc., prepared under the direction of the Joint Committee on Printing, of the House & Senate, pursuant to an Act of the 52nd Congress of the United States, 1893, 1923), Vol. XVIII, pp. 9299-9303.

SEPTEMBER 5. Mother Teresa of Calcutta. Feb. 3, 1994, at the National Prayer Breakfast, Washington, D.C. "National Prayer Breakfast - Mother Teresa Defends Life," Christian American (Chesapeake, VA: The Christian Coalition, Mar. 1994), Vol. 5, No. 1, p. 29. "Mother Teresa Condemns Abortion At National Prayer Breakfast" The Dallas/Fort Worth Heritage (Dallas, TX: The Dallas/Fort Worth Heritage, Mar. 1994), Vol. 2, No. 9, p. 6.

SEPTEMBER 6. Webster, Daniel. Jun. 17, 1825, in an oration celebrating the 50th anniversary of the Battle of Bunker Hill. David Josiah Brewer, World's Best Orations (St. Louis: F.P. Kaiser, 1901), Vol. 10, pp. 3828-3846. Ronald Reid, ed., Three Centuries of American Rhetorical Discourse - An Anthology & a Review (Prospect Heights, IL: Waveland Press, Inc., 1988), p. 213.

SEPTEMBER 7. Adams, John. Sept. 7, 1774, in a letter to his wife Abigail relating the events of the First Continental Congress. John & Abigail Adams, Vol. I, pp. 23-24. Charles Francis Adams (son of John Quincy Adams & grandson of John Adams), ed., Letters of John Adams - Addressed To His Wife (Boston: Charles C. Little & James Brown, 1841), Vol. I, pp. 23-24. Edmund Fuller & David E. Green, God in the White House - The Faiths of American Presidents (NY: Crown Publishers, Inc., 1968), pp. 21-22. L.H. Butterfield, Marc Frielander, & Mary-Jo King, eds., The Book of Abigail & John - Selected Letters of The Adams Family 1762-1784 (Cambridge, Massachusetts & London, England: Harvard University Press, 1975), p. 76. Phyllis Lee Levin, Abigail Adams (NY: St. Martin's Press, 1987), p. 55.

SEPTEMBER 8. Lincoln, Abraham. Apr. 14, 1865, Ford's Theatre, his last words. Miner, Lincoln, p. 52. Peter Marshall & David Manuel, The Glory of America (Bloomington, MN: Garborg's Heart 'N Home, Inc., 1991), 4.14.

SEPTEMBER 9. California, State of. 1849, Constitution, Preamble. Constitutions of the United States - National & State (Dobbs Ferry, NY: Oceana Publications, Inc., published for Legislative Drafting Research Fund of Columbia University, Release 96-4, Issued Nov. 1996), Vol. 1, California(Nov. 1996), p. 1. Charles E. Rice, The Supreme Court & Public Prayer (NY: Fordham University Press, 1964), p. 168; "Hearings, Prayers in Public Schools & Other Matters," Committee on the Judiciary, U.S. Senate (87th Cong., 2nd Sess.), 1962, pp. 268 et seq.

SEPTEMBER 10. Story, Joseph. 1844. Vidal v. Girard's Executors, 43 U.S. 126, 132 (1844), pp. 198, 205-206. William W. Story, Life & Letters of Judge Story, Vol. II, Chap. XII. Stephen Abbott Northrop, D.D., A Cloud of Witnesses (Portland, OR: American Heritage Ministries, 1987; Mantle Ministries, 228 Still Ridge, Bulverde, TX), p. 434.

SEPTEMBER 11. President George W. Bush, statements issued from Barksdale Air Force Base in Louisiana, Tuesday, Sept. 11, 2001, 1:30pm EDT, & later that evening in a national address from the Oval Office. Sept. 11th. The date, Sept. 11, 1777. The Continental Congress was being forced to evacuate Philadelphia, as the British had just won the Battle of Brandywine, forcing Washington's 10,000 troops to retreat. In addition to this desperate situation, Congress was made aware that there was a shortage of Bibles due to the interruption of trade with the King's printers in England. Congress voted to import Bibles from Scotland or Holland into different parts of the Union, stating: "The use of the Bible is so universal and its importance so great...it was resolved accordingly to direct said Committee of Commerce to import 20,000 copies of the Bible." Congress, Continental. Sept. 11, 1777. Robert Flood, The Rebirth of America Philadelphia: Arthur S. DeMoss Foundation, 1986), p. 39. Journals of the Continental Congress 1774-1789 (Washington, D.C.: Government Printing Office, 1905), book 146, Vol. VIII, pp. 731-735. Journal of the American Congress, 1774-1788 (Washington: 1823), Vol. II, pp. 261-262. Tim LaHaye, Faith of Our Founding Fathers (Brentwood, TN: Wolgemuth & Hyatt, Publishers, Inc., 1987), p. 96. Benjamin Franklin Morris, The Christian Life & Character of the Civil Institutions of the United States (Philadelphia, PA: G.W. Childs, 1864), pp. 215-216. Gary DeMar, America's Christian History: The Untold Story (Atlanta, GA: American Vision Publishers, Inc., 1993), pp. 47-48. D.P. Diffine, Ph.D., One Nation Under God - How Close a Separation? (Searcy, AR: Harding University, Belden Center for Private Enterprise Education, 6th edition, 1992), p. 2.

SEPTEMBER 12. Cooley, Thomas. 1898, Thomas Cooley, The General Principles of Constitutional Law in the United States of America (Boston: 1898), pp. 224-225. Charles E. Rice, The Supreme Court & Public Prayer (NY: Fordham University Press, 1964), p. 47. John Whitehead, The Rights of Religious Persons in Public Education (Wheaton, IL: Crossway Books, Good News Publishers, 1991), p. 46.

SEPTEMBER 13. Key, Francis Scott. Tim LaHaye, Faith of Our Founding Fathers (Brentwood, TN: Wolgemuth & Hyatt, Publishers, Inc., 1987), p. 95. Charles Wallis, ed., Our American Heritage (NY: Harper & Row, Publishers, Inc., 1970), p. 144. D.P. Diffine, Ph.D., One Nation Under God - How Close a Separation? (Searcy, AR: Harding University, Belden Center for Private Enterprise Education, 6th edition, 1992), p. 17.

SEPTEMBER 14. Harvard, John. 1642. Old South Leaflets. Peter Marshall & David Manuel, The Glory of America (Bloomington, MN: Garborg's Heart'N Home, Inc., 1991), 9.28. "New England's First Fruits in Respect to the Progress of Learning in the College at Cambridge in Massachusetts Bay," in Verna M. Hall, comp., & Rosalie J. Slater, developer, Teaching & Learning America's Christian History (San Francisco: Foundation for American

Christian Education, 1975), frontpiece. Peter G. Mode, ed., Sourcebook & Bibliography Guide for American Church History (Menasha, WI: George Banta Publishing Co., 1920), pp. 73-74. Pat Robertson, America's Dates With Destiny (Nashville, TN: Thomas Nelson Publishers, 1986), pp. 43-44.

SEPTEMBER 15. Taft, William Howard. Nov. 7, 1912, in a Proclamation of a National Day of Thanksgiving. A Compilation of the Messages & Papers of the Presidents 20 vols. (NY: Bureau of National Literature, Inc., prepared under the direction of the Joint Committee on Printing, of the House & Senate, pursuant to an Act of the 52nd Congress of the United States, 1893, 1923), Vol. XVI, pp. 7764-7765.

SEPTEMBER 16. Bradford, William. 1650, in his work titled, The History of Plymouth Plantation 1608-1650 (Boston, MA:: Massachusetts Historical Society, 1856; Boston, MA: Wright & Potter Printing Co., 1898, 1901, from Original Manuscript, Library of Congress Rare Book Collection, Washington, D.C.; rendered in Modern English, Harold Paget, 1909; NY: Russell & Russell, 1968; NY: Random House, Inc., Modern Library College edition, 1981; San Antonio, TX: American Heritage Classics, Mantle Ministries, 228 Still Ridge, Bulverde, TX, 1988), p. 21. Jordan D. Fiore, ed., Mourt's Relation: A Journal of the Pilgrims of Plymouth (Plymouth, MA: Plymouth Rock Foundation, 1841, 1865, 1985), pp. 10-11. William T. Davis, ed., History of Plymouth Plantation (NY: Charles Scribner's Sons, 1908), p. 46. The Annals of America, 20 vols. (Chicago, IL: Encyclopedia Britannica, 1968), Vol. 1, p. 66. Verna M. Hall, comp., Christian History of the Constitution of the United States of America (San Francisco: Foundation for American Christian Education, 1976), p. 193. Marshall Foster & Mary-Elaine Swanson, The American Covenant - The Untold Story (Roseburg, OR: Foundation for Christian Self-Government, 1981; Thousand Oaks, CA: The Mayflower Institute, 1983, 1992), p. 11. Gary DeMar, America's Christian History: The Untold Story (Atlanta, GA: American Vision Publishers, Inc., 1993), pp. 34-35.

SEPTEMBER 17. United States Constitution. Sept. 17, 1787. Charles W. Eliot, LL.D., ed., American Historical Documents 1000-1904 (NY: P.F. Collier & Son Co., The Harvard Classics, 1910), Vol. 43, p. 205. Gary DeMar, God & Government - A Biblical & Historical Study (Atlanta, GA: American Vision Press, 1982), pp. 163, 172. Holy Bible. 1760-1805. Donald S. Lutz & Charles S. Hyneman, "The Relative Influence of European Writers on Late Eighteenth-Century American Political Thought," American Political Science Review 189 (1984): 189-197. (Courtesy of Dr. Wayne House of Dallas Theological Seminary.) John Eidsmoe, Christianity & the Constitution - The Faith of Our Founding Fathers (Grand Rapids, MI: Baker Book House, A Mott Media Book, 1987; 6th printing, 1993), pp. 51-53. Origins of American Constitutionalism, (1987). Stephen K. McDowell & Mark A. Beliles, America's Providential History (Charlottesville, VA: Providence Press, 1988), p. 156. Holy Bible (during the period 1760-1805), was the source for 34 % of all quotations cited by our Founding Fathers. After reviewing an estimated 15,000 items, including newspaper articles, pamphlets, books, monographs, etc., Professors Donald S. Lutz & Charles S. Hyneman, in their work "The Relative Influence of European Writers on Late Eighteenth-Century American Political Thought" published in the American Political Science Review, revealed that the Bible, especially the book of Deuteronomy, contributed 34 % of all quotations used by our Founding Fathers. The other main sources cited include: Baron Charles Montesquieu 8.3 %, Sir William Blackstone 7.9 %, John Locke 2.9 %, David Hume 2.7 %, Plutarch 1.5 %, Beccaria 1.5 %, Trenchard & Gordon 1.4 %, Delolme 1.4 %, Samuel von Pufendorf 1.3 %, Cicero 1.2 %, Hugo Grotius .9 %, Shakespeare .8 %, Vattel .5 %, etc. These additional sources as well took 60 % of their quotes directly from the Bible. Direct & indirect citations combined reveal that 94 % of all quotations referenced by the Founding Fathers are derived from the Bible.

SEPTEMBER 18. Langdon, John. Oct. 21, 1785, John Langdon, as President (Governor) of New Hampshire, made an official Proclamation for a General Thanksgiving. Tim LaHaye, Faith of Our Founding Fathers (Brentwood, TN: Wolgemuth & Hyatt, Publishers, Inc., 1987), pp. 165-166.

SEPTEMBER 19. Washington, George. Sept. 19, 1796, Farewell Address, published in the American Daily Advertiser, Philadelphia, Sept., 1796. James D. Richardson (U.S. Representative from Tennessee), ed., A Compilation of the Messages & Papers of the Presidents 1789-1897, 10 vols. (Washington, D.C.: U.S. Government Printing Office, published by Authority of Congress, 1897, 1899; Washington, D.C.: Bureau of National Literature & Art, 1789-1902, 11 vols., 1907, 1910), Vol. 1, p. 213-224, Sept. 17, 1796. John Clement Fitzpatrick, ed., The Writings of George Washington, from the Original Manuscript Sources 1749-1799, 39 vols. (Washington, D.C.: U.S. Government Printing Office, 1931-1944), Vol. 35, p. 229. William Barclay Allen, ed., George Washington - A Collection (Indianapolis: Liberty Classics, Liberty Fund, Inc., 7440 N. Shadeland, Indianapolis, IN 46250, 1988; based almost entirely on materials reproduced from The Writings of George Washington from the original manuscript sources, 1745-1799), pp. 512-527. Charles W. Eliot, LL.D., ed., American Historical Documents 1000-1904 (NY: P.F. Collier & Son Co., The Harvard Classics, 1910), Vol. 43, pp. 250-266..

SEPTEMBER 20. Ames, Fisher. Sept. 20, 1789, in an article published in Palladium magazine. D. James Kennedy,

"The Great Deception " (Ft. Lauderdale, FL: Coral Ridge Ministries, 1989; 1993), p. 3.

SEPTEMBER 21. Coolidge, (John) Calvin. Sept. 21, 1924, address to the Holy Name Society, Washington, D.C. Calvin Coolidge, Foundations of the Republic - Speeches & Addresses (NY: Charles Scribner's Sons, 1926), pp. 103-112.

SEPTEMBER 22. Hale, Everett. 1897, in "Challenge to the Youth of Boston." Charles Wallis, ed., Our American Heritage (NY: Harper & Row, Publishers, Inc., 1970), p. 186.

SEPTEMBER 23. McGuffey, William Holmes. William Ellery Channing, "Religion The Only Basis of Society" William Holmes McGuffey, McGuffey's Fifth Eclectic Reader (Cincinnati & New York: Van Antwerp, Bragg & Co., revised edition, 1879), lesson XCIII, pp. 284-286.

SEPTEMBER 24. Marshall, John. 1819, in the case of McCulloch v. Maryland, 4 Wheaton 316, 431. John Bartlett, Bartlett's Familiar Quotations (Boston: Little, Brown and Co., 1855, 1980), p. 402. Chief Justice John Marshall, in a letter to Jasper Adams, May 9, 1833, JSAC, p. 139. Photo Copies of Jasper Adams' handwritten notes were included with his printed copies of the sermon: The Relation of Christianity to Civil Government in the United States: Sermon preached in St. Michael's Church, Charleston, Feb. 13, 1833 By Rev. J. Adams, Charleston, Printed by A. E. Miller, No.4 Broad-street, 1833. Courtesy of the William L. Clements Library, University of Michigan. "May 9, 1833, Chief Justice Marshall to the Author, Richmond May 9th, 1833. Reverend Sir, I am much indebted to you for the copy of your valuable sermon on the relation of Christianity to civil government preached before the convention of the Protestant Episcopal Church in Charleston, on the 13th of Feby. last. I have read it with great attention & advantage. The documents annexed to the sermon certainly go far in sustaining the proposition which it is your purpose to establish. One great object of the colonial charters was avowedly the propagation of the Christian faith. Means have been employed to accomplish this object, & those means have been used by government. No person, I believe, questions the importance of religion to the happiness of man even during his existence in this world. It has at all times employed his most serious meditation, & had a decided influence on his conduct. The American population is entirely Christian, & with us, Christianity & Religion are identified. It would be strange, indeed, if with such a people, our institutions did not presuppose Christianity, & did not often refer to it, & exhibit relations with it. Legislation on the subject is admitted to require great delicacy, because freedom sic of conscience & respect for our religion both claim our most serious regard. You have allowed their full influence to both. With very great respect, I am Sir, your Obedt., J. Marshall. Rev. J. Adams, Charleston, Adams's Notes, pages 2-3, http:// members.tripod.com/~candst/jaspltrs.htm D. James Kennedy, "The Bible and the Constitution " (Fort Lauderdale, FL: Coral Ridge Ministries), p. 4. Liberty and Justice for All (Virginia Beach, VA: Regent University, 1993), p. 7.

SEPTEMBER 25. U.S. Congress. Sept. 25, 1789, the First Amendment. Michael J. Malbin, Religion & Politics - The Intentions of the Authors of the First Amendment (Washington: 1978). William Miller, The First Liberty - Religion & the American Republic (NY: 1986). Linda DePauw, et al., eds., Documentary History of the First Federal Congress... (Baltimore: 1972 & following) (work in progress). M.E. Bradford, Religion & The Framers: The Biographical Evidence (Marlborough, NH: The Plymouth Rock Foundation, 1991), p. 12. Edwin S. Gaustad, Neither King nor Prelate - Religion & the New Nation, 1776-1826 (Grand Rapids, MI: William B. Eerdmans Publishing Co., 1993), pp. 157-158. George Mason, in his previously proposed wording to be considered for the First Amendment. Kate Mason Rowland, The Life of George Mason (New York: G.P. Putnam's Sons, 1892), Vol. I, p. 244.

SEPTEMBER 26. Harvard University. 1636. Old South Leaflets. Benjamin Pierce, A History of Harvard University (Cambridge, MA: Brown, Shattuck, & Co., 1833), Appendix, p. 5. Peter G. Mode, ed., Sourcebook & Biographical Guide for American Church History (Menasha, WI: George Banta Publishing Co., 1921), pp. 74-75. Robert Flood, The Rebirth of America (Philadelphia: Arthur S. DeMoss Foundation, 1986), p. 41. "Our Christian Heritage," Letter from Plymouth Rock (Marlborough, NH: The Plymouth Rock Foundation), p. 2. Pat Robertson, America's Dates With Destiny (Nashville, TN: Thomas Nelson Publishers, 1986), pp. 44-45. Gary DeMar, America's Christian History: The Untold Story (Atlanta, GA: American Vision Publishers, Inc., 1993), p. 40. Rosalie J. Slater, "New England's First Fruits, 1643," Teaching & Learning America's Christian History (San Francisco: Foundation for Christian Education, 1980), p. vii. Stephen McDowell & Mark Beliles, "The Providential Perspective" (Charlottesville, VA: The Providence Foundation, P.O. Box 6759, Charlottesville, Va. 22906, Jan. 1994), Vol. 9, No. 1, p. 3. D.P. Diffine, Ph.D., One Nation Under God - How Close a Separation? (Searcy, AR: Harding University, Belden Center for Private Enterprise Education, 6th edition, 1992), p. 4.

SEPTEMBER 27. Adams, Samuel. 1750, statement. William V. Wells, The Life & Public Services of Samuel Adams (Boston: Little, Brown & Co., 1865). Rosalie J. Slater, Teaching & Learning America's Christian History (San Francisco: Foundation for American Christian Education, 1975). Peter Marshall & David Manuel, The Glory of America (Bloomington, MN: Garborg's Heart'N Home, Inc., 1991), 11.3. Stephen McDowell & Mark Beliles,

"The Providential Perspective" (Charlottesville, VA: The Providence Foundation, P.O. Box 6759, Charlottesville, Va. 22906, Jan. 1994), Vol. 9, No. 1, p. 5.

SEPTEMBER 28. Pasteur, Louis. John Hudson Tiner, Louis Pasteur - Founder of Modern Medicine (Milford, Michigan: Mott Media, Inc., 1990), p. 90.

SEPTEMBER 29. 1622, Bradford, William, the account of Squanto's death. William Bradford (Governor of Plymouth Colony), The History of Plymouth Plantation 1608-1650 (Boston, MA:: Massachusetts Historical Society, 1856; Boston, Massachusetts: Wright & Potter Printing Co., 1898, from original manuscript; rendered in Modern English, Harold Paget, 1909; NY: Russell & Russell, 1968; San Antonio, TX: American Heritage Classics, Mantle Ministries, 228 Still Ridge, Bulverde, TX, 1988), pp. 109-110.

SEPTEMBER 30. Franklin, Benjamin. 1739. Benjamin Franklin, The Autobiography of Benjamin Franklin (NY: Books, Inc., 1791), p. 146. Benjamin Franklin, Autobiography, 1771-75 (Reprinted Garden City, NY: Garden City Publishing Co., Inc., 1916), Vol. 1, pp. 191-192. John Pollack, George Whitefield & the Great Awakening (Garden City New Jersey: Doubleday & Co., 1972), p. 117. John Eidsmoe, Christianity & The Constitution - The Faith of Our Founding Fathers (Grand Rapids, MI: Baker Book House, 1987), p. 204. Tim LaHaye, Faith of Our Founding Fathers (Brentwood, TN: Wolgemuth & Hyatt, Publishers, Inc., 1987), p. 116. Peter Marshall & David Manuel, The Glory of America (Bloomington, MN: Garborg's Heart 'N Home, 1991), 12.18.

OCTOBER 1. Muhlenberg, John Peter Gabriel. William Holmes McGuffey, McGuffey's Fifth Eclectic Reader (Cincinnati & New York: Van Antwerp, Bragg & Co., revised ed., 1879), lesson LXV, pp. 200-204.

OCTOBER 2. Toynbee, Arnold Joseph. Mar. 30, 1956, comment recorded in Collier's. James Beasely Simpson. Best Quotes of '54, '55, '56 (NY: Thomas Y. Crowell Co., 1957), p. 352.

OCTOBER 3. Washington, George. Oct. 3, 1789, from the city of New York, President issued a Proclamation of a National Day of Thanksgiving. Jared Sparks, ed., The Writings of George Washington 12 vols. (Boston: American Stationer's Co., 1837, NY: F. Andrew's, 1834-1847), Vol. XII, p. 119. James D. Richardson, ed., A Compilation of the Messages & Papers of the Presidents 1789-1897, 10 vols. (Washington, D.C.: U.S. Government Printing Office, published by Authority of Congress, 1897, 1899; Washington, D.C.: Bureau of National Literature & Art, 1789-1902, 11 vols., 1907, 1910), Vol. 1, p. 64. William J. Johnson, George Washington - The Christian (St. Paul, MN: William J. Johnson, Merriam Park, Feb. 23, 1919; Nashville, TN: Abingdon Press, 1919; reprinted Milford, MI: Mott Media, 1976; reprinted Arlington Heights, IL: Christian Liberty Press, 502 West Euclid Ave., Arlington Heights, IL., 60004, 1992), pp. 172-174. William Barclay Allen, ed., George Washington - A Collection (Indianapolis: Liberty Classics, Liberty Fund, Inc., 7440 N. Shadeland, Indianapolis, IN 46250, 1988; based on The Writings of George Washington from original manuscript sources, 1745-1799/John Clement Fitzpatrick, editor), pp. 534-353. John Clement Fitzpatrick, ed., The Writings of George Washington, from the Original Manuscript Sources 1749-1799, 39 vols. (Washington, D.C.: U.S. Government Printing Office, 1931-1944). John F. Schroeder, ed., Maxims of Washington (Mt. Vernon: Mt. Vernon Ladies' Association, 1942), pp. 275, 287. Anson Phelps Stokes & Leo Pfeffer, Church & State in the United States, 3 vols. (NY: Harper & Brothers, 1950), p. 87. John Eidsmoe, Christianity & the Constitution - The Faith of Our Founding Fathers (Grand Rapids, MI: Baker Book House, A Mott Media Book, 1987, 6th printing 1993), p. 118. Gary DeMar, The Biblical Worldview (Atlanta, GA: An American Vision Publication - American Vision, Inc., 1992), Vol. 8, No. 12, p. 8. D.P. Diffine, Ph.D., One Nation Under God - How Close a Separation? (Searcy, AR: Harding University, Belden Center for Private Enterprise Education, 6th edition, 1992), p. 9.

OCTOBER 4. Reagan, Ronald. 1983, Proclamation of a National "Year of the Bible." The Bible - The Book that Shaped a Nation. David R. Shepherd, ed., Ronald Reagan: In God I Trust (Wheaton, IL: Tyndale House Publishers, Inc., 1984), pp. 86-87.

OCTOBER 5. Edwards, Jonathan. JUKES-EDWARDS A STUDY IN EDUCATION AND HEREDITY BY A.E. WINSHIP, LITT.D. HARRISBURG, PA.: R.L. Myers & Co. 1900. G.P. Putnam's Sons, New York, reprinted this study in "The Jukes." http://books.jibble.org/1/5/6/2/15623/15623-8/Jukes-EdwardsbyAEWinship-0.html Marshall Foster, Winning the Battle for the 21st Century (Thousand Oaks, CA: Mayflower Institute, 1993), p. 39.

OCTOBER 6. 1862, Lincoln, Abraham, in conversation with Eliza Gurney & three other Quakers. John G. Nicolay & John Hay, eds., The Complete Works of Abraham Lincoln: Speeches, Letters & State Papers (1905). William J. Johnson, Abraham Lincoln, the Christian (NY: Abingdon Press, 1913), p. 97.

OCTOBER 7. Muhlenberg, Henry Melchior. Henry Melchior Muhlenberg, The Notebook of a Colonial Clergyman, translated & ed., by Theodore G. Tappert & John W. Doberstern (Philadelphia: Fortress Press, 1975), p. 195. Lucille Johnston, Celebrations of a Nation (Arlington, VA: The Year of Thanksgiving Foundation, 1987), p. 87.

OCTOBER 8. Rickenbacker, Edward Vernon "Eddie". http://richthofen.com/rickenbacker/ Jessie Clayton Adams, More Than Money (San Antonio, TX: The Naylor Co., 1953), p. 22. Courtesy of the personal library of Mike Gross.

Captain Edward Vernon Rickenbacker, Seven Came Through (NY: Doubleday, Doran Company, Inc., 1943).
OCTOBER 9. Cass, Lewis. Tryon Edwards, D.D., The New Dictionary of Thoughts - A Cyclopedia of Quotations (Garden City, NY: Hanover House, 1852; revised & enlarged by C.H. Catrevas, Ralph Emerson Browns & Jonathan Edwards descendent, along with Tryon, of Jonathan Edwards (1703-1758), president of Princeton, 1891; The Standard Book Co., 1955, 1963), p. 90.
OCTOBER 10. Columbus, Christopher. Oct. 8, 10, 12, 16, 28, Nov. 6, 27, Dec. 12, 16, 22, 24, 1492, in his Journal of the First Voyage (El Libro de la Primera Navegacion), as recounted in Bartolome' de Las Casas' abstract, translated into English by Samuel Eliot Morison, Journals & Other Documents on the Life & Voyages of Christopher Columbus (NY: Heritage Press, 1963), pp. 65, 72. John Bartlett, Bartlett's Familiar Quotations (Boston: Little, Brown & Co., 1855, 1980), pp. 150-151. John Eidsmoe, Columbus & Cortez, Conquerors for Christ (Green Forest, AR: New Leaf Press, 1992), pp. 85-86. Bjorn Landstrom, Columbus (NY: The Macmillan Co., 1966), pp. 66-75. Peter Marshall & David Manual, The Light & the Glory (Old Tappan, NJ: Fleming H. Revell Co., 1977), p. 42.
OCTOBER 11. Adams, John. Oct. 11, 1798, in a letter to the officers of the First Brigade of the Third Division of the Militia of Massachusetts. Charles Francis Adams (son of John Quincy Adams & grandson of John Adams), ed., The Works of John Adams - Second President of the United States: with a Life of the Author, Notes, & Illustration (Boston: Little, Brown, & Co., 1854), Vol. IX, pp. 228-229. Charles E. Rice, The Supreme Court & Public Prayer (NY: Fordham University Press, 1964), p. 47. Senator A. Willis Robertson, "Report on Prayers in Public Schools & Other Matters, Senate Committee on the Judiciary (87th Congress, 2nd Session), 1962, 32. Richard John Neuhaus, The Naked Public Square (Grand Rapids, MI: William B. Eerdman Publishing Co., 1984), p. 95. War on Religious Freedom (Virginia Beach, Virginia: Freedom Council, 1984), p. 1. A. James Reichley, Religion in American Public Life (Washington, D.C.: The Brookings Institute, 1985), p. 105. Pat Robertson, America's Dates With Destiny (Nashville, TN: 1986), pp. 93-95. Charles Colson, Kingdoms in Conflict (Grand Rapids, MI: Zondervan Publishing House, 1987), pp. 47, 120. Tim LaHaye, Faith of Our Founding Fathers (Brentwood, TN: Wolgemuth & Hyatt, Publishers, Inc., 1987), p. 194. John Eidsmoe, Christianity & the Constitution - The Faith of Our Founding Fathers (Grand Rapids, MI: Baker Book House, A Mott Media Book, 1987; 6th printing, 1993), pp. 273, 292, 381. Gary DeMar, "Is the Constitution Christian?" (Atlanta, GA: The Biblical Worldview, An American Vision Publication - American Vision, Inc., Dec. 1989), p. 2. Peter Marshall & David Manuel, The Glory of America (Bloomington, MN: Garborg's Heart 'N Home, 1991), 8.11. Kerby Anderson, "Christian Roots of the Declaration " (Dallas, TX: Freedom Club Report, Jul. 1993), p. 6. Rush H. Limbaugh III, See, I Told You So (NY: reprinted by permission of Pocket Books, a division of Simon & Schuster Inc., 1993), pp. 73-76. Stephen McDowell & Mark Beliles, "The Providential Perspective " (Charlottesville, VA: The Providence Foundation, P.O. Box 6759, Charlottesville, Va. 22906, Jan. 1994), Vol. 9, No. 1, p. 4.
OCTOBER 12. Columbus, Christopher. Oct. 8, 10, 12, 16, 28, Nov. 6, 27, Dec. 12, 16, 22, 24, 1492, in his Journal of the First Voyage (El Libro de la Primera Navegacion), as recounted in Bartolome' de Las Casas' abstract, translated into English by Samuel Eliot Morison, Journals & Other Documents on the Life & Voyages of Christopher Columbus (NY: Heritage Press, 1963), pp. 65, 72. John Bartlett, Bartlett's Familiar Quotations (Boston: Little, Brown & Co., 1855, 1980), pp. 150-151. John Eidsmoe, Columbus & Cortez, Conquerors for Christ (Green Forest, AR: New Leaf Press, 1992), pp. 85-86. Bjorn Landstrom, Columbus (NY: The Macmillan Co., 1966), pp. 66-75. Peter Marshall & David Manual, The Light & the Glory (Old Tappan, NJ: Fleming H. Revell Co., 1977), p. 42.
OCTOBER 13. Thatcher, Margaret Hilda. Feb. 5, 1996, in New York City, prior to her trip to Utah where she addressed the U.K. - Utah Festival, in an interview with Joseph A. Cannon, titled "The Conservative Vision of Margaret Thatcher," published in Human Events - The National Conservative Weekly, (Potomac, Maryland: Human Events Publishing, Inc., 7811 Montrose Road, Potomac, MD, 20854, 1-800-787-7557; Eagle Publishing, Inc.), Mar. 29, 1996, Vol. 52, No. 12, pp. 12-14.
OCTOBER 14. Penn, William. The World Book Encyclopedia, 18 vols. (Chicago, IL: Field Enterprises, Inc., 1957; W.F. Quarrie & Co., 8 vols., 1917; World Book, Inc., 22 vols., 1989), Vol. 13, pp. 6181-6183, 6192-6195. William Penn, From his writing No Cross, No Crown, written while imprisoned in Tower of London for 8 months. Thomas Pyrn Cope, ed., Passages from the Life and Writings of William Penn (Philadelphia: Friends Bookstore, 1882).
OCTOBER 15. Madison, James. Oct. 15, 1788. Robert Rutland, ed., The Papers of James Madison (Chicago: University of Chicago Press, 1973), Vol. VIII, p. 293. Senate Confirmation Hearings of Clarence Thomas, Sept. 10, 1991. http://www.issues2000.org/Court/Clarence_Thomas_Government_Reform.htm
OCTOBER 16. Brown, John. Statement by John Brown. Richard O. Boyer, The Legend of John Brown (NY: Alfred A. Knopf, 1973), p. 314. Peter Marshall & David Manuel, From Sea to Shining Sea (Old Tappan, N.J.: Fleming H. Revell Co., 1986), p. 402.

OCTOBER 17. Washington, George. Oct. 18, 1777, in communicating to his brother, John Augustine Washington, the capitulation of British General Burgoyne's army at Saratoga. Jared Sparks, ed., The Writings of George Washington 12 vols. (Boston: American Stationer's Co., 1837; NY: F. Andrew's, 1834-1847), Vol. V, p. 103. William J. Johnson, George Washington - The Christian (St. Paul, MN: William J. Johnson, Merriam Park, Feb. 23, 1919; Nashville, T: Abingdon Press, 1919; reprinted Milford, MI: Mott Media, 1976; reprinted Arlington Heights, IL: Christian Liberty Press, 502 West Euclid Ave., Arlington Heights, IL., 60004, 1992), p. 100.

OCTOBER 18. Winslow, Edward. Young's Chronicles, p. 350. Peter Marshall & David Manuel, The Glory of America (Bloomington, MN: Garborg's Heart'N Home, Inc., 1991), 10.18.

OCTOBER 19. Washington, George. Oct. 20, 1781, order after the capitulation of Yorktown. Horace W. Smith, Orderly Book of the Siege of Yorktown (1865), p, 47. William J. Johnson, George Washington - The Christian (St. Paul, MN: William J. Johnson, Merriam Park, Feb. 23, 1919; Nashville, TN: Abingdon Press, 1919; reprinted Milford, MI: Mott Media, 1976; reprinted Arlington Heights, IL: Christian Liberty Press, 502 West Euclid Ave., Arlington Heights, IL., 60004, 1992), p. 134. William Barclay Allen, ed., George Washington - A Collection (Indianapolis: Liberty Classics, Liberty Fund, Inc., 7440 N. Shadeland, Indianapolis, IN 46250, 1988; based almost entirely on materials from The Writings of George Washington from the original manuscript sources, 1745-1799/ John Clement Fitzpatrick, p. 198. John Clement Fitzpatrick, ed., The Writings of George Washington, from the Original Manuscript Sources 1749-1799, 39 vols. (Washington, D.C.: U.S. Government Printing Office, 1931-1944).

OCTOBER 20. Hoover, Herbert Clark. "Our Christian Heritage," Letter from Plymouth Rock (Marlborough, NH: The Plymouth Rock Foundation), p. 7.

OCTOBER 21. Nelson, Horatio. Oct. 21, 1805, his dying words. The World Book Encyclopedia, 18 vols. (Chicago, IL: Field Enterprises, Inc., 1957; W.F. Quarrie & Co., 8 vols., 1917; World Book, Inc., 22 vols., 1989), Vol. 12, p. 5495.

OCTOBER 22. Texas, Declaration of Independence of. Mar. 2, 1836, in General Convention at the Town of Washington. Printed by Baker & Bordens, San Felipe de Austin. Historical Documents Co., (8 North Preston Street, Philadelphia, Pa. 19104), 1977.

OCTOBER 23. Wilson, Woodrow. Oct. 23, 1913, Proclamation of a National Day of Thanksgiving & Prayer. A Compilation of the Messages & Papers of the Presidents 20 vols. (NY: Bureau of National Literature, Inc., prepared under direction of the Joint Committee on Printing, of the House & Senate, pursuant to an Act of the 52nd Congress of the United States, 1893, 1923), Vol. XVI, p. 7902-7903.

OCTOBER 24. Romulo, Carlos Pea. General of the Philippines, quoted by President Ronald Reagan, Feb. 2, 1984, at a National Prayer Breakfast. David R. Shepherd, ed., Ronald Reagan: In God I Trust (Wheaton, IL: Tyndale House Publishers, Inc., 1984), pp. 73-75.

OCTOBER 25. Cleveland, Grover. Oct. 25, 1887, Proclamation of a National Day of Thanksgiving & Prayer. James D. Richardson (U.S. Representative from Tennessee), ed., A Compilation of the Messages & Papers of the Presidents 1789-1897, 10 vols. (Washington, D.C.: U.S. Government Printing Office, published by Authority of Congress, 1897, 1899; Washington, D.C.: Bureau of National Literature & Art, 1789-1902, 11 vols., 1907, 1910), Vol. 8, pp. 571-572.

OCTOBER 26. Boston Tea Party. 1774, the Provincial Congress of Massachusetts gave charge to the Minutemen of the Massachusetts Militia by the Provincial Congress of Massachusetts. Richard Frothingham, Rise of the Republic of the United States (Boston: Little, Brown & Co., 1872), p. 393.

OCTOBER 27. Roosevelt, Theodore. 1909. Noah Brooks, Men of Achievement-Statesmen (NY: Charles Scribner's Sons, 1904), p. 317. George Grant, Third Time Around (Brentwood, TN: Wolgemuth & Hyatt, Inc., 1991), p. 118. George Grant, The Quick & the Dead (Wheaton, IL: Crossway, 1981), p. 134. John Eidsmoe, Columbus & Cortez, Conquerors for Christ (Green Forest, AR: New Leaf Press, 1992), pp. 296-297.

OCTOBER 28. Bartholdi, Frederic Auguste. Statement as sculptor of the Statue of Liberty. Frederic Auguste Bartholdi, The Statue of Liberty Enlightening the World. (NY: North American Review, Published for the benefit of the Pedestal Fund, 1885).

OCTOBER 29. Hoover, Herbert Clark. Oct. 18, 1931, in an address beginning a nation-wide drive to aid the private relief agencies during the Great Depression. Herbert Hoover, The Memoirs of Herbert Hoover - The Great Depression 1929-1941 (NY: The MacMillan Co., 1952), p. 151.

OCTOBER 30. Adams, John. to Thomas Jefferson. R.K. Arnold, ed., Adams to Jefferson/Jefferson to Adams-A Dialogue from their Correspondence (San Francisco: Jerico Press, 1975), pp. 330-1.

OCTOBER 31. Luther, Martin. Statement. Robert Flood, The Rebirth of America (Philadelphia: Arthur S. DeMoss Foundation, 1986), p. 127.

NOVEMBER 1. Adams, John. Nov. 1800, in a letter to his wife, Abigail Adams. John Adams, John Adam's Prayer (Washington, D.C.: White House Collection). John Bartlett, Bartlett's Familiar Quotations (Boston: Little, Brown & Co., 1855, 1980), p. 382. Charles Fadiman, ed., The American Treasury (NY: Harper & Brothers, Publishers, 1955), p. 317.

NOVEMBER 2. 1783, Washington, George. Farewell Orders to the Armies of the United States issued from Rock Hill, near Princeton. Jared Sparks, ed., The Writings of George Washington 12 vols. (Boston: American Stationer's Co., 1837; NY: F. Andrew's, 1834-1847), Vol. VIII, pp. 492-496. William J. Johnson, George Washington - The Christian (St. Paul, MN: William J. Johnson, Merriam Park, Feb. 23, 1919; Nashville, TN: Abingdon Press, 1919; reprinted Milford, MI: Mott Media, 1976; reprinted Arlington Heights, IL: Christian Liberty Press, 502 West Euclid Ave., Arlington Heights, IL., 60004, 1992), pp. 143-144. William Barclay Allen, ed., George Washington - A Collection (Indianapolis: Liberty Classics, Liberty Fund, Inc., 7440 N. Shadeland, Indianapolis, IN 46250, 1988; based almost entirely on materials reproduced from The Writings of George Washington from the original manuscript sources, 1745-1799/John Clement Fitzpatrick, editor), pp. 266-271. John Clement Fitzpatrick, ed., The Writings of George Washington, from the Original Manuscript Sources 1749-1799, 39 vols. (Washington, D.C.: U.S. Government Printing Office, 1931-1944). Saxe Commins, ed., The Basic Writings of George Washington (NY: Random House, 1948), complete work, pp. 499-502. Charles Wallis, ed., Our American Heritage (NY: Harper & Row, Publishers, Inc., 1970), p. 130.

NOVEMBER 3. Coolidge, (John) Calvin. Nov. 3, 1924, in a Radio Address from the White House to the Nation. Calvin Coolidge, Foundations of the Republic - Speeches & Addresses (NY: Charles Scribner's Sons, 1926), pp. 173-179.

NOVEMBER 4. Carroll, Charles. Nov. 4, 1800, in a letter to James McHenry. Bernard C. Steiner, The Life & Correspondence of James McHenry (Cleveland: The Burrows Brothers, 1907), 475. Cathy Adams, "The Faith of Our Founding Fathers - A Tribute to Our Country's Foundation " (Dallas, TX: Texas Eagle Forum, P.O. Box 872098, 75287; 214-250-0734, 214-380-2853 Fax), Vol. 2, No. 6, p. 1.

NOVEMBER 5. 1775(circa),, Adams, Abigail, in a letter to her friend, Mercy Warren. Warren-Adams Letters, 1743-1777 (Massachusetts Historical Society Collections), Vol. I, p. 72. L.H. Butterfield, ed., Adams Family Correspondence (Cambridge, MA: The Belknap Press of Harvard University Press, 1963), Vol. I, p. 323. Edmund Fuller & David E. Green, God in the White House - The Faiths of American Presidents (NY: Crown Publishers, Inc., 1968), p. 22. Jan Payne Pierce, The Patriot Primer III (Fletcher, NC: New Puritan Library, Inc., 1987), p. 44.

NOVEMBER 6. Williams, George. Young Men's Christian Association. Stephen Abbott Northrop, D.D., A Cloud of Witnesses (Portland, OR: American Heritage Ministries, 1987; Mantle Ministries, 228 Still Ridge, Bulverde, TX), p. 508.

NOVEMBER 7. Graham, William Franklin "Billy ". May 2, 1996, in his speech titled "The Hope for America," delivered upon his acceptance of the Congressional Gold Medal, presented during the celebration of the National Day of Prayer, Washington, D.C. (Compliments of Billy Graham Assoc., A. Larry Ross, Director of Media/Public Relations, 4835 LBJ Freeway, Suite 800, Dallas, TX, 75244, USA, 214-387-0700, Fax 214-387-0755.)

NOVEMBER 8. Lewis & Clark Expedition 1804, Reuben Gold Thwaites, based on journals kept by Captains Meriwether Lewis & William Clark, "Rocky Mountain Explorations," (D. Appleton & Co.) The World Book Encyclopedia (Chicago: Field Enterprises, Inc., 1957), Vol. 10, pages 4393-4395. http://www.pbs.org/lewisandclark/index.html http://www.lewis-clark.org/index.html

NOVEMBER 9. Eisenhower, Dwight David. Nov. 9, 1954, to the first National Conference on the Spiritual Foundation of American Democracy in a luncheon meeting at the Sheraton-Carlton Hotel in Washington, DC. Public Papers of the Presidents - Dwight D. Eisenhower, 1954 - Containing Public Messages, Speeches, & Statements of the President, Jan. 1 to Dec. 31, 1954 (Washington, DC: U.S. Government Printing Office, 1960), Item 327, p. 1029-31.

NOVEMBER 10. Livingstone, David. As described by Henry Morton Stanley. Stephen Abbott Northrop, D.D., A Cloud of Witnesses (Portland, OR: American Heritage Ministries, 1987; Mantle Ministries, 228 Still Ridge, Bulverde, TX), p. 287.

NOVEMBER 11. Harding, Warren Gamaliel. Nov. 4, 1921, Proclamation declaring Armistice Day a legal public holiday. A Compilation of the Messages & Papers of the Presidents 20 vols. (NY: Bureau of National Literature, Inc., prepared under the direction of the Joint Committee on Printing, of the House & Senate, pursuant to an Act of the 52nd Congress of the United States, 1893, 1923), Vol. XVIII, pp. 9005-9006. Tomb of the Unknown Soldier. No. 11, 1932, inscription on back panel. Thomas Vorwerk, The Unknown Soldier (Springfield, MO: Pentecostal Evangel, Jun. 28, 1992), p. 12.

NOVEMBER 12. Bradford, William. Nov. 12, 1620, The History of Plymouth Plantation 1608-1650 (Boston, MA: Massachusetts Historical Society, 1856; Boston, MA: Wright & Potter Printing Co., 1898, 1901, from the Original Manuscript, Library of Congress Rare Book Collection, Washington, D.C.; rendered in Modern English, Harold Paget, 1909; NY: Russell & Russell, 1968; NY: Random House, Inc., Modern Library College edition, 1981; San Antonio, TX: American Heritage Classics, Mantle Ministries, 228 Still Ridge, Bulverde, TX, 1988), ch. 9, p. 64. John Bartlett, Bartlett's Familiar Quotations (Boston: Little, Brown & Co., 1855, 1980), p. 265.

NOVEMBER 13. Sergeant George Hutchings of the First Battalion Fifth Marine Division, Charlie Company, recipient of the Purple Heart. George Hutchings, 400 Tumulty, Ballwin, MO 63021, (636) 394-0310, georgeeaglewings@aol.com.

NOVEMBER 14. Washington, Booker Taliaferro. Up From Slavery (1904). Bob Cutshall, More Light for the Day (Minneapolis, MN: Northwestern Products, Inc., 1991), 1.20. Perry Tanksley, To Love is to Give (Jackson, MS: Allgood Books, Box 1329; Parthenon Press, 201 8th Ave., S., Nashville, TN, 1972), p. 43.

NOVEMBER 15. Witherspoon, John. May 17, 1776, in his sermon titled, "The Dominion of Providence over the Passions of Men" delivered at The College of New Jersey (Princeton). Varnum Lansing Collins, President Witherspoon (NY: Arno Press & The New York Times, 1969), I:197-98. John Eidsmoe, Christianity & the Constitution - The Faith of Our Founding Fathers (Grand Rapids, MI: Baker Book House, A Mott Media Book, 1987, 6th printing 1993), p. 85. William W. Woodward, The Works of the Rev. John Witherspoon (Philadelphia: 1802), Vol. III, p. 46. Peter Marshall & David Manuel, The Light & the Glory (Old Tappan, NJ: Fleming H. Revell Co., 1977), p. 296. Stephen McDowell & Mark Beliles, "The Providential Perspective" (Charlottesville, VA: The Providence Foundation, P.O. Box 6759, Charlottesville, Va. 22906, Jan. 1994), Vol. 9, No. 1, p. 7. William Safire, ed., Lend Me Your Ears - Great Speeches in History (NY: W.W. Norton & Co. 1992), p. 429.

NOVEMBER 16. Smith, Samuel Francis. 1832, patriotic hymn, My Country 'Tis Of Thee. Patriotic Anthology, p. 480. Peter Marshall & David Manuel, The Glory of America (Bloomington, MN: Garborg's Heart'N Home, Inc., 1991), 2.2. Hugo Frey, ed., America Sings (NY: Robbins Music Corporation, 1935), p. 104. D.P. Diffine, Ph.D., One Nation Under God - How Close a Separation? (Searcy, AR: Harding University, Belden Center for Private Enterprise Education, 6th edition, 1992), p. 11. http://en2.wikipedia.org/wiki/God_Save_the_Queen

NOVEMBER 17. Elizabeth I, Queen of England. Speaking to her ladies regarding her epitaph. John Bartlett, Bartlett's Familiar Quotations (Boston: Little, Brown & Co., 1855, 1980), p. 164.

NOVEMBER 18. Watts, J.C. Feb. 4, 1997, Tuesday, Library of Congress, Washington, D.C., in the televised Republican response to President Clinton's State of the Union Address. Arthur, Chester Alan. Sept. 22, 1881, in a Proclamation of a National Day of Humiliation & Mourning. James D. Richardson, ed., A Compilation of the Messages & Papers of the Presidents 1789-1897, 10 vols. (Washington, D.C.: U.S. Government Printing Office, published by Authority of Congress, 1897, 1899; Washington, D.C.: Bureau of National Literature & Art, 1789-1902, 11 vols., 1907, 1910), Vol. VIII, p. 34.

NOVEMBER 19. 1863, Lincoln, Abraham, Gettysburg Address, commemorating the field where 50,000 men died in the Battle of Gettysburg, Jul. 1-3, 1863. Engraved in stone in the Lincoln Memorial in Washington, D.C. John Bartlett, Bartlett's Familiar Quotations (Boston: Little, Brown & Co., 1855, 1980), p. 523. Charles W. Eliot, LL.D., ed., American Historical Documents 1000-1904 (NY: P.F. Collier & Son Co., The Harvard Classics, 1910), Vol. 43, p. 441. The World Book Encyclopedia, 18 vols. (Chicago, IL: Field Enterprises, Inc., 1957; W.F. Quarrie & Co., 8 vols., 1917; World Book, Inc., 22 vols., 1989), Vol. 7, p. 2982. Henry Steele Commager, ed., Documents of American History, 2 vols. (NY: F.S. Crofts & Co., 1934; Appleton-Century-Crofts, Inc., 1948, 6th edition, 1958; Englewood Cliffs, NJ: Prentice Hall, Inc., 9th edition, 1973), p. 228. Frederick C. Packard, Jr., ed., Are You an American? - Great Americans Speak (NY: Charles Scribner's Sons, 1951), pp. 32-33. Roy P. Basler, ed., The Collected Works of Abraham Lincoln, 9 vols. (New Brunswick, NJ: Rutgers University Press, 1953), Vol. 1. Daniel Boorstin, Jr., ed., An American Primer (Chicago: U. of Chicago Press, 1966), p. 418. Lillian W. Kay, ed., The Ground on Which We Stand - Basic Documents of American History (NY: Franklin Watts., Inc, 1969), pp. 197-198.

NOVEMBER 20. Byrd, Robert. Jul. 27, 1962, in a message delivered in Congress by United States Senator from West Virginia two days after the Supreme Court declared prayer in schools unconstitutional. Robert Flood, The Rebirth of America (Philadelphia: Arthur S. DeMoss Foundation, 1986), pp. 66-69.

NOVEMBER 21. Dwight, Timothy. Jul. 4, 1798, as president of Yale College, in an address delivered at New Haven, titled, "The Duty of Americans, at the Present Crisis, Illustrated in a Discourse, Preached on the Fourth of Jul., 1798." (#Ital original). The Annals of America, 20 vols. (Chicago, IL: Encyclopedia Britannica, 1968, 1977), Vol. 4, pp. 33-39. Peter Marshall & David Manuel, The Glory of America (Bloomington, MN: Garborg's Heart 'N Home, Inc., 1991), 1.11. Peter Marshall & David Manuel, From Sea to Shining Sea (Old Tappan, NJ: Fleming H.

Revell Co., 1986). Barton, Bruce. Statement. Tryon Edwards, D.D., The New Dictionary of Thoughts - A Cyclopedia of Quotations (Garden City, NY: Hanover House, 1852; revised & enlarged by C.H. Catrevas, Ralph Emerson Browns & Jonathan Edwards descendent, along with Tryon, of Jonathan Edwards (1703-1758), president of Princeton, 1891; The Standard Book Co., 1955, 1963), pp. 46-47.

NOVEMBER 22. Kennedy, John Fitzgerald. Nov. 22, 1963, the conclusion to the speech he had prepared to give at the Dallas Trade Mart, before he was assassinated. Congressional Record, 88th Congress, 1st Session, pp. 22823-22824. The Annals of America, 20 vols. (Chicago, IL: Encyclopedia Britannica, 1968), Vol. XVIII, p. 201. Peter Marshall & David Manuel, The Glory of America (Bloomington, MN: Garborg's Heart'N Home, Inc., 1991), 11.22.

NOVEMBER 23. Pierce, Franklin. Mar. 4, 1853, Inaugural Address, delivered on the steps of the Capitol building. James D. Richardson (U.S. Representative from Tennessee), ed., A Compilation of the Messages & Papers of the Presidents 1789-1897, 10 vols. (Washington, D.C.: U.S. Government Printing Office, published by Authority of Congress, 1897, 1899; Washington, D.C.: Bureau of National Literature & Art, 1789-1902, 11 vols., 1907, 1910), Vol. 5, pp. 197-203. Benjamin Franklin Morris, The Christian Life & Character of the Civil Institutions of the United States (Philadelphia: George W. Childs, 1864), p. 609. Inaugural Addresses of the Presidents of the United States - From George Washington 1789 to Richard Milhous Nixon 1969 (Washington, D.C.: U.S. Government Printing Office; 91st Congress, 1st Session, House Document 91-142, 1969), pp. 103-109. Davis Newton Lott, The Inaugural Addresses of the American Presidents (NY: Holt, Rinehart & Winston, 1961), pp. 104, 107, 108. Charles E. Rice, The Supreme Court & Public Prayer (NY: Fordham University Press, 1964), pp. 183-184. Arthur Schlesinger, ed., The Chief Executive (NY: Chelsea House Pub., 1965), pp. 113-114, 117, 118. Benjamin Weiss, God in American History: A Documentation of America's Religious Heritage (Grand Rapids, MI: Zondervan, 1966), p. 86. Willard Cantelon, Money Master of the World (Plainfield, NJ: Logos International, 1976), p. 120. J. Michael Sharman, J.D., Faith of the Fathers (Culpepper, Virginia: Victory Pub., 1995), pp. 53-54.

NOVEMBER 24. Knox, John. Inscription on the Reformation Monument in Geneva, Switzerland. John Bartlett, Bartlett's Familiar Quotations (Boston: Little, Brown & Co., 1855, 1980), p. 162.

NOVEMBER 25. Truth, Sojourner. Page Smith, The Nation Comes of Age (NY: McGraw-Hill Book Co., 1981), Vol. 4, p. 660. Peter Marshall & David Manuel, The Glory of America (Bloomington, MN: Garborg's Heart'N Home, Inc., 1991), 11.26.

NOVEMBER 26. Washington, George. Oct. 3, 1789, from the city of New York, President issued a Proclamation of a National Day of Thanksgiving. Jared Sparks, ed., The Writings of George Washington 12 vols. (Boston: American Stationer's Co., 1837, NY: F. Andrew's, 1834-1847), Vol. XII, p. 119. James D. Richardson (U.S. Representative from Tennessee), ed., A Compilation of the Messages & Papers of the Presidents 1789-1897, 10 vols. (Washington, D.C.: U.S. Government Printing Office, published by Authority of Congress, 1897, 1899; Washington, D.C.: Bureau of National Literature & Art, 1789-1902, 11 vols., 1907, 1910), Vol. 1, p. 64. William J. Johnson, George Washington - The Christian (St. Paul, MN: William J. Johnson, Merriam Park, Feb. 23, 1919; Nashville, TN: Abingdon Press, 1919; reprinted Milford, MI: Mott Media, 1976; reprinted Arlington Heights, IL: Christian Liberty Press, 502 West Euclid Ave., Arlington Heights, IL., 60004, 1992), pp. 172-174. William Barclay Allen, ed., George Washington - A Collection (Indianapolis: Liberty Classics, Liberty Fund, Inc., 7440 N. Shadeland, Indianapolis, IN 46250, 1988; based almost entirely on materials reproduced from The Writings of George Washington from the original manuscript sources, 1745-1799/John Clement Fitzpatrick, editor), pp. 534-353. John Clement Fitzpatrick, ed., The Writings of George Washington, from the Original Manuscript Sources 1749-1799, 39 vols. (Washington, D.C.: U.S. Government Printing Office, 1931-1944). John F. Schroeder, ed., Maxims of Washington (Mt. Vernon: Mt. Vernon Ladies' Association, 1942), pp. 275, 287. Anson Phelps Stokes & Leo Pfeffer, Church & State in the United States, 3 vols. (NY: Harper & Brothers, 1950), p. 87. Pat Robertson, America's Dates with Destiny (Nashville: Thomas Nelson Publishers, 1986), p. 112. Tim LaHaye, Faith of Our Founding Fathers (Brentwood, TN: Wolgemuth & Hyatt, Publishers, Inc., 1987), pp. 104-106. John Eidsmoe, Christianity & the Constitution - The Faith of Our Founding Fathers (Grand Rapids, MI: Baker Book House, A Mott Media Book, 1987, 6th printing 1993), p. 118. Gary DeMar, The Biblical Worldview (Atlanta, GA: An American Vision Publication - American Vision, Inc., 1992), Vol. 8, No. 12, p. 8. D.P. Diffine, Ph.D., One Nation Under God - How Close a Separation? (Searcy, AR: Harding University, Belden Center for Private Enterprise Education, 6th edition, 1992), p. 9. Gary DeMar, America's Christian History: The Untold Story (Atlanta, GA: American Vision Publishers, Inc., 1993), pp. 76-77.

NOVEMBER 27. Truman, Harry S. Nov. 29, 1948, in a personal letter to Dr. Chaim Weizmann, President of the State of Israel. Harry S. Truman, Memoirs by Harry S. Truman - Volume Two: Years of Trial & Hope (Garden City, NY: Doubleday & Co., Inc., 1956), pp. 168-169.

NOVEMBER 28. Warren, James. Jun. 16, 1775, in a Resolution of the Provincial Congress of Massachusetts, James Warren, president. Copied from original, printed courtesy Essex Institute, Salem, Massachusetts. Verna M. Hall, The Christian History of the American Revolution (San Francisco, CA: Foundation For American Christian Education, 1976), p. 410.

NOVEMBER 29. Lewis, "C.S." Clive Staples. 1952, in: Mere Christianity. Carroll E. Simcox, comp., 4400 Quotations for Christian Communicators (Grand Rapids, MI: Baker Book House, 1991), p. 207.

NOVEMBER 30. Twain, Mark. Innocents Abroad, or the New Pilgrim's Progress, p. 513. Stephen Abbott Northrop, D.D., A Cloud of Witnesses (Portland, OR: American Heritage Ministries, 1987; Mantle Ministries, 228 Still Ridge, Bulverde, TX), pp. 88-89.

DECEMBER 1. Lincoln, Abraham. Dec. 1, 1862, in concluding his Second Annual Message to Congress. John Bartlett, Bartlett's Familiar Quotations (Boston: Little, Brown & Co., 1863, 1980), pp. 520-524. John G. Nicolay & John Hay, eds., The Complete Works of Abraham Lincoln: Speeches, Letters & State Papers (1905), Vol. V, p. 537. James D. Richardson (U.S. Representative from Tennessee), ed., A Compilation of the Messages & Papers of the Presidents 1789-1897, 10 vols. (Washington, D.C.: U.S. Government Printing Office, published by Authority of Congress, 1897, 1899; Washington, D.C.: Bureau of National Literature & Art, 1789-1902, 11 vols., 1907, 1910), Vol. VI, p. 142. Pat Robertson, America's Dates With Destiny (Nashville, TN: Thomas Nelson Publishers, 1986), p. 157. Peter Marshall & David Manuel, The Glory of America (Bloomington, MN: Garborg's Heart 'N Home, Inc., 1991), 12.1.

DECEMBER 2. Cortez, Hernando. 1519, to the Tabascan tribe in Mexico. Francisco Lopez de Gomara, Cortez: The Life of the Conqueror by His Secretary (Berkeley: U. of California Press, 1552, 1964), ch. 23, p. 51. John Eidsmoe, Columbus & Cortez, Conquerors for Christ (Green Forest, AR: New Leaf Press, 1992), p. 173.

DECEMBER 3. Jefferson, Thomas. Dec. 3, 1803, Treaty with the Kaskaskia Indians, 1806 with the Wyandotte Indians, & 1807 Cherokee Indians. Costanzo, Federal Aid to Education & Religious Liberty, 36 U. of Det. L.J., 1, 15 (1958). Charles E. Rice, The Supreme Court & Public Prayer (NY: Fordham University Press, 1964), p. 64. Daniel L. Driesbach, Real Threat & Mere Shadow: Religious Liberty & the First Amendment (Westchester, IL: Crossway Books, 1987), p. 127. Richard Peters, ed., The Public Statutes at Large of the United States of America (Boston: Charles C. Little & James Brown, 1846), A Treaty Between the United States & the Kaskaskia Tribe of Indians, 23 Dec. 1803, Art. III, Vol. VII, pp. 78-79., Treaty with the Wyandots, etc., 1805, Vol. VII, Art. IV, p. 88, Treaty with the Cherokees, 1806, vol. VII, Art. II, p. 102. Robert L. Cord, Separation of Church & State (NY: Lambeta Press, 1982), p. 39. "A Treaty Between the United States of America & the Kaskaskian Tribe of Indians." 7 Stat. 78-9 (1846). Daniel L. Driesbach, Real Threat & Mere Shadow - Religious Liberty & the First Amendment (Westchester, IL: Crossway Books, 1987), p. 127.

DECEMBER 4. Father Jacques Marquette. Dec. 4, 1674. Founded settlement which was to become Chicago. The Jesuit Relations, Vol. LIX. Henry Steele Commager & Allan Nevins, The Heritage of America - Readings in American History (Boston: D.C. Heath & Co., 1949), pp. 14-19. World Book Encyclopedia - 18 Volumes (Chicago: Field Enterprises, Inc., 1957),Vol. 11, p. 4817.

DECEMBER 5. Williamson, Hugh. John Neal, Trinity College Historical Society Papers, Series 13 (NY: AMS Press, 1915), pp. 62-63. Tim LaHaye, Faith of Our Founding Fathers (Brentwood, TN: Wolgemuth & Hyatt, Publishers, Inc., 1987), p. 182.

DECEMBER 6. Saint Nicholas. Erik Brady, "St. Nick," USA Today, Dec. 23, 1997, pp. 1A-2A. Alberto Carosa, "How the Nordic Figure of Father Christmas bounced back home to the south," The Wanderer, St. Paul, MN, Dec. 25, 1997, Vol. 130, No. 52.

DECEMBER 7. Franklin D. Roosevelt's Pearl Harbor Speech (Dec. 8, 1941), http://dizzy.library.arizona.edu/images/USS_Arizona/links.shtml To the Congress of the United States: Yesterday, Dec. 7, 1941 - a date which will live in infamy - the United States of America was suddenly and deliberately attacked by naval and air forces of the Empire of Japan. The United States was at peace with that nation and, at the solicitation of Japan, was still in conversation with the government and its emperor looking toward the maintenance of peace in the Pacific. Indeed, one hour after Japanese air squadrons had commenced bombing in Oahu, the Japanese ambassador to the United States and his colleagues delivered to the Secretary of State a formal reply to a recent American message. While this reply stated that it seemed useless to continue the existing diplomatic negotiations, it contained no threat or hint of war or armed attack. It will be recorded that the distance of Hawaii from Japan makes it obvious that the attack was deliberately planned many days or even weeks ago. During the intervening time, the Japanese government has deliberately sought to deceive the United States by false statements and expressions of hope for continued peace. The attack yesterday on the Hawaiian Islands has caused severe damage to American naval and military forces. Very many American lives have been lost. In addition, American ships have been reported torpedoed on the high seas between

San Francisco and Honolulu. Yesterday, the Japanese government also launched an attack against Malaya. Last night, Japanese forces attacked Hong Kong. Last night, Japanese forces attacked Guam. Last night, Japanese forces attacked the Philippine Islands. Last night, the Japanese attacked Wake Island. This morning, the Japanese attacked Midway Island. Japan has, therefore, undertaken a surprise offensive extending throughout the Pacific area. The facts of yesterday speak for themselves. The people of the United States have already formed their opinions and well understand the implications to the very life and safety of our nation. As commander in chief of the Army and Navy, I have directed that all measures be taken for our defense. Always will we remember the character of the onslaught against us. No matter how long it may take us to overcome this premeditated invasion, the American people in their righteous might will win through to absolute victory. I believe I interpret the will of the Congress and of the people when I assert that we will not only defend ourselves to the uttermost, but will make very certain that this form of treachery shall never endanger us again. Hostilities exist. There is no blinking at the fact that that our people, our territory and our interests are in grave danger. With confidence in our armed forces - with the unbounding determination of our people - we will gain the inevitable triumph - so help us God. I ask that the Congress declare that since the unprovoked and dastardly attack by Japan on Sunday, Dec. 7, a state of war has existed between the U.S. and the Japanese empire.

DECEMBER 8. Lincoln, Abraham. Dec. 8, 1863, Mar. 26, 1864, in Proclamations of Amnesty & Pardon to the participants of the Confederate insurrection; also Sept. 7, 1867, May 29, 1865, in Proclamations of Amnesty & Pardon issued by President Andrew Johnson. Charles W. Eliot, LL.D., ed., American Historical Documents 1000-1904 (NY: P.F. Collier & Son Co., The Harvard Classics, 1910), Vol. 43, p. 443. James D. Richardson, ed., A Compilation of the Messages & Papers of the Presidents 1789-1897, 10 vols. (Washington, D.C.: U.S. Government Printing Office, published by Authority of Congress, 1897, 1899; Washington, D.C.: Bureau of National Literature & Art, 1789-1902, 11 vols., 1907, 1910), Vol. VI, pp. 213-215, 310-311, 548-549.

DECEMBER 9. Harrison, Benjamin. Dec. 9, 1891, Third Annual Message. James D. Richardson (U.S. Rep.TN), ed., A Compilation of the Messages & Papers of the Presidents 1789-1897, 10 vols. (Washington, D.C.: U.S. Government Printing Office, published by Authority of Congress, 1897, 1899; Washington, D.C.: Bureau of National Literature & Art, 1789-1902, 11 vols., 1907, 1910), Vol. IX, pp. 188, 198.

DECEMBER 10. Grant, Ulysses S. Dec. 1, 1873, Fifth Annual Message. James D. Richardson, ed., A Compilation of the Messages and Papers of the Presidents 1789-1897, 10 vols. (Washington, D.C.: U.S. Government Printing Office, 1897, 1899; Washington, D.C.: Bureau of National Literature & Art, 1789-1902, 11 vols., 1907, 1910), Vol. 7, p. 240. U.S. Congress. Apr. 20, 1898, Joint Resolution recognizing the independence of Cuba and declaring war with Spain. Charles W. Eliot, LL. D., ed., American Historical Documents - 1000-1904 (New York: The Harvard Classics, P.F. Collier & Son Co., 1910), Vol. 43, p. 467. McKinley, William. Jul. 6, 1898, Proclamation of a National Day of Thanksgiving. James D. Richardson, ed., A Compilation of the Messages and Papers of the Presidents 1789-1897, 10 vols. (Washington, D.C.: U.S. Government Printing Office, 1899; Washington, D.C.: Bureau of National Literature and Art, 1789-1902, 11 vols., 1907, 1910), Vol. X, pp. 213-214. A Compilation of the Messages and Papers of the Presidents 20 vols. (New York: Bureau of National Literature, Inc., 1893, 1923), Vol. XIII, pp. 6573-6574.

DECEMBER 11. Solzhenitsyn, Alexander. Jun. 30, 1975, while speaking in Washington, D.C. Society, Nov.-Dec. 1975. The Annals of America, 20 vols. (Chicago, IL: Encyclopedia Britannica, 1968), Vol. 20, pp. 174-182.

DECEMBER 12. Pennsylvania State Constitution 1776, Frame of Government, Chapter 2, Section 10. The Constitutions of the Several Independent States of America (Boston: Norman & Bowen, 1785), p. 81. S.E. Morison, ed., Sources & Documents Illustrating the American Revolution 1764-1788 & the Formation of the Federal Constitution (NY: Oxford University Press, 1923), p. 166. Benjamin Franklin Morris, The Christian Life & Character of the Civil Institutions of the United States (Philadelphia, PA: L. Johnson & Co., 1863; George W. Childs, 1864), p. 233.

DECEMBER 13. Brooks, Phillips. 1867, wrote his famous song, O Little Town of Bethlehem. John Bartlett, Bartlett's Familiar Quotations (Boston: Little, Brown & Co., 1855, 1980), p. 619.

DECEMBER 14. Washington, George. Saturday, Dec. 14, 1799, at about eleven o'clock in the evening, in speaking his final words to his secretary, Tobias Lear. Mason L. Weems, The Life of General Washington (1808), p. 170. William J. Johnson, George Washington - The Christian (St. Paul, MN: William J. Johnson, Merriam Park, Feb. 23, 1919; Nashville, TN: Abingdon Press, 1919; reprinted Milford, MI: Mott Media, 1976; reprinted Arlington Heights, IL: Christian Liberty Press, 502 West Euclid Ave., Arlington Heights, IL, 60004, 1992), p. 234. D. James Kennedy, "The Faith of George Washington" (Fort Lauderdale, Florida: Coral Ridge Ministries), p. 10.

DECEMBER 15. 1791, First Amendment, U.S. Constitution. Henry B. Watson, The Key to the Constitution of the

United States (Alexandria, VA: Patriotic Education Inc., 1988), p. 34. Jan. 23, 1808, letter to Samuel Miller, Thomas Jefferson. Jefferson Writings, Merrill D. Peterson, ed., (NY: Literary Classics of the United States, Inc., 1984), pp. 1186-1187. Thomas Jefferson Randolph, ed., Memoirs, Correspondence, and Private Papers of Thomas Jefferson, 4 vols, (London & Charlottesville, VA 1829, Vol. IV, p. 106.

DECEMBER 16. Boston Tea Party. 1773, in a unanimous declaration by the men of Marlborough, Massachusetts. Charles E. Kistler, This Nation Under God (Boston: Richard G. Badger, The Gorham Press, 1924), p. 56.

DECEMBER 17. Beethoven, Ludwig van. Statement recorded by Nathan Haskell Dole, A Score of Musical Composers. Stephen Abbott Northrop, D.D., A Cloud of Witnesses (Portland, OR: American Heritage Ministries, 1987; Mantle Ministries, 228 Still Ridge, Bulverde, TX), p. 29. U.S. Supreme Court. 1948, Justice Frankfurter, McCollum v. Board of Education of School District Number 71, 333 U.S. 203, 236 (1948). Elizabeth Ridenour, Public Schools - Bible Curriculum (Greensboro, N.C.: National Council On Bible Curriculum, 1996), p. 13, 14-15, 28, 42. Robert K. Skolrood, The National Legal Foundation, letter to National Council on the Bible Curriculum in Public Schools, Sept. 13, 1994, p. 2.

DECEMBER 18. Wesley, Charles. 1753, Hark the Herald Angels Sing. John Bartlett, Bartlett's Familiar Quotations (Boston: Little, Brown & Co., 1855, 1980), p. 350. Herbert V. Prochnow, 5100 Quotations for Speakers & Writers (Grand Rapids, MI: Baker Book House, 1992), p. 519.

DECEMBER 19. Washington, George. In a letter written from Valley Forge to John Banister, dated Apr. 21, 1778. William Barclay Allen, ed., George Washington - A Collection (Indianapolis: Liberty Classics, Liberty Fund, Inc., 7440 N. Shadeland, Indianapolis, IN 46250, 1988; based almost entirely on materials reproduced from The writings of George Washington from the original manuscript sources, 1745-1799/John Clement Fitzpatrick, editor), p. 103. John Clement Fitzpatrick, ed., The Writings of George Washington, from the Original Manuscript Sources 1749-1799, 39 vols. (Washington, D.C.: U.S. Government Printing Office, 1931-1944). Douglas S. Freeman, George Washington - A Biography vols. I-VII (NY: Charles Scribner's Sons, 1948), Vol. IV, p. 621.

DECEMBER 20. Bennett, William J., The Death of Outrage-Bill Clinton & the Assault on American Ideals (NY: Touchstone, Rockefeller Ctr, 1230 Ave. of the Americas, NY, NY 10020, 1998), p. 139.

DECEMBER 21. Newton, John. Robert Flood, The Rebirth of America Philadelphia: Arthur S. DeMoss Foundation, 1986), pp. 178-179.

DECEMBER 22. Eisenhower, Dwight. Dec. 22, 1944, "Orders of the Day" during the Battle of the Bulge. Diary, Office C-in-C, Book XIV, p. 1910. Dwight D. Eisenhower, Crusade in Europe (Garden City, NY: Doubleday & Co., Inc., 1948), p. 355.

DECEMBER 23. Paine, Thomas. Dec. 23, 1776. The American Crisis. "Common Sense" Thomas Paine - 1776 (Reston, VA: Intercessors For America, Jul./Aug. 1993), Vol. 20, No. 7/8, p. 1.

DECEMBER 24. Columbus, Christopher. Oct. 8, 10, 12, 16, 28, Nov. 6, 27, Dec. 12, 16, 22, 24, 1492, Journal of the First Voyage (El Libro de la Primera Navegacion), as recounted in Bartolome' de Las Casas' abstract, translated into English by Samuel Eliot Morison, Journals & Other Documents on the Life & Voyages of Christopher Columbus (NY: Heritage Press, 1963), pp. 65, 72. John Bartlett, Bartlett's Familiar Quotations (Boston: Little, Brown & Co., 1855, 1980), pp. 150-151. John Eidsmoe, Columbus & Cortez, Conquerors for Christ (Green Forest, AR: New Leaf Press, 1992), pp. 85-86. Bjorn Landstrom, Columbus (NY: The Macmillan Co., 1966), pp. 66-75.

DECEMBER 25. Washington, George. Mar. 9, 1781, from Newport, Rhode Island, to William Gordon. Jared Sparks, ed., The Writings of George Washington 12 vols. (Boston: American Stationer's Co., 1837; NY: F. Andrew's, 1834-1847), Vol. VII, p. 449. William J. Johnson, George Washington - The Christian (St. Paul, MN: William J. Johnson, Merriam Park, Feb. 23, 1919; Nashville, TN: Abingdon Press, 1919; reprinted Milford, MI: Mott Media, 1976; reprinted Arlington Heights, IL: Christian Liberty Press, 502 West Euclid Ave., Arlington Heights, IL., 60004, 1992), p. 133.

DECEMBER 26. Logan, John Alexander. Decoration Day, 1886, in an oration at Riverside Park in New York. Stephen Abbott Northrop, D.D., A Cloud of Witnesses (Portland, OR: American Heritage Ministries, 1987; Mantle Ministries, 228 Still Ridge, Bulverde, TX), p. 290.

DECEMBER 27. Kepler, Johann. Sir David Brewster, biography. Stephen Abbott Northrop, D.D., A Cloud of Witnesses (Portland, OR: American Heritage Ministries, 1987; Mantle Ministries, 228 Still Ridge, Bulverde, TX), p. 266. Henry M. Morris, Men of Science - Men of God (El Cajon, CA: Master Books, Creation Life Publishers, Inc., 1990), pp. 11-13.

DECEMBER 28. Wilson, Woodrow. May 11, 1918, Proclamation of a National Day of Humiliation, Prayer & Fasting. A Compilation of the Messages & Papers of the Presidents 20 vols. (NY: Bureau of National Literature, Inc., under the Joint Committee on Printing, of the House & Senate, pursuant to an Act of the 52nd Congress of the United States, 1893, 1923), Vol. XVII, pp. 8495-8496.

DECEMBER 29. Texas, State of. Aug. 27, 1845, Constitution, Preamble. Journals of the Convention, Assembled at the City of Austin on the Fourth of Jul., 1845, for the purpose of framing a Constitution for the State of Texas (Austin, TX: Miner & Cruger, Printers to the Convention, 1845; A Facsimile Reproduction of the 1845 Edition with a Preface by Mary Bell Hart, Shoal Creek Publishers, 1974), p. 338. Texas, State of. 1876, Constitution, Article I, Section 4. Charles E. Rice, The Supreme Court & Public Prayer (NY: Fordham University Press, 1964), p. 175; "Hearings, Prayers in Public Schools & Other Matters," Committee on the Judiciary, U.S. Senate (87th Cong., 2nd Sess.), 1962, pp. 268 et seq.

DECEMBER 30. Kipling, (Joseph) Rudyard. In his Ballad of East & West. Lewis C. Henry, Best Quotations For All Occasions (Greenwich, CONN: Fawcett Publications, Inc., 1961), p. 33.

DECEMBER 31. King, Martin Luther, Jr. Dec. 31, 1955, in an address at Montgomery, AL. Carroll E. Simcox, comp., 4400 Quotations for Christian Communicators (Grand Rapids, MI: Baker Book House, 1991), p. 49. John F. Kennedy, Dec. 17, 1962, Remarks upon lighting the National Community Christmas Tree at the Pageant of Peace Ceremonies on the Ellipse, delivered over television and radio at 5:15 p.m..

Printed in the United States
33442LVS00002B/349-351

9 780965 355780